"For how easy this book is to read, the dens͈ Reading this book is like eating something completely delicious and later realizing that it was half cauliflower. Rehor and Schiffman use such delightful candor and direct language to explain their research that readers might not even notice they are reading a methods section until they are deep into it. With this auspicious beginning, *Women and Kink* delivers the authors' original data supported with others' research in a writing style so smooth that it is lovely to read. *Women and Kink* covers various aspects of kink from sex, pain, the mind, spirituality, and safety to consent, exhibitionism, role play, fetishes, and money. Together, Rehor and Schiffman explore the ways in which women engage in kink, and a wide range of respondents' relationship statuses and reasons for participating in kink. Fascinating for academic and popular interest readers, *Women and Kink* makes a significant contribution to our understandings about what women think about kink, and how they feel about and practice kink over time—all in a refreshingly straightforward read."

Dr. Elisabeth Sheff, author of The Polyamorists Next Door, Stories from the Polycule, When Someone You Love is Polyamorous, and Children in Polyamorous Families

"This book contributes to the literature by discussing interesting and groundbreaking research on kink in WOMEN, an understudied population. It provides a window into a world that is often misunderstood and mischaracterized. This is a great read for any therapist by illuminating the experiences and giving voice to the women who engage in kink behaviors."

Rose Hartzell-Cushanick, PhD, EdS, LMFT, AASECT-certified Sex Therapist Supervisor at San Diego Sexual Medicine and Adjunct Professor at San Diego State University, CA, USA

"Jennifer! Julia! A heartfelt thanks for making these courageous retellings available for learning, growth and enjoyment. May this groundbreaking work lead the way for people everywhere to speak to their concerns, desires, turn-ons, and ways of life in ways that affirm them and help them make sense of their relationships, their communities and their world. Thank you both for this precious gift of a book."

Mike Giancola, LMFT, Licensed Marriage and Family Therapist focusing on sexual health, San Diego, CA, USA

Women and Kink

Based on original research from nearly 1,600 women from the kink community, this book takes you on a journey into the motivations, meanings, and benefits of kink, in these women's own words.

Women and Kink presents a diverse range of personal and intimate stories about life, love, relationships, kink, sex, self-discovery, growth, resilience, community, and more. The book offers insight into the breadth of the kink community, with chapters discussing different aspects of kink and forms of engagement, both individually and within relationships. Filled throughout with personal vignettes and examples, the authors provide commentary, reflection questions, and thought-provoking considerations to readers who are looking to explore a new area of their life.

By exploring personal stories of love, alternative sexualities, and reasons for participating in the "unconventional," the book supports and empowers each reader to build a relationship and life that best suits their needs. It is also an illuminating resource for sex therapists, counselors, and other mental health professionals interested in developing a kink-affirmative practice.

Jennifer Rehor is a Licensed Marriage and Family Therapist, AASECT-Certified Sex Therapist, and Clinical Supervisor. She is the owner and founder of Affirming Therapy Center (ATC) in San Diego, CA, USA.

Julia Schiffman is an Associate Clinical Social Worker, Sex Educator, and Community Activist. She specializes in sex therapy, and she works with LGBTQ couples and non-monogamous/polyamorous families in her San Diego, CA, USA private practice.

Women and Kink

Relationships, Reasons, and Stories

JENNIFER REHOR AND JULIA SCHIFFMAN

Routledge
Taylor & Francis Group
NEW YORK AND LONDON

First published 2022
by Routledge
605 Third Avenue, New York, NY 10158

and by Routledge
2 Park Square, Milton Park, Abingdon, Oxon, OX14 4RN

Routledge is an imprint of the Taylor & Francis Group, an informa business

© 2022 Jennifer Rehor and Julia Schiffman

All rights reserved. No part of this book may be reprinted or reproduced or utilised in any form or by any electronic, mechanical, or other means, now known or hereafter invented, including photocopying and recording, or in any information storage or retrieval system, without permission in writing from the publishers.

Trademark notice: Product or corporate names may be trademarks or registered trademarks, and are used only for identification and explanation without intent to infringe.

Library of Congress Cataloging-in-Publication Data
Names: Rehor, Jennifer, author. | Schiffman, Julia, author.
Title: Women and kink: relationships, reasons, and stories/Jennifer Rehor and Julia Schiffman.
Description: New York, NY: Routledge, 2021. | Includes bibliographical references and index.
Identifiers: LCCN 2021002061 (print) | LCCN 2021002062 (ebook) | ISBN 9780367187729 (hardback) | ISBN 9780367187736 (paperback) | ISBN 9780429274640 (ebook)
Subjects: LCSH: Paraphilias–Psychological aspects. | Women–Sexual behavior. | Women–Psychology.
Classification: LCC HQ71 .R39 2021 (print) | LCC HQ71 (ebook) | DDC 155.3/33–dc23
LC record available at https://lccn.loc.gov/2021002061
LC ebook record available at https://lccn.loc.gov/2021002062

ISBN: 978-0-367-18772-9 (hbk)
ISBN: 978-0-367-18773-6 (pbk)
ISBN: 978-0-429-27464-0 (ebk)

Typeset in Dante and Avenir
by Deanta Global Publishing Services, Chennai, India

In Memory of John "Roadkill" McConnell
Of all the friendship, passion, respect, and wisdom you shared with us over the years, two ideas burn most brightly: "Stay true to who you are," a lifelong journey as we all continue to grow and learn, and "You must find the beauty in the world," a sentiment we too-easily forget but have taken to heart.
We know you would have found beauty in these stories of women finding who they are, and we will be forever sad that we lost the chance to have long conversations about the ideas that sprang from them.
Your beautiful soul is missed.

Contents

    Authors   xii
    Acknowledgments   xv

1   Introduction   1

    The Research   2
    Background   2
    Methods   5
    Results   6
    Comments about Aspects of and Engagement with Kink   9
    Comments about Relationship Status   10
    Comments about Reasons for Participating   10
    Comments about Stories   11
    Discussion   11
    Definitions   11
    Points of Interest   12
    Notes   13

2   Aspects of Kink   14

    Kink and Sex   15
    Kink and Pain   21
    Kink and the Mind   24
    Kink and Spirituality   27
    Kink and Community   28

Kink and Safety 35
Kink and Consent 38
Kink and Exhibitionism/Voyeurism 41
Kink and Role Play 48
Kink and Fetish 52
Kink and Money 60
What Does This Mean? 64
Notes 65

3 Engagement with Kink   66

Kink as (Mostly) Fantasy 67
New to Kink 68
Kink as Private 70
I'm Not Kinky! 72
Kink is beyond Novelty 73
Self-Identity Includes Kink 75
Kink over Time 80
What Does This Mean? 83

4 Relationship Status   85

Relationships without Formal Commitments 87
Power-Dynamic Relationships 91
Non-Monogamy: Relationships with More Than One Partner 97
On the Topic of Marriage 104
Additional Chosen Families 113
What Does This Mean? 115

5 Reasons for Participating in Kink   117

Personal Reasons 119
Relational Reasons 129
Sexual Reasons 137
What Does This Mean? 144

6 Stories   146

Story #1 147
Story #2 149
Story #3 151
Story #4 154
Story #5 155
Story #6 156

Story #7   159
Story #8   161
Story #9   163
Story #10   165
What Does It All Mean?   174

7   Conclusion   175

The Problem with Labels   176
The Joys with Research   178
Sample Size   181
Final Thoughts   181
Note   182

Appendix A: The Survey   183
Appendix B: Additional Sensual, Erotic, and Sexual Behaviors   201
Appendix C: Exhibitionistic Behaviors   206
Appendix D: Additional Forms of Erotica   212
Appendix E: Additional Role-Play Scenarios   214
Appendix F: Additional Fetishes   221

Resources   230
References   232
Index   234

Authors

Jennifer Rehor, LMFT, CST

Jennifer Rehor is a Licensed Marriage and Family Therapist (LMFT), an AASECT-Certified Sex Therapist (CST), and a Clinical Supervisor. She received a master's degree in Psychology/Marriage and Family Therapy from Brandman University and a master's degree in Human Sexuality from San Francisco State University. Jennifer has been a guest lecturer for cultural competency in working with kinky clients at various universities' Marriage and Family Therapy programs, as well as an Adjunct Faculty Instructor at Alliant International University, teaching their graduate-level Sex Therapy course.

Jennifer is the founder and owner of Affirming Therapy Center (ATC) in San Diego, California, a group private practice with a team of sex-positive clinicians who are committed to serving people of gender, sexual, and relationship diversity (GSRD), including LGBTQ, heterosexual, kink, BDSM, sex work/adult industry, single, monogamy, non-monogamy, swinging, polyamory, and a variety of relationship dynamics and family configurations. At ATC, Jennifer offers individual therapy and couples counseling, helping adults with anxiety, depression, relationships, sexual health, life transitions, and personal growth, and to increase intimacy and sexual satisfaction.

As a polyamorous, kinky, bisexual woman with a traditional and religious upbringing, Jennifer understands both liberal and conservative perspectives. And as a first-generation American and a Sephardic Jew with roots in Egypt, Syria, Turkey, Greece, Italy, Spain, and Portugal, she appreciates the diversity found within and between cultures. With a curious mind and a penchant for travel, Jennifer enjoys learning about people from all over the world.

Jennifer's personal involvement with kink began in 2003, when she started attending workshops, play-parties, and full-emersion kinky weekend retreats. Throughout this journey, she has identified as a top, bottom, switch, masochist, sensualist, Mistress, little girl, pet, toy, pin-up girl, pet owner, nudist, submissive, brat, model, rope bunny, and kinkster. She knows what it's like to perform vaudeville at furry conventions, have a submissive boi-toy, belly dance at Renaissance Faires, splosh with friends, and give classes on the art of liquid latex. Each role, activity, and connection has contributed to a deeper understanding of her spirit. And although Jennifer enjoys hosting Nyotaimori parties, receiving the gift of service-oriented submission, wearing latex at fetish events, and playing at local dungeons across the country and the world—these experiences do not entirely define her identity. She also enjoys attending theater, volunteering at a children's ballet studio, photography, performing on stage, taking dance classes, and gardening.

Driven by this rich tapestry of insight and experiences, Jennifer is most passionate about normalizing sexual behaviors, fostering an understanding that *different* is not necessarily *wrong*, and giving people permission to pursue and explore their own desires, aspirations, dreams, and ultimately, themselves.

Julia Schiffman, ASW

Julia Schiffman is a Registered Associate Clinical Social Worker (ASW), Psychotherapist, Sex Educator, and Community Activist. Julia earned her bachelor's degree from the University of San Diego in Theology and Religious Studies with an emphasis in Eastern Religion and earned her master's of Social Work from the University of Southern California. She received a dual-track certificate of completion in Sex Therapy and Sexuality Education from the Sexual Health Certificate Program (SHCP) at the University of Michigan. Julia has lectured at many events and international conferences on topics such as kink basics, polyamory relationship dynamics, and awareness of and treatment for domestic and interpersonal violence specific to LGBTQ relationships.

In San Diego, California, Julia provides therapy services in her private practice where she focuses on trauma-informed and interpersonal issues with individuals, couples, and non-monogamous/polyamorous families. The population she serves are those from GSRD backgrounds, including kink,

BDSM, sex work/adult industry, LGBTQ, and non-monogamy. For more than a decade, she has volunteered for various causes, including the San Diego LGBT Community Center, local kink organizations, and as the Outreach Coordinator and Board Member for the Center for Positive Sexuality.

Julia's calling to become a social worker is driven by the desire to provide resources and connections to those in need. She believes there is always something to learn from others and, from the moment she learned of Jennifer's research, she knew she had to help tell these women's stories. Julia is a lesbian, kinky, polyamorous woman who is a switch, a professional sugar baby, and owned by a couple as their pet. She is currently in a triad with a cisgender straight man and cisgender lesbian woman and has a Dom.

Julia finds the opportunity to co-author this book with Jennifer as the perfect chance to create a resource for women, written by hundreds of women, that shows—as she already knows—there is more than one way to have a relationship, experience sex, and engage in kink.

Acknowledgments

There are many people who make this world a better place through charm, creativity, knowledge, persistence, patience, laughter, tears, and a host of other fine qualities. While writing this book about relationships, we took some time to reflect on each connection we have made with others, and the lasting effects these connections accord. We have grown emotionally and intellectually because of their influence on our lives.

Much gratitude goes to Dr. Carrington at San Francisco State University, whose support and advice are still appreciated years after the research project launched; and to the thesis committee along with the SXS Cohort of 2008–2010, for all of the feedback, critique, and review of the research project, as well as friendships and engaging discussions both inside and outside of the classroom.

We would like to thank CARAS (Community-Academic Consortium for Research on Alternative Sexualities) for providing the spark of inspiration for this research project and for formally endorsing this work.

We would also like to show our immense gratitude to Thomas Rehor for his intellectual banter and constructive criticism and for providing extensive technical and writing assistance. We appreciate the countless hours that you contributed to this project, together with your creativity and willingness to debate ideas, from big-picture questions to some obscure details that bordered on the minutiae.

A special thank you goes to Katie Mercer for providing the initial coded data through MAXQDA. You gave us a starting point to sort through what once seemed like an insurmountable amount of data.

We are grateful to Michael Giancola and Andrew Pari for providing preliminary reviews of the manuscript, along with thoughtful comments, feedback, and words of encouragement.

We were both fortunate enough to be taken under the wing of Dr. John McConnell, a kink-knowledgeable, seasoned Psychologist and Licensed Marriage and Family Therapist. As difficult as it is for clients to find kink-knowledgeable therapists, it is even more challenging to find kink-aware supervisors! We appreciate all of your guidance and invaluable insights.

We'd like to thank our sex therapy supervisors from the American Association of Sexuality Educators, Counselors and Therapists (AASECT), including Doug Braun-Harvey, Dr. Rose Hartzell-Cushanik, and Kimberly Jackson, and each of our California Board of Behavioral Sciences (BBS) supervisors, including Stephanie Andrews, Adam Beer, Mark Brewer, Kathleen Burns, Marilyn Cornell, Erick Frank, Dr. Anne Goshen, Jamie Julian, and Kate Webb; you all have helped shape us as therapists. We have much appreciation for our colleagues from The Sexual Health Consultation Group (hosted by The Harvey Institute), whose collaboration and knowledge have impacted the work we do and the way we view sexual health and wellness.

The clinicians at Affirming Therapy Center (ATC)—Penelope "Nel" Mercer, Sandra Koellmann, Jake Ryan, and Jesse Jones—and future ATC clinicians: your passion and dedication for working with clients from Gender, Sexual, and Relationship Diversity within the framework of positive Sexual Health and Wellness is making such a difference in this world. Collaborating with you and working alongside you is an immense honor and a privilege.

A thoughtful and heartfelt appreciation is extended to the Theology and Religious Studies Department at the University of San Diego for the constant reminder to stay curious about the world, try on the shoes of others, and that there are many paths up the mountain to get to the same destination. The loving support and persistent cheering from Lavada Rogers helped make this project a reality. Thank you, Hercules Liotard, for your discipline, protocol, structure, aftercare, and praise throughout the entire process.

We are thankful for our Sexology predecessors, who paved the way for this field of research and inquiry, and to all of our colleagues whom we've met at conferences, workshops, meetings, and classes, too numerous to mention here, but whose unique perspectives and provocative conversations influenced this research and our ways of thinking.

Special thanks go to Clare Ashworth, Ellie Duncan, and Heather Evans—our incredible editorial team at Routledge/Taylor & Francis. You have been a dream to work with. Gina Ogden is eternally appreciated for connecting us with our publisher.

We are forever grateful for the support, patience, and encouragement of our family, partners, friends, loves, mentors, play-partners, communities, and "framily."

Thank you to each of the organizers who approved recruitment efforts from their members, which made this study possible, including Behind Closed Doors, Beyond Vanilla, Church Street Fetish Fair, Club X, Desire Leather Women, Fetish Fair Fleamarket, FetLife.com, GLLA Weekend, LA-RAWW, Leather Fleamarket & Play Party, Lifestyle Alternatives Centre of Palm, Montreal Fetish Weekend, NLA-Dallas, Society of Janus, South Florida Munch, The Northeast Spanking Society, The Red Chair, TSR Network, Tulsa Dungeon Society, Twisted Tryst, and www.ardorotica.com.

And lastly, we would like to thank each and every one of the women who contributed to the substance of this project, without whom this book would not exist. We sincerely hope we did right by you. May your words and lives help other people to feel more accepted, validated, loved, and, dare we say, *normal*.

Introduction 1

Kink is about sexual interests—that's how the media portrays it—but at its core, the process of exploring kink is about discovering who you are and what you want, of searching for and reaching for ways of getting more "life" out of your life, of moving past traditional social boundaries, and realizing aspects of yourself in creative, playful, and meaningful ways.

Women and Kink utilizes scientific research and explores the responses study participants gave regarding their relationship status, their reasons for participating in bondage, discipline, dominance, submission, sadism, and masochism (BDSM), and open-ended "is there anything else you'd like to add" prompts. This book brings to light a variety of ideas and experiences of kinky women, illuminates the tremendous diversity of relationship structures that differ from common social norms, illustrates reasons why women engage in kink activities, and shares some of their intimate stories. The responses these women provide are thoughtful, provocative, and inspiring. These women speak unabashedly about their sensual, erotic, and sexual lives, giving us all a glimpse into what they do, why they do it, whom they do it with, and so much more.

We hope their personal stories will inspire those of you who are curious, those who are just entering the kink world, and those who are more experienced but want to learn from others. We also hope these stories captivate you, tantalize you, and embolden you, and help you realize how very similar and very unique we all are. With so many stories from so many women, *Women and Kink* compellingly demonstrates that we all have choices in how we create our own realities and relationships.

The Research

In 2010–2011, survey results from 1,580 women from the kink community were gathered, and the quantitative data about their erotic, sensual, and sexual behaviors were analyzed and published in the *Archives of Sexual Behavior* (Rehor, 2015). As part of this same study, qualitative data were collected including fill-in responses for questions with open-ended prompts.

Before we share the qualitative results of the study explored in this book, we'd like to briefly describe the Kinky Women Research Study, provide a context for the research, explain the methods for gathering data, and discuss the general analysis.

Background

The following is written by the senior researcher on this project, Jennifer Rehor, and is for all the other sex-geeks out there!

In 2008, I was enrolled in San Francisco State University's Human Sexuality Studies program. As a part of the graduate program, students must complete a research-based thesis project. We were encouraged to pick a topic in the first semester in order to begin the research process promptly. I started with a project that I was not passionate about, but that could be completed in my two-year timeline. The following summer, I attended a conference by Community-Academic Consortium for Research on Alternative Sexualities (CARAS) and I was so inspired by the work of these researchers! That is when I realized that my research must include some form of "alternative sexualities" and that my time in school would be pointless if I did not accomplish something wonderful, something captivating to my heart and my mind.

My academic advisor encouraged me to spend the summer reviewing the literature in the field as it pertains to kink. I gathered articles on all sorts of interesting topics: sadism, masochism, fetishism, dominance, submission, BDSM, kink, and many others. What caught my attention was a gap in the literature, specifically about women.

Essentially, all of the quantitative articles at the time were based almost entirely on male participants. I could find only a couple of articles that analyzed kink behaviors of women. Much of the seminal work about kink took place prior to the internet and, understandably, study participants were difficult to find, even more so female participants. Due to this lack of female respondents, there was an assumption in the academic literature that very few women actually enjoy kink for their own sensual, erotic, and sexual pleasure.

Through my own personal experiences, I knew that these behaviors were not a male-only phenomenon. At that time, I had been participating in women-only weekend-long kink events annually for the previous six years. As a matter of fact, I had seen more women in a swimming pool at these weekend kink events than had been included in the pool of women in all these quantitative studies, COMBINED.

So, I wondered, if these assumptions about women and kink were true, how could we account for women-only kink events or organizations?

At that moment, I realized, "I know what my research must be about."

That epiphany sparked a journey that taught me, energized me, pushed me, and allowed me to grow. In 2010, I launched a survey and collected knowledge from 1,361 women, young and old, happy and sad, from here and from there, and cherished their lives and loves. My endeavor delayed graduation by one full academic year, but having a thesis project that impassioned me was worth the wait. By 2011, I completed, defended, and published my thesis, *The Occurrence of Unconventional Sexual Behaviors of Women* (Rehor, 2011). While writing my thesis, I kept the survey open for a couple more months and gathered an additional 219 participants.

Essentially, the purpose of my thesis was twofold. Firstly, I wanted to officially debunk the myths that kink is a male-only phenomenon and that women participate only for one of only two reasons: either for financial gain or at the request of their male partner (Breslow et al., 1985; Spengler, as cited by Moser & Levitt, 1987: 332). (In academia, even if we know a phenomenon to be true, we need to document it in a research paper and add it to the body of literature.) Secondly, I wanted to contribute to the knowledge about kink behaviors in an exploratory way.

After completing my degree, I re-analyzed the data to include the additional 219 participants and submitted a journal article about my research, titled "Sensual, Erotic, and Sexual Behaviors of Women from the 'Kink' Community," to the *Archives of Sexual Behavior*, where it was published two years later (Rehor, 2015). The focus of this article is the specific activities of women who participate in kink, which lays a solid foundation for understanding this remarkable phenomenon.

By this time, I had embarked upon a career path to becoming a Psychotherapist. My goals shifted as I went back to school for a second master's degree, completed the requirements for becoming a licensed marriage and family therapist, and attended the additional training to become a couple's therapist and an American Association of Sexuality Educators, Counselors, and Therapists (AASECT) certified sex therapist.

I had reached the milestones I set out for myself personally and professionally, and I was happy.

One day, I was telling a dear friend about my research and explained that, besides the data points I'd already published, I had thousands of quotations from the women in my survey. I had allowed and encouraged the participants to elaborate on their answers, to clarify their ideas, or to just write what they wanted. And they did. These women wrote a lot, more than I had time to organize and understand, about how they connect in play, in romance, in love, in sex, in friendship, and in community.

My friend smiled and said, "It's like you have a treasure chest in your closet, waiting to be discovered and shared!" I have information—important information—from my survey that was not included in my thesis or my published article, information that was not readily quantifiable, easily counted, or categorized. I have candid stories that women told about themselves, their lives, and their loves.

In the back of my mind, something kept tickling me. "They told you their stories. They told you their stories *because those stories are important*. You have to share their stories!"

I realized I wasn't finished. I still had an unopened treasure chest. It was time for the treasure to come out of the closet.

World Sexual Health Day—San Diego 2017—is where I met Julia. We chatted a bit at the event, then walked across the street to a local munch (social event), where we learned more about each other's goals and aspirations. We are both sex therapists and we have the same passion for understanding and working with kink. I told her of my hidden treasure chest and my dream of sharing it. To my surprise, she offered to help me write the book. Her enthusiasm, open-mindedness, candidness, and curiosity sold me on the idea of co-authoring this book.

A few months later, an e-mail from a colleague was posted on a professional listserv, inviting Sexologists to meet with a publisher, Routledge, Taylor & Francis, at the AASECT conference that Julia and I were already planning to attend. We developed and presented our proposal and, to our delight, it was approved.

We opened my treasure chest together.

The real work began.

Julia and I began sifting through the stories—each unique—to find commonality and difference, to organize and categorize the thousands of narratives into a compendium that could reach out to the whole world.

We are proud, overjoyed, and humbled to present these stories of women and kink.

Methods

This project was approved by the Internal Review Board of San Francisco State University. It was also endorsed by the CARAS Research Advisory Committee (RAC) program.

This study was designed to be community-based research (seeking a non-clinical, non-criminal sample). Therefore, the sample was specifically focused on recruiting people who were at least familiar enough with the kink community to either attend a kink event or be involved in a kink-related online forum. Administrators of several groups listed on an online kink-related event directory were contacted by e-mail with a request for permission to recruit participants. Approvals were received from 21 kink-related community organizations. Then, with the organizers' permission, flyers were sent to their events and posted online with a link to the online survey.

The survey instrument[1] developed for this study was based primarily on previous research. The inclusion criteria questions were: "Do you consent to take the survey?", "Are you female?", and "Are you at least over 18 years old?"

The demographic questions were "In what year were you born?", "In which state do you reside? (If outside the USA, in which country do you reside?)", and "What is your current relationship status?" Potentially, the survey could be answered by women anywhere in the world.

The survey included a list of 126 forms of erotic activities—a broader spectrum of human sexual behavior than documented in previous studies, and included activities that may be unique to females and therefore had never been documented in the academic literature (such as breast play).

These activities were categorized into the following seven sub-categories:

- 62 BDSM behaviors (including physical and psychological stimuli)
- 10 role-play scenarios
- 5 exhibitionistic behaviors
- 5 fetishistic behaviors
- 8 forms of erotica
- 24 overt sexual activities
- 12 miscellaneous erotic activities

First and foremost, quantitative questions were asked (something that has a yes or no response and easily countable). For example, "Did you ever get your hair brushed by someone else for your own pleasure?" is a yes or no answer; there is no judgment involved, nor is there a subjective element of, "How much did you like it?" Importantly, such questions can be asked again in the future to see how people change.

The activities must be willingly participated in and must be for sensual or erotic purposes. And for every question asked, there was an option for free-text responses.

It was anticipated that there would be some ambiguous areas. For example, is a voyeur a participant or an observer? If a mistress orders a submissive to spank the mistress for the benefit of the submissive, who is having the activity done to whom? The best way to handle this was to include an abundance of free-text boxes in the survey to allow participants to clarify their particular situation.

Results

Who participated in the study?
  Here is the basic demographic information:

- All respondents indicated they were female and over the age of 18
- Age range from 19 to 72 years
- Mean age of 35 years, with a standard deviation of 10
- Approximately 80% from the US (from 48 of the 50 US states)
- Approximately 20% from countries outside of the US, including Australia, Austria, Belgium, Brazil, Canada, Czech Republic, Ecuador, England, Finland, France, Germany, India, Ireland, Japan, Mexico, Netherlands, New Zealand, Scotland, Switzerland, and Wales

There were three hypotheses that the study examined.

- Hypothesis 1: Kink behaviors are a male-only phenomenon
- Hypothesis 2: Women participate in kink behaviors for one of only two reasons: either for financial gain or at the request of their male partner
- Hypothesis 3: Women from the kink community participate in a wide variety of sensual, erotic, and sexual activities

Hypothesis 1 and hypothesis 2 directly challenged the assumptions from previous research. The third hypothesis was exploratory and intended to contribute to the understanding of what women from the kink community do for their own sensual, erotic, and sexual pleasure.

Let's review the three hypotheses individually.

Hypothesis 1: *Kink behaviors are a male-only phenomenon.* If kink behaviors are a male-only phenomenon, the following criteria must be met:

- Recruitment efforts will produce few, if any, female respondents
- The female respondents will indicate that they participate in these activities exclusively with men
- None of the female respondents will state that kink behaviors are a necessary requirement in order to attain an orgasm
- None of the respondents will have paid money to someone for participating in kink behaviors

This study recruited 1,580 women to participate in the survey.

More than half of the women participated in behaviors with other women. Nearly 8% reported that they can "ONLY attain an orgasm by participating in these (BDSM) activities." Some of these women have even paid someone else to perform kink behaviors.

The hypothesis that kink behaviors are a male-only phenomenon is **rejected**.

Hypothesis 2: *Women participate in kink behaviors for one of only two reasons: either for financial gain or at the request of their male partner.* In order for this hypothesis to be true, the following criteria must be met:

- Most of the women who respond to the study will indicate that they have been paid for participating in kink behaviors
- The only two reasons why the respondents have participated in kink behaviors will be "for money" or "at the request of a male partner"

In this study, less than 10% of the respondents indicated they had been paid money in the previous 12 months to perform kink-related activities.

When asked about their PRIMARY reason for participating in these activities, less than 2% participated for money and less than 20% participated at the request of a male partner, while 70% participated for self-discovery/personal pleasure.

In fact, 94% of the women indicated at least one reason other than for money or at the request of a male partner when combining the primary reason and other reasons for participating in kink activities.

The hypothesis that women participate in kink behaviors for one of only two reasons: either for financial gain or at the request of their male partner is **rejected**.

Hypothesis 3: *Women from the kink community participate in a wide variety of sensual, erotic, and sexual activities.* In order for this hypothesis to be true, the following criterion must be met:

- The women who respond to the study will indicate that they have engaged in an assortment of kink activities

This hypothesis is exploratory and descriptive and was addressed by analyzing various aspects of the data.

Of the 126 erotic activities listed, these women stated that they willingly participated in an average of 57 activities (with a standard deviation of 22). The range of activities participated in is from 1 to 121. These numbers do not include the additional activities from the "other" answers the women provided.[2]

The hypothesis that women from the kink community participate in a wide variety of sensual, erotic, and sexual activities is **supported**.

A little side note: Richard von Krafft-Ebing, a seminal sex researcher in the late 1800s, famously said (well, famous to sex researchers), "with opportunity for the natural satisfaction of the sexual instinct, every expression of it that does not correspond with the purpose of nature—i.e., propagation—must be regarded as perverse" (von Krafft-Ebing, 1906). Meaning, unless you are having sex to reproduce, you are a pervert.

In all fairness, the term "perverse" may not have had the same connotations that it does today.

Well, when we compiled a list of ALL the activities these women participated in and ranked them by "participation in any form," coitus (penetrating vagina with penis) didn't even make the top 20 list. Instead, coitus came in at #22, with 79.18% of the women stating that they have willingly participated in this activity.

For those of you who are curious, the list of categories of the top 20 erotic stimuli/behaviors willingly participated in (whether as the person doing the activity, having it done to them, and/or observing) by the women in the survey is as follows:

1. Touching (caress, cuddle, massage, tickle)
2. Kissing, licking, sucking
3. Spanking
4. Hair pulling

5. Biting
6. Scratching/leaving marks/abrasion
7. Use bondage toys (chains, gags, cuffs, rope, etc.)
8. Moderate bondage (can't get out on own/with mobility)
9. Masturbation (solo)
10. Cunnilingus (stimulating woman's genitals with mouth)
11. Light bondage (able to get out if you wanted to)
12. Paddling
13. Breast play (slap, clothespins, etc.)
14. Hand job (stimulating genitals with hands/fingers)
15. Flogging
16. Fellatio (stimulating man's genitals with mouth)
17. Grooming (shaving, manicure, pedicure, brush hair, etc.)
18. Stimulating anus with fingers or penis
19. Genital play (slap, kick, clothespins, etc.)
20. Ice play

As you can see, the activities with the highest response from the entire survey were touching and kissing, licking, and sucking.

This background gives some context for the data collection and purpose of the study. To learn more about the various activities that were analyzed in the study, please refer to the published thesis (Rehor, 2011) and the article in *Archives of Sexual Behavior* (Rehor, 2015).

But now, let's focus our attention on the comments provided in the various fill-in responses that comprise the rest of this book, including aspects of kink, level of engagement with kink, relationship status, reasons for participating in kink, and personal stories.

Comments about Aspects of and Engagement with Kink

The survey instrument offered two non-guided, open-ended opportunities to provide additional information:

- "For the activities you checked in the previous section, if there is anything else about your experiences that you would like to add, please do so below."
- "If there is anything else you'd like to add or clarify about your sexual lifestyle, please do so below."

In this book, we also analyze responses from the free-text answers to prompts found within the survey in regard to exhibitionistic behaviors, voyeuristic behaviors, forms of erotica, role-play scenarios, and fetishes.

The responses to these prompts contain such deep, meaningful content, glimpses into the lives of these women, what they hold dear, their heartaches, triumphs, and lessons learned along the way.

These responses are used for Chapter 2 (Aspects of Kink) and Chapter 3 (Engagement with Kink).

Comments about Relationship Status

We inquired into the women's relationship status, listing what seemed to be sufficient choices, shown below.

- "What is your current relationship status?"

The choices were: single (never married/domestic partnership), divorced/separated, widowed, casual BDSM relationship(s)/play partner(s), long-term relationship, married/domestic partner, monogamous, polyamorous/open relationship/polyfidelity, swingers, BDSM family, 24/7 BDSM relationship. The women could select as many as required to best define their relationship.

As with all the questions, there was an "Other" text box. The other relationship statuses were extensive and profound.

Many of our respondents clarified that their relationships do not fit nicely into a single or even multiple boxes. Over 10% of the respondents wanted to tell us more—that even with all of these new boxes, their relationships still didn't quite fit. So, they provided detail in the "other, please explain" category.

"What is your current relationship status?" was originally included as a basic demographic question, yet it turned into an unintended finding. The variation in relationship styles became apparent when people were given the opportunity to describe their unique situations.

This topic will be examined in Chapter 4.

Comments about Reasons for Participating

We wanted to learn more about the women's motivations for participating in kink behaviors.

- "What was your PRIMARY reason for participating in your most recent activity from the previous section?"

- "What other reason(s) (if any) did you participate in your most recent activity from the previous section?"

For these two questions, there were six choices and an optional fill-in textbox. The PRIMARY reason allowed for one answer to be selected, while the "other reason(s)" question allowed for participants to select as many answers as needed.

A discussion of the combined responses from the fill-in boxes for these two questions constitutes Chapter 5.

Comments about Stories

The stories found in Chapter 6 are assembled from some of the more extensive and detailed remarks from any of the open-ended prompts throughout the survey.

In Chapter 7, we review what we have learned and discovered, and offer final thoughts for our readers and friends.

Discussion

Beyond behaviors are meanings. Analyzing a list of behaviors is important in its own right: it gives us a starting point to discuss what it is that people do. But, there's so much more to be revealed! And that is what we found in the thousands of free-text responses we explored.

As we stated before, kink, at its core, is a tool, a process of exploring ourselves. It is adventure, discovery, surprises, changes, life, love, lust, relationships, a beginning, a transformation, an ending, and anything else.

The quotations in the pages of the following chapters honor hundreds of women's perspectives, experiences, and knowledge. Each voice is special in its own right, but collectively, they articulate the extraordinary opportunities to explore ourselves and our world around us.

Definitions

Kink behaviors: unconventional sensual, erotic, and sexual behaviors including BDSM-related behaviors (physical and psychological stimuli including bondage, discipline, dominance, submission, sadism, and masochism), exhibitionism (arousal by being observed by others), voyeurism (arousal by observing others), and fetishism (arousal by objects).

Kink community: the organizations representing people who have an interest in kink behaviors. These organizations provide physical or online spaces for adults with similar interests to meet, discuss, support, educate, and/or interact and may also be known as BDSM, Fetish, Leather, Sadomasochistic, Sadism and Masochism (aka S&M, SM, or S/M), Alt Sex, and Alternative Sexuality, among others.

Kink: referencing kink behaviors or the kink community.

Kinky: (of a person, outlook, or object) affiliated with kink behaviors or the kink community.

Munch: a casual and informal social event for people who are interested in meeting other people with similar kinky interests, but where overt kink behaviors do not occur.

Play: engaging in specific kink behaviors in an arranged place and time, which may or may not include overt sexual activities. In the swinger community, "play" generally refers to engaging in overt sexual activity.

Play partner: a person who someone plays with. Play partners can be people who just met at an event, casual "friends with benefits" where the "benefits" are exclusively kink activities, or close intimate friends, to name a few.

The Scene: either the kink community (e.g., "I'm new to the scene") or a specific time when people are engaging in kink activities (e.g., "I'm still smiling as I think about the scene we did last night").

Vanilla: people or activities considered more conventional than those involved in kink. The idea is that "vanilla" is a plain flavor compared to other spices.

Points of Interest

Women and Kink contains an abundance of quotations from the hundreds of women who participated in our study. Each quotation has depth, meaning, and importance to the woman who wrote it. As you read these women's messages, ponder the ideas and consider the emotions and desires condensed in the words. Discover for yourself if those ideas also describe you.

Notice in some quotations the purposeful use of uppercase and lowercase. Within the kink community, titles such as "Master," "Mistress," "Owner," and their pronouns are typically capitalized, while titles such as "slave," "submissive," "pet," and their pronouns are lowercase—even at the beginning of a sentence. This is one method that people use to express respect and authority, and to differentiate their roles.

Many terms, abbreviations, and acronyms used by participants of our survey in their free-text answers may have multiple meanings. We did not define or explain any of these, as doing so would be assumptive. Our readers are encouraged to decide these meanings for themselves.

We left spelling and grammatical irregularities, unusual wording, and ambiguous expressions unchanged, and only made very minor spelling, grammatical, and punctuation corrections (in order to improve readability). In all cases, we were mindful to keep the original intent of their responses intact.

Content Warning: While we did redact some identifying information (for anonymity), we were intentional in keeping these women's voices uncensored. Therefore, there may be terms, phrases, and ideas that are uncomfortable, offensive, triggering, or disturbing for some of our readers. Additionally, some activities and behaviors may be illegal in certain jurisdictions; we do not know the legal implications and neither condone nor encourage any illegal activities and behaviors.

While we were diligent about not re-using quotations within the book, on rare occasions the same quotation is used more than once in order to illustrate a specific idea. If there were opportunities to expand on an idea or introduce a new concept, but doing so was not supported by the women's words or would take away from the spirit of their voices, we kept the commentary on track with the responses.

When we needed to understand what specific words or phrases mean, we used the *Cambridge Dictionary* as a starting point if there was no other authoritative source available.

So, let's take a deep breath, open our treasure chest together and see what's hidden inside!

Notes

1 The entire survey is included in Appendix A.
2 A detailed list of these additional behaviors is in Appendix B.

Aspects of Kink 2

"It's important to have an understanding regarding what someone's mindset is to BDSM. There is so much more than the actual physical activities that transpire."

Kink is an abundance of qualities, facets, ideas, beliefs, and complexities. It is people united in communities and still possessing conflicting ideas and behaviors. It is what you expect and what you never dare dream.

The women in our study do not enjoy kink in a vacuum, disconnected, acting out a bad script in a grainy film. Rather, kink is intertwined in their lives, loves, passions, philosophies, professions, and adventures, in the sacred and in the mundane, in their hearts and in their souls. Kink allows them to be as alive as they can be while not being part of themselves at all, both intimate and detached. And more, and less.

Media depictions about kink are sensationalized and would have us believe that kink is only about sex. While sex is certainly one aspect of kink, our study's participants teach us that kink can also pertain to pain, the mind, spirituality, community, safety, consent, exhibitionism, voyeurism, role play, fetishes, and money.

You didn't expect that, did you?

Well, neither did we!

These women detailed, explained, expanded, and clarified the particular features of and ways of thinking about kink, in all its intricacies.

And that is where our adventure begins.

Kink and Sex

> "Although fully capable of orgasms without s/m it is similar to oatmeal without brown sugar. It satisfies a need but does nothing for the appetite."

It's true that we have sex to reproduce, but most of us engage in sexual behaviors for pleasure far, far more often than for reproduction. Therefore, we are going to go out on a limb and assert that we have sex mostly because it brings us pleasure.

But before we do, we must point out that there is not a good definition of "sexual activity." The *Cambridge Dictionary* states that sex (as an activity) is "physical activity between people involving sexual organs," and it defines a sex organ as "a part of the body involved in the production of babies, such as the vagina or penis" (*Cambridge Dictionary*, n.d.).

Yikes. Based on that, plants and animals don't reproduce and kissing is not a sexual activity.

What a limiting way to think about sex!

Okay, out on another limb for us! We are going to assert that sexual activity is any activity that causes sensations of eroticism. Yes, we know that erotic means "relating to sexual desire or pleasure," according to the *Cambridge Dictionary* (n.d.), but our definition allows each of us to decide what is and isn't sexual and erotic. Like happiness, sadness, and any other emotion, sexuality and eroticism are subjective, so we will not attempt to refine them further.

Add to this ambiguity that there is not a good definition of kink everyone can agree on and that engaging in kink is just as subjective an experience as sex is.

> "BDSM is really very sexual for me ... the whole male dominating me is a HUGE turn on for me. I enjoy the service aspect of being submissive."

> "BDSM is not necessarily about sex."

> "My sex life is pretty 'vanilla'—very little (if any) role play or props, but still mostly satisfying. Interestingly, it is my husband who prefers to keep it on the more boring side, as he's not very adventurous."

> "I really like to wear a strap-on and fuck my husband, ;)"

> "... For poly folks, I think that there's a lot more blending of kink and sex than is really clear in this survey. For me (and most of my partners), it's really about having kinky sex, not 'being kinky.'"

We can see that, for some of these women, kink and sex almost always go together. Others state that kink is optional during sex or that, while they do not require kink for sexual gratification, it amplifies the intensity of a sexual encounter.

This introduces us to the topics of women's sexual pleasure, kink as an enhancement for sex, and kink without sex, important ideas because all of these perspectives come together to make up a more intricate picture of women's pleasure. Let's look at them in more detail.

Women Enjoy Sex

Let's re-read that: Women Enjoy Sex. This should not be new news to you (but if it is, that's okay … we have a lot to learn in this section!). Before we talk about the connection between kink and sex, we need to take a look at this foundational idea that many women partake in, derive pleasure from, and experience joy during sexual activities.

> "… Sex is nice and pleasure is good for you. A crazy notion to some. Still a revolutionary idea for myself sometimes …"

> "I am extremely sexually active and am very conscious and attracted to my male counterparts at work, however since I am the senior analyst and we are forbidden to date, you see I have to develop all kinds of scenarios at work just to relax which then, creates another issue, I need to really get off. So, I have sex as often as 20 times a week with men in other parts of the building, sometimes in the building but most often in their cars, I love sex and obviously am good enough at it that we both cum at the same time, which I find to be very advantageous, for me, we can both leave and go home."

> "I don't know what you're going to do with this survey, but I'd love you to get the word out that women can love sex at any age. I'm 55 years old, and no fashion model by any means. My husband is not a super-hunk, either. But we can still go to it. He will often lie naked in bed and ask me to disrobe beside the bed and give him a hard-on just by standing there, not by touching him. As soon as he's at attention, I'll suck that cock to make it harder, and then he'll pound me until my eyeballs roll back in my head. Sometimes, we'll head into the shower, me still covered in cum, and wash each other off. All the touching usually puts us back in the mood, and I'll suck him again in the shower, and we'll have sex again, often without returning to the bedroom. We're both more patient,

tender, lovers than we were when we married 30 years ago. Then, sex was about quantity. Now, it's about quality. I'm just an ordinary woman, and if I can still love sex after all these years, any woman can."

How these women find sex, have sex, and enjoy sex is invigorating to read!

These women slip us a message of hope and a frame of reference to understand that sex can be discovered, rediscovered, explored, and enjoyed at any age. They tell us that women's sexual enjoyment changes due to personal, biological, or environmental circumstances. It is as though these women are sexual chameleons. What a lovely ability to have!

Kink as an Enhancement for Sex

Kink activities can enhance sexual satisfaction, orgasms, and desire; they can embellish the experience and enjoyment of sex and promote feelings of fulfillment.

> "For me 'vanilla' (plain) sex is like Tofu … yeah it works, it will nourish you (certainly better than nothing), but without soy sauce or teriyaki sauce or SOMETHING, it is well … tofu. Need I say more?"
>
> "I am able to reach orgasm without BDSM; however, the sex is far better and more fulfilling. I feel myself longing for it when it is not present during sex."
>
> "It's the best form of foreplay known to man/woman. If more couples did kink I think the woman in her 40s suffering from lowered libido would be mostly cured. Sex, vanilla sex is so far off base as to what really turns a woman on. SO fuck off base ;-)"
>
> "I really enjoy getting fucked with a knife held to my throat, stories where my blood ends up slowly pooling around me whispered into my ear, then being ordered to come."
>
> "I love to be tied up and spanked. I also love my Hitachi Magic Wand. I love to use it almost daily … I am heteroflexible. Not turned on by all women, but certain women turn my crank. I am curious, but haven't been with a woman yet. I would love to be in a polyamorous relationship as I need more than one sexual outlet. I masturbate almost daily with my Hitachi Magic wand. I love sex, I love cock worship and spanking. I have safe sex and have managed to stay STD free. I keep a masturbation

journal to keep track of when I masturbate, what was I thinking about when masturbating and why I felt the need to do it. It has helped me tremendously, I now know I have 5–6 different kinds of orgasms and what I am doing when I produced them."

There are women who state that they need something special in order to orgasm, to get aroused, to have sexual enjoyment. For these women, that something special is kink.

"I have never had a successful sexual encounter that did not include some form of BDSM activity, even if it was only fantasy to bring on orgasm. 'Vanilla' sex is not something that works for me."

"… Not all bdsm is sexual for me, but during sex I have to include some bdsm elements (even if it's just choking, spanking, rough sex, or calling me a slut) in order for me to orgasm. I enjoy BDSM without sex, but I don't enjoy or get off on sex without some bdsm in it."

"Orgasm is difficult for me under all circumstances. So, answering questions about 'do you NEED this activity in order to achieve orgasm' are not very relevant. There is no specific activity that I do that I *require* in order to get off, but generally there must be some element that has some flavor of power exchange in which my partner has power (perceived or real) over me."

And while the following two women don't mention whether kink was necessary for orgasm specifically, they do state how important it is for their sexual satisfaction.

"My sex life may be odd and on the kinky side … (though I do straight sex, it really doesn't do it for me, i'd rather have the power exchange aspect) … I consider my sex life to be extremely healthy."

"I was born this way. My submissive eyes found dominant eyes along the way, i have seldom had vanilla sex in my life, i would rather go without. The internet made it possible to find many like myself, always nice to know one is not that odd, lol."

Does "kink as an enhancement for sex" intrigue you?

Do people need to experiment with scores of kink behaviors in order to find sexual satisfaction? No, not at all. You simply should be aware that such behaviors are not so uncommon and can be helpful for some people to better enjoy their sex lives.

A word about "vanilla sex." Vanilla sex is used by some people to mean sex that is uninteresting to them, too routine and predictable, or too conforming to their culture's expectations.

But consider that, as soon as you pull your partner's hair, talk dirty to them, kiss, tickle, or pinch them, you've engaged in kink. Consider also the situation in which vanilla sex is someone's peak erotic turn-on …

Kink without Sex

While kink may be synonymous with sex for some people, this is not the case for everyone. It's possible to enjoy kink and to enjoy sex, just not mixed together, and sometimes kink is completely unrelated to sex.

Separating kink and sex may not be for any particular reason, any more than some people don't enjoy wine and cheese at the same time. They didn't make a conscious decision to not enjoy it together; they just don't.

> "I don't always look at it as sex … many times just as fun but sensual."
>
> "I do not have sex with my BDSM play partners."
>
> "As I said before, I do not mix BDSM with sexual activity. I do have sex with my 24/7 slave but that is usually when I feel horny nothing to do with BDSM play. Usually after a session of BDSM he is so deep in subspace that sex is totally out of the question. Maybe the next morning!!!!"
>
> "This leaves my situation undescribed. I am in a sexually monogamous relationship with my wife and owner yet i have a very intense non-sexual D/s relationship with one girl and an even more intense S&m relationship with another. None of my play is casual."
>
> "I usually separate sexual intercourse from BDSM—I don't have sex with most of my BDSM play partners, nor do I have extremely kinky sex with the people who I do have sex with. BDSM is a different release for me in and of itself, even though it is clearly sexual and I've orgasmed during it."

Sex isn't necessarily the focus of kink activities and relationships and, for some people, that distinction is very important.

> "I engage in many of the activities that were listed, not for reasons of sexual gratification, but because they offer satisfaction in other ways."

> "I never orgasm, so these activities have no bearing on my ability to do so."

> "… I'd like to point out that the pleasure of BDSM isn't simply that of sexuality (though of course that is the basis). BDSM has the ability, if done right, to create a relationship more steeped in trust than any vanilla one I have experienced …"

> "Please, please remember that living IS NOT ALL ABOUT SEX. Many people incorporate BDSM into their lives, but SEX is not the main motivation. Having a stable caring relationship is far more important. i feel that the focus of many of these surveys on the sexual aspect whilst ignoring the myriad other factors involved when two or twenty folk join their lives is a big issue in folk becoming depressed/disillusioned/fearful when they for any reason cannot 'perform.'"

There you have it: opportunities to experience and explore kink, even when sex isn't present. Sometimes sexual intercourse never happens, even with a long-term partner. And actually, a few women talk about being celibate (choosing not to have intercourse) or remaining virgins while exploring kink.

> "I entered the lifestyle as a virgin, and have remained so for the two years I have been out doing scenes at dungeons. I've found that's something of a rarity."

> "For me, kissing is the most intimate activity—though this is in the context of never having had intercourse with a man. Even were I to, though, I think it would be second place to (tongue-in-mouth) kissing."

> "i was a virgin until I was 23 years old. I had this wonderful bf who did not pressure me about sex. He was 26. Together we discovered magazines and films about power exchange/bdsm … It has been 21 years now and we are still 'mistress and slave' and we have not ever had vaginal or oral sex …"

> "I have taken a vow of chastity based on my religion until marriage. I therefore, do not have any type of sex and verbalize that as a hard limit before playing with anyone. I find that the BDSM community is a safe place in which to be a virgin because I can still experience sexual

> pleasure, but do not have to worry about people violating my vow due to the importance of respecting safe-words and limits."

> "I have been celibate (non-penetrative intercourse for 14 months), [and,] before a lover of a couple of times, I was celibate for 3 years. It has been an important to conscious choice, to choose to be celibate to get to know myself as a sexual human being. (sensual celibacy is another choice in our sexual life.) I look forward to transitioning, however I know that as a choice it is powerful."

We hope we have unhooked for you the idea that kink and sex are necessarily interchangeable ideas.

What do you do with this information? Where do you go from here?

There are no rules to this game except those you choose for yourself, based on your personality, expectations, desires, lifestyle, and many other factors. These rules might change daily or never. You have choices. We encourage you to explore them, if that is your desire.

Kink and Pain

> "Giving pain (if my partner wishes to receive it) is something I enjoy, but ONLY when I know my partner wants to play in that manner. So, I am not sadistic in that I don't experience pleasure from giving pain whether its well-received or not."

Since kink is an umbrella term that includes BDSM (bondage, discipline, dominance, submission, sadism, and masochism) as well as other unconventional sexual behaviors, we want to take a moment to break apart the sadism and masochism (S/M) elements.

Sadism is the feeling of pleasure by giving pain. Masochism is the feeling of pleasure by receiving pain. There is an interesting relationship between pain and pleasure.

People generally tend to avoid situations that create pain for themselves and tend to seek out situations that create pleasure. This is known as the "pain pleasure principle" in Psychology and there is a reward system in our brains and bodies that is described by this principle.

Yet, sometimes pain is associated with sensual, erotic, and sexual pleasures. Don't believe us? Well, just look at the responses below.

> "I like: sensation play, pain play. I like to see the other person respond to the pain I give …"

> "The spanking thing, I love the physical sensation of it. I also like pretty rough nipple play. It feels good to me. I'm not a masochist, actually, and wouldn't like them so much if it just plain hurt."

> "I thrive on sensations. Especially pain. While it can be fair to make assumptions based on what a survey asks, it can be very hard to understand various kinks unless you go deeper. For example, just because I said I have received flogging for pleasure, you never specifically ask how intense the flogging was. Some want it so light that I would barely be able to feel it and others enjoy breaking skin or being knocked off their feet by the force of a blow. I also really enjoy seeing bruises after a play session."

These women echo the connection between pain and pleasure.

> "I think I've finally found the title that fits me the best out of all the options given. Sadomasochist. I've realized that I love pain. I adore it. I love being in both physical and emotional pain and love putting others in that pain because I know how wonderful it can be. The clarity it gives me is something that I can find no other way. When you are in pain, you can't worry about whether or not you'll have time to do laundry on Wednesday or if you remembered to turn off the stove. In a world where everyone is going a mile a minute and my thoughts are sometimes two or three steps ahead of me, pain forces me to slow down. I have to focus on my breathing. I can hear my heartbeat in my ears. It makes me remember that I'm human, not some machine that needs to keep running and running and running in order to keep up with everyone else."

> "… BDSM play for me is almost always about cathartic pain and in those cases I have never ever developed a romantic attachment. It is only when that person crosses the line into something gentle and loving in a clearly sexual context, not a friendly hug or something, that I've been drawn into hoping for more than friendship. I am a masochist, but I'm not, in some respects, a 'sexual' masochist in that pain alone gives me sexual pleasure. It's a very different kind of pleasure, which 'may' involve sexual contact or arousal, but does not need to, to be good in its own right … Just last night I wanted play for pleasure, but it was the male top's idea to engage in play with a 'misery stick' or 'evil stick' and he had a great time,

and I had only a few moments of being where I wanted to be. I never got to cry or anything like I really need, so it wasn't the most fulfilling experience, but I'm still glad I did it and glad he enjoyed our time together. I care about him as a friend very deeply."

Sometimes, the use of controlled pain can help alleviate chronic pain, as evidenced by the following two accounts.

"As a means of managing symptoms of fibromyalgia … Prefer 'stinging' and 'pinching' type of pain/torture to 'thudding' type of pain/torture. Also find this type of play very successful in managing symptoms of fibromyalgia."

"I enjoy getting inside their head, and walking them on the line of orgasm—and by denying them release, I can get their endorphins going, when I flog them, or what is considered erotic torture. Erotic tease and denial. Power Exchange for me. Imagine being able to make someone have an orgasm, with a flick of a finger. Now that is power! That's the best description, I think, of what energy goes on, within their head, and why some people can take so much, when flogged, spanked, or whipped. The pain becomes pleasure, as the endorphins are released. That's also why some of us have been using flogging on people with Fibromyalgia, to help ease their pain. By confusing the brain, and making it a sort of biofeedback, it does seem to help, as long as you're not turning their skin black and blue!"

Imagine that! Using pain to manage symptoms of pain. For anyone looking for a research topic, this is an area worthy of further exploration.

However, there is a myth that some level of pain must be involved to be considered "kink." No … pain is only one subset of what goes into kink. Some people specify that they do not enjoy pain but do enjoy other elements of kink play.

"i don't like real pain however so it is always controlled with 'safe' words."

"I have role played as the villain and the victim and find both roles enjoyable however I am not submissive and rarely can tolerate receiving pain."

"BD/SM activities are pleasurable for me in that I get to give and receive sensation. Humiliation, servitude, and the like do not excite me … Additionally, I do not enjoy receiving pain—I am not masochistic, by which I mean I do not need pain to feel pleasure or to achieve orgasm. In fact, BD/SM activities do not excite me enough to orgasm, by themselves. I play because it allows me to

(1) connect with others in an intimate way,
(2) help others experience pleasure through play and through the sensations I can evoke for them, and
(3) receive pleasure and attention from many partners other than my primary partner (who is my husband)"

What are your thoughts about the connection between pain and pleasure? Is pain something to be prevented at all costs, or something to relish in? Does some pain feel better than other pain?

Think about the popularity of tattoos, piercings, and other body modifications that may have a beautiful combination of pain with pleasure—both during (as the endorphins kick in) and afterwards (enjoying the body art in how it looks, feels, or is noticed).

But even if the example of body modification doesn't resonate with you, have you ever studied for hours and hours until you felt mentally worn out, just to get a good grade on a test? (Repeat uncountable times throughout your education.) Have you ever practiced so hard for a sporting competition or a performance until you were tired and sore?

You sought out activities that were not particularly pleasant because you wanted the pleasurable results (in these examples, a sense of accomplishment). You didn't blame your coach or teacher for causing your discomfort; on the contrary, you appreciated all the effort they put into your training.

Let's not forget hickeys, love-bites, and tickling!

Pain and pleasure are subjective qualities that vary between people. You can decide for yourself whether to explore pain for pleasure, pain to relieve chronic pain, or pain as a sensation to be avoided. You get to tune in to your own body and determine what feels good to you.

Kink and the Mind

"It's a mental rather than physical state that is more arousing."

There are people for whom the most important sex organ is between the ears, not the legs. Their sexuality is influenced more by mental stimulation than physical stimulation, and how they feel about someone or about the relationship can affect their ability to feel stimulated.

> "Not really BDSM, but D/s (Dominant/submissive) which means to us: not only pain but also mindplay etc."

> "To me it's about feeling incredibly wanted."

> "For me, having a 'Head Space' prior to physical activities is necessary for me to actually enjoy them. Being mentally in that place of existing as someone else's property, and being owned allows me to do anything they ask of me."

The mental stimulation can come from the element of Power Exchange (which typically refers to elements of authority and control being intentionally given to or received by each person).

> "Most of the benefit to any of these experiences comes in the form of mental stimulation. Power exchange requires thinking and creativity, which is very important for me sexually. The physical side of things is really just a manifestation of the mental side."

> "It is first off an exchange of power. For the purpose of the role one person is in control and the other submits. If it is at the dungeon it is just a scene that both agree to. If it is/becomes a relationship then outside of our kink activities both have equal say in daily living. It is really a give and take thing. This is very general because of the nature of any two persons. True that only one can be the leader, but leaders listen to opinions. My favorite way of saying it is: 'one hand washes the other.'"

> "You went into detail much more on physical forms of 'kink' and less in the psychological forms. for me, kink doesn't work (i don't become my submissive, happy self) unless there's a psychological transfer of power to my partner. the mental transition has to happen before or near the beginning of the physical for kink to be enjoyable for me."

Kink activities can create altered mental states. Some of the women describe a rush, release of chemicals in the body such as endorphins, and the sensation can feel like a floaty, infinite space. This experience is commonly referred to as headspace with many variations such as domspace, subspace, topspace, bottomspace, puppyspace, and littlespace.

Notice how these women describe the ways that kink makes them excited or relaxed, releases endorphins, diminishes awareness, and alters mental clarity, among other things.

> "Intensity of experience generates an altered state. Playing on this edge, exploring the altered state, very intimate and human. the final frontier!"

> "i love the thrill of it, the endorphins, the release, the submitting of ego and self."

> "All the activities that I partake in are about letting go of control. Once I let go, I am unaware of anything else happening around me, so if others are there, they are not in my consciousness."

> "Being the doer/instigator with willing participants gives me such a rush—I have permission to do the nasty fun things roiling in my mind. The more reaction I can stimulate, the higher I can fly."

> "My favorite sexual activities include getting tied up with my legs spread while my throat, pussy and ass get fucked. This always involves me taking so much pain that it sends me deep into that alternate reality where the pain stops hurting and I begin to float. I love to include being choked until I pass out (blood chokes, not air blocks), and then come to while still being fucked and/or beaten."

> "While I do have toys I prefer (either b/c of my skill with said object, or the response it usually elicits), such as single-tailed whips (snake whip, bullwhip, etc.), knives/claws, and breath play, the toys and methods, while fun, are just tools to accomplish an end. My favorite BDSM activity has less to do with a specific tool or methodology; more than anything what I enjoy is the 'high' in my partner that I am able to generate, often referred to as 'flying.' The look in their eyes, the way their body responds, the way they lose all sense of their surroundings and are enveloped in the endorphin and adrenaline rush that overcomes them; this is a HUGE turn-on for me."

Within these altered mental states, the experience can become contemplative and reflective.

> "It allows for time when your mind is able to let go of all the other things in your life."

> "I like how it takes me deep inside myself. I can be almost meditative."

Intense encounters influence our mental state and, ultimately, it's our mind that leads and guides our body through these emotional and sexual experiences.

If you are inclined, try this experiment: instead of initiating an emotional or sexual experience with physical foreplay, try mental foreplay. Set aside time for you to fantasize and plan what might be, who you might want to share this with, and what you hope to feel by doing something in a new or different way.

We think you will discover new aspects of yourself. And that should be a no-brainer!

Kink and Spirituality

> "My participation in BDSM culture has led me on a very intense personal journey of self-discovery that verges on the spiritualistic …"

What exactly is spirituality? This is one of those concepts that means different things to different people. So, we referenced the *Cambridge Dictionary* to find "Spiritual" listed as "relating to deep feelings and beliefs, especially religious beliefs" (*Cambridge Dictionary*, n.d.). Some women speak about how kink and sexuality are a part of their spiritual or religious practices including worship, rituals, ceremonies, and redemption.

> "I find my submission liberating, freeing, spiritually supreme."
>
> "Ritual (pagan sexuality) is an important part of my sexuality too."
>
> "Also, for me, kink is often a spiritual and religious practice (I am Wiccan), so I often set up situations of religious kink. In particular, I seek sexual submission to my Goddess, so some of my most common fantasies involve sexually engaging with other people because She wants me to."
>
> "This is who i am and how i operate, it is not always for pleasure, but more so for self-fulfillment. This life is a very spiritual one for me and is what makes me content and happy."
>
> "Sex Magic, when it happens, is really sacred and I've had visions as a result. It happens on occasion when everything lines up just right. Sometimes it doesn't involve hardcore, in fact more often than not … but when it happens I consider it a gift from the Goddess which makes the scenario far more profound and intimate."

> "Achieving the ultimate orgasm is as close to heaven, I feel, you can get. Discovering and exploring your body is essential to that."

> "... Spanking is redemptive for me. It is as if I am atoning for my sexual activities that involve bdsm. I pay the price of doing kinky things by being spanked. It is an arousing activity. It settles me down ... Also, my Dom is very aroused by giving His pain to me, which in turn pleases me."

Those last two examples may have been more metaphoric than literal, though we are not sure. When someone says that something is "close to heaven," do they mean it in the religious sense? Or, is it just a figure of speech?

And what do you think about the idea of spanking as a way of earning redemption and atonement? Do you think these are based on religious beliefs (such as the use of self-flagellation for discipline and purification purposes found in some religious contexts), or are these ideas that are tools for creating a scene?

Taking a step back, kink can be a connection to other parts of an individual, their practices, and worldviews. Kink can also be the method, practice, or ritual to access a set of beliefs and value systems.

Sometimes, it seems like the whole purpose of engaging in unconventional sensual, erotic, and sexual behavior—that is, kink—is to titillate the senses. But we see that kink also gives people the opportunity to connect to themselves in a deeper and more intimate manner, a way to find the happiness that is already inside them, an important expression of their spirit.

Were you surprised to learn that sex and kink can have such a profound purpose for some people? Is it hard to imagine incorporating religious dogma with sensual pleasure? Do the ways these women integrate spirituality in their lives and sex lives resonate with you? In all cases, what have you learned about yourself as you consider these ideas?

Kink and Community

> "I know we like to keep our lifestyle a bit mysterious and sinister, but I feel infinitely safer in a dungeon than I do in a vanilla bar! BDSM women are some of the most interesting people I have met anywhere, and they are frequently some of the most educated."

Let's talk about the kink community ... Well, for starters, there isn't one. Wait, what?

What we mean is that there is not ONE governing body of the kink community, but rather there are many organizations that, together, create a network of communities. These communities might be based on location, interest, or other commonalities. They bring together a group of people who have at least one thing in common: an interest in kink. These communities can involve open discussions, parties, social events, online interactions, and other activities and resources.

The two authors of this book have collectively attended community events in dozens of US cities and in a few countries outside of the United States. What do these events have in common? At these events, there is an opportunity for learning and teaching, with a focus on event participation. The people attending are remarkably creative, they enjoy a sense of sharing and belonging, and they manifest a sense of openness and exploration. Yet, each community and event is different in some ways—there are nuances in these differences, sometimes as subtle as the ambiance.

Some communities are very casual, such as a Kink BBQ on a Hawaiian island where everyone comes as they are—in shorts, tank tops, and sandals—and some are very high protocol, such as a D/s dinner event where each submissive receives specific training beforehand and the Masters and Mistresses are in black-tie attire.

Some events are based on certain preferences or fetishes. There are people who enjoy wearing latex and walking the red carpet at Fetish Weekends and there are people who enjoy wearing latex who take over a small hotel in a quaint Swiss village every year since the 1970s. There are munches, leather events, furry conventions, and masked balls. There are small group gatherings and large national and international events. There are contests, weekend retreats, camping trips, street fairs, and events catered to kink-industry professionals.

A local kink venue (known as a "dungeon") might host a weekly or monthly event where the only overt play involves spankings, and only spankings. Dungeons may host femme-dom nights, male-dom nights, women-only events, men-only events, gender-queer events, and pansexual events. There are themed events and crossover events (for example, blending swinger members with BDSM members). A dungeon might have events every day in the week or only once per year.

And, of course, there's the online community, a place where people can exchange ideas, learn about others and themselves, study new skills through educational videos, and most importantly, know that they're not the only ones with an interest in kink—all from the comfort of their own home or from the palm of their hand (mobile device). Many groups and events are based on location, interests, and other common features such as relationship styles, nationality, culture, religion, and philosophies.

At the time that this book's research was conducted in 2010, "more than 650,000 members of FetLife, an online social networking site serving participants in the kink community (http://fetlife.com retrieved 12/29/10) ... had more than 2,000 upcoming kink-related events announced and more than 22,000 groups available for those knowledgeable and curious about kink behaviors." (Rehor, 2011). Compare that to 2020 (the time of this book's writing), and the numbers have increased considerably. FetLife grew to have over 9.1 million members, 902,000 upcoming events, and 143,000 groups (FetLife, 2020).

The interest in and acceptance of kink continues to grow!

And there are many ways of getting involved in the kink community. Some people may attend one event per year, and others are involved in organizing community events, outreach, and educational programs on an ongoing basis.

There are regional similarities and differences in activities, rules, and culture of the communities.

> "... Also, it bears a mention, there is a huge difference in kink culture between where I came from *(Redacted)* [City A] and the Midwest where I am now. People here are much more closed, private, and much more like users rather than community members. In *(Redacted)* [City A] ... there are munches and play parties in every small to medium size city, and they are all linked by leader co-operation and members who regularly travel to the events around them. It therefore shocked me to find that *(Redacted)* [City B] has a very small munch and no play parties (other than small private ones for close friends)."

> "I have to say that I've found most of the people in the BDSM community (in the Midwest, anyway) to be some of the sanest, most welcoming, open-minded, and good-natured people I have ever met. I have been in many types of relationships (casual, formal) and find my relationships with those in the BDSM community to be the most satisfying (sexually and platonically) of my life; by contrast, my heterosexual/monogamous & 'vanilla' relationships have been fraught with control issues, abuse, untreated & unacknowledged mental illness, closed-mindedness, judgmental attitudes, deception, substance abuse/impulse control issues—the very aspects of dysfunctional relationships that those not of the BDSM orientation & outside of the BDSM community claim are inherently and unavoidably present in BDSM/poly relationships. I've also found women

to be much more respected, protected, and revered in the BDSM community than in society as a whole …"

As with all communities, there are areas of overlap with other groups.

"It is interesting to see how this lifestyle evolves over time, and especially how closely straight and glbti individuals associate."

"This community is not about swinging for sex. Many are monogamous to their partners. There is a lot of fun stuff to do in the community but because I am not a pain slut I don't get much of anything [but] TLC happening to me. I am here for the sensation play, emotional peaks and friendships. Sex is rare for some of us, like me."

A note about the idea of protection: throughout the book, the women use terms such as "under the protection of," "provide protection," "protect me," etc. Without further elaboration, "protection" could mean that the protector acts as a bodyguard, vets potential new playmates, monitors scenes to make sure they are not damaging, or something entirely different.

One benefit of participating in the community is the ability to learn from other people, which is helpful for those who want to grow their knowledge, improve their skills, practice techniques, and cultivate creativity within a particular area or craft.

"Learning new bondage techniques."

"To practice on someone familiar that was present (needle play)."

"Have participated in some activities (as indicated in responses), but still at a novice level. Need more experience (perhaps some training)."

"I performed my first cbt (cock and ball torture) after meeting at a munch and enjoy bondage & learned new knots to use, was very hot."

"I am a bisexual switch (take both the top and bottom roles) who has played and learned in the BDSM scene for 6 years. I am active in the leather community—do a lot of volunteering."

"I have entered a relationship with a Master and his slave. He wants to train his slave in bisexuality through me. (I am in a sub role then). The Master may use me as well. The deal is that I do not do any sexual things with Him, only with her, the slave. In return He teaches me more specific and difficult bondage tricks. It is a learning agreement."

> "I am a medical professional with a doctorate in my field. However, I've learned as much within the bdsm community as I have in my professional life. I believe that anything worth doing is worth doing exceptionally well. In that way BDSM is similar to anything else in life. There will be a bell curve and some will be better trained, better skilled, 'naturals,' while others fall in the middle and some fall on the incompetent/ignorant end of the curve. I consider it my job, as one that likely falls in the middle, to continue to study and learn from those with more experience/insight than I, while helping to guide those that are newer or less knowledgeable."

When we learn and gain new skills, we are able to teach others.

> "I have been active in the Lifestyle for 7 some years. My partner is my submissive and we live a 24/7 D/s lifestyle as well as are deeply involved in the community as a teacher, educator, event staff member and group leader."

> "I also teach various subjects on alternative sexuality at events around the country."

> "I like to teach women to squirt and recruit new women to being bi and being in the lifestyle. I have taught 100's of women to squirt."

Another important aspect of the kink community is socializing through attending events. Participating in an activity with people who share beliefs, ideas, and interests can be anything from a fun afternoon to a profound, life-altering experience. It can give us a sense of belonging and can create lifelong friendships.

> "I was on a Kinky Organization's float in the Gay Pride Parade."

> "I have only been in the scene about three years, I have found LOTS of wonderful people in the scene who have been kind, interesting, intelligent and FUN."

> "I have had mostly positive experiences, both privately and in public scenes."

> "All of my experiences at big events have been so wonderful! There is a strong sense of community and all of the people I've met are such good people. It's truly a wonderful lifestyle."

> "I would also like to note that I am very involved in the social and public aspects of the lifestyle including, but not limited to attending munches, socials, support groups, play parties, and conventions, and myself organizing socials, munches, and play parties."

> "I also helped co-run a local TNG group for a year and a half a few years ago. I do wonder if there are differences in the answers that you get based on how into the local scene people are as the more you are around things the more you see and may want to try … or even have the opportunity to try."

Meeting people and creating connections provide value in people's lives. For these women, having shared spaces to express various facets of themselves becomes one of the central elements of the kink community.

Many people note that attending an event and meeting other like-minded people creates a sense of acceptance and support and helps them to feel less alone.

> "… be with likeminded [people] who are informed and do not judge on your kink, hence not feeling like a freak."

> "I am relieved to have finally allowed myself to express this part of me. For so many years I kept my desires hidden from everyone thinking that there would never be a way to actually participate. Although stepping out into the community was very difficult, it has been one of the best decisions of my life. Thank goodness for the internet!"

These four individuals echo the role that community has in contributing to their acceptance of themselves.

> "I love bondage and blindfolds with someone I trust. not into humiliation. as a BBW, I've been put down enough in vanilla life. It took me years to feel sexy just the way I am, but now I love myself and the acceptance of the D/s community has helped me become self-confident …"

> "Don't knock it, until you try it. The stigma and stereotypes surrounding individuals in the kink community are still very prevalent. As a lesbian domme in the community, it's nice to be a part of a group of people who have great respect for the strength in women rather than pigeonholing people because of labels."

> "I am kind of new to this life and have found that in this community the people are there to support you in things you want to try and do not force you to try thing[s] you don't want to. I have found great friends and will probably keep trying things because I have found a safe place to do it."

> "Sometimes the emotional aftermath of such intense play sessions can be a bit hard to deal with. The things we enjoy in the kink community are mostly frowned on by society. The fact that we have been told from birth that these things are taboo and make you a 'bad person' can be a bit daunting after engaging in them. It's very important to have friends in the community that can help support you as well as have a partner that understands and is respectful of limits and experience level. Without proper support, there can be seriously dangerous psychological side effects of some of the things people participate in. There are healthy ways to enjoy and express sexuality regardless of the kink level."

And yet, some people may enjoy kink activities without an interest in participating in the community.

> "I am not very active in any kink subculture."

With any luck, we've confused you enough that you are pondering exactly what the kink community might be.

There are people who involve themselves in kink communities because it gives them a place to hide themselves and to reveal themselves, to learn and to teach, to be with those who are the same and with those who are different, to find comfort and to find stimulation, to organize events, and to casually engage.

The idea is that you find what you want, where you want, and how you want, and you surround yourself with people who understand that about you. Your kink community might just be your neighbor you share a glass of wine with as you discuss topics such as pre-colonial attitudes toward bilateral orchiectomy as a method to enhance a falsetto upper register in opera singers, or it might be the anonymity of participating in your town's Gay Pride parade with thousands of other community members.

If you haven't already attended a kink event, how do you imagine you would feel going to one? What kind of community are you drawn to? Are there types of events that have more interest to you? Would you enjoy a casual social event, a hands-on training course in a specific skill, or a big dress-up Fetish Ball?

What would you hope to see, learn, and do when attending an event within the community?

Of course, we are not encouraging or discouraging your involvement in any communities. We are merely alerting you to their existence and purpose, should you be curious.

Kink and Safety

> "I do these things in a safe manner and maintain my desire above all else."

Safety is important in almost everything we do. We lock the doors at night, double-check the oven to ensure it is turned off, and buy health insurance. The more physical the activity, the more safety becomes a concern. Bicyclists wear helmets, drivers wear seatbelts, and construction workers wear steel-toed shoes. And, consider all the protective gear worn by sports players, coupled with professional referees monitoring the game with medical experts readily available.

For many kink activities, safety measures are an important consideration. Numerous workshops in the kink community that are geared toward improving skills will discuss safety as a primary component in the training. For example, schooling in new rope bondage techniques should always include instruction on how to quickly get someone out of those knots (such as the use of safety scissors and quick-release knotting techniques).

A well-known motto used in the kink community is SSC—safe, sane, and consensual. According to urban legend, this acronym came from the American "Safe and Sane Fourth of July" fireworks campaign. The basic tenants of SSC are that all activities are considered "safe" or done with sufficient safety precautions, that everyone involved has the capacity to consent to the activities, and that everyone involved does in fact consent.

> "I have been involved in the lifestyle for 9 years and truly enjoy all I have learned. I also want to add that in all scenarios the most focused thing on my mind other than the responses I want to elicit is Safety. Very important for many reasons. I also as a Dominant REFUSE to take mind altering Anything. That includes alcohol, drugs, and I will not play if I am in Sleep deprivation. I do not want to break my toy."

> "For other people, just to take very much care, use the safe, sane and consensual thought process when choosing a play partner. Make sure you have a safe call in place when meeting new people, and make sure when playing, you have a safeword and that it will be honored, as best."
>
> "… All activities are always done using SSC guidelines (safe, sane, consensual). There are always boundaries that are set, that way things don't get to a point that is uncomfortable for either party. There's always a safe word (yellow is slow down, red is stop), and I only play with people who know what they're doing (how to safely hurt me without causing any harm or damage). And I'm never forced into doing anything, even when I'm submissive. It's all done with my permission and is done to me because I want it to be. I always know that with a word I can stop whatever is going on at any time …"
>
> "Everything we do is safe, completely consensual and we have a 'safe word' we can use to stop a scene or play at ANY time. If we're using gags, we have a tune we can hum to stop the scene …"

You might be wondering, what do they mean by "using a safe word"? A safe word is a word or phrase that is established by the participants ahead of time, with the idea that, if the safe word is said, the other players will check-in with that player in order to make necessary adjustments or stop the scene. The safe word typically isn't a word such as "stop!" because sometimes we want to be able to engage in a struggle using normal exclamations and expletives without actually stopping the scene. Rather, it's a word that normally would not be spoken during such an activity, like "banana," "platypus," or "supercalifragilisticexpialidocious!"

Safety is also mentioned as it pertains to sexual activities—including precautions for unwanted pregnancy and sexually transmitted diseases or infections (STD/STI).

> "Always ask for current STD test and use condoms … if no testing … and a multiple partner person won't take a chance."
>
> "My sexual exploits have always been consensual and condoms have always and will always be used with anyone who is not a long-term partner."
>
> "I only engage in the activities checked with consenting partners and always take precautions against pregnancy, STI's and other potential issues. I will play casually with almost anyone, but if sex is involved I

prefer to know my partner pretty well and/or be in a relationship with them."

"I may be monogamous but, in my last relationship, my girlfriend was not—she's polyamorous. We broke up not because she had a boyfriend (too) but because she and her boyfriend were not willing to practice safe(r) oral sex when attending their sex parties. Sexual safety is extremely important to me."

In addition to the idea of safe, sane, and consensual practices, another concept incorporated into the kink community is risk-aware consensual kink (RACK). Underlying RACK is the view that it is irresponsible and unrealistic to think that everything we do is 100% safe. Just like any other activity, it is important instead to be aware of potential risks and to do what is necessary to take appropriate precautions.

"I strictly abide by SSC and RACK principles and would never engage in any BDSM activity that I did not feel competent and skilled in. On multiple occasions, I have requested the supervision and mentoring of more experienced community members and have generally found those individuals to be very open to assisting and guiding me as I learn."

Sometimes, an awareness of the risk outweighs the desire to participate.

"just that auto asphyxiation is a heck of a risk, so I can't do this except as fantasy …"

RACK was created to acknowledge that no activity is without risk and, indeed, sometimes, bad things do happen.

"I really wish I had never allowed myself to be whipped. I could've used a safe word, but refused due to inexperience and fear of rejection."

"I have been physically hurt requiring emergency surgery because I was inexperienced and trusting. There are a ton of fake Doms out there preying on individuals who want to explore, but don't know the rules and true meaning of submission."

"I think that people coming into the scene are vulnerable to the myths of BDSM. [With] the community and its heightened sense of morals, communication and being open. No, people are people. There are those who use newbies who come into the community. [For example,] a Dom I

> know puts on newbie munches and bingo, within weeks he's 'protecting' said newbie [and] will [be] getting her to blow his cock in the dungeon but keeping her out of the hands of the 'predators' ... Cough ... [So,] keep your vanilla standards and expectations until someone has proven themselves worthy of your service and submission."

> "I have recently started playing with another dom which i've found surprisingly exciting. He compliments me perfectly when we're in a group situation and we don't need to talk to know what we want each other to do with our toys; however, it's made things challenging when we're with each other one on one. In fact, we've both managed to hurt each other on numerous occasions because there's no fear (when we let go) of hurting a submissive playmate since neither of us are submissive and we tend to fight back sometimes quite violently. This is leading me to believe that there's a good reason why subs and doms generally work with their polar opposites and don't end up with each other."

What does all this talk about safety mean? It's not that kink is inherently dangerous, but rather that the players and rules can be ad hoc and there is no authoritative body that regulates skillsets. Because the participants care about themselves, their friends and partners, and their kink activity, they put a high premium on safety.

A special note of caution: just because something is agreed upon by everyone participating in an activity does not make it ethical, moral, or legal. Please, for any activity you engage in, use your common sense. Ultimately, we must accept responsibility for our own safety and do our best to provide for the safety of others.

Kink and Consent

> "i wouldn't do those things to someone that didn't give consent."

On first blush, the concept of consent is simple to understand. But as we look at the complexities of humans and human culture, we will find that consent is difficult to universally define and that there are no simple answers.

The *Cambridge Dictionary* states that consent means "permission or agreement," "to agree to do something, or to allow someone to do something" (*Cambridge Dictionary*, n.d.). And, the National Coalition for Sexual Freedom (NCSF) differentiates kink from abuse by the idea that consent is "freely given" in kink activities, as opposed to abuse which is when actions to or with others are "without their informed and freely given consent" (NCSF, 1998).

But given the variation in cultural, social, and personal ideas about ways to convey agreement, how do we find a common understanding of knowing when permission is given freely?

When we feel compelled to act due to peer-pressure, have we freely consented? If we find intense sexual pleasure in surrendering power to another such that we find we cannot say "No" due to the impending orgasm, are we still freely consenting? If we agree to something after a sip of wine, are we freely consenting? How about after two glasses of wine? Ten glasses? We can probably all think of situations in which we did something we didn't want to do, but believed the alternative was worse. Was that freely-given consent?

Giving or declining consent is not always verbal and not always straightforward. There are cultures in which a person must be asked three times before consent is given; it is not that they are cajoled into acceptance; it is simply their custom. There are cultures in which a question is answered "Please" to mean "Yes" and "Thank you" to mean "No." There are cultures in which lingering eye contact grants approval and looking away signals refusal.

The best solution we can offer is that all parties must do their best to act in good faith, knowing that even a simple "Yes" or "No" might be only part of an answer. We must communicate. We must pay attention to body language, social circumstances, and personal differences.

Now that we've given you pause to wonder how consent is communicated and understood, let's look at how the women in our survey deal with consent in kink activities.

> "I would never do something at someone's request unless I fully wanted to as well."

> "All of my experiences have been positive, and in the context of either fully consensual single events or fully consensual monogamous relationships ..."

> "I want it known that most women I have met in BDSM own their sexuality and desires. Every BDSM act I have ever participated in was of my own free will and consent ..."

> "It's important, as a submissive, for those outside the lifestyle to realize that submissives and slaves—particularly female—are doing it for our own pleasure. It does not constitute as abuse—it is a consensual, desired behavior. Although many female subs/slaves have had some sexual

traumas, not all of us have gone through things like rape or incest. There are many of us who are 'well-adjusted' and psychologically sound with no trauma that still are drawn to service or being a bottom in some form. The stigma of female subs/slaves as being damaged psychologically, emotionally or formerly abused is frustrating and the stereotype that female sub/slaves are meek, overpowered doormats is highly inaccurate. Many of us are powerful and assertive in the vanilla world. Submitting is simply a desire, not a forced situation. I hope in the future that the vanilla world can understand the consensuality and commonality of this type of behavior for further acceptance. Being persecuted or looked down upon for sexual preferences is unfair and hurtful, as everyone is sexual and everyone has their tastes. There is no 'right' or 'wrong' sexuality—unfortunately the media and society seem to think so."

The ability to say "no," "not now," or "not any more" is an important part of giving consent. "Yes" today does not necessarily mean "Yes" forever; or even tomorrow, or two minutes from now.

Communication in any situation is always important.

"Often there is no formal requests among friends. We know or have an idea about what others would like and just initiate. If someone doesn't like that activity, or isn't into it at that time, they are expected to say so. Sometimes they are willing to try it anyway, or we do something completely different."

"Power exchange is consensual. So, if I do something at the request of a male partner it is REALLY still for my own personal pleasure. A Master or Dominant is given the power by the slave or sub. Said slave/sub can refuse or take back their own power at any time."

There are situations where there may not be overt conversations, but rather, implied expectations within the relationship.

"As someone that is owned, these are requirements, not requests."

"Under the order of my Master … it wasn't a request, there was no choice in the matter."

One way of ensuring that consent is given is through open and honest conversations where everyone involved can state their own wants, needs, boundaries, and hard-limits. Yet, as you can see from the above examples, the concept of consent can be more complicated than this. Sometimes, there are no overt conversations. Consent can be implied, can be for a specific amount of time, or can be part of a relationship agreement.

For many people, the idea of consent is essential to the sense of bodily autonomy and freedom. It is a topic worth exploring for each relationship, among partners, and for yourself.

How do you incorporate the element of consent in your relationships? Do you have open conversations? Do you use explicit or implicit language? What about non-verbal cues, tone of voice, facial expressions, and body language? Or is it a combination of these and other ways of communicating?

Conversely, are there situations in your life where you don't want your partner to ask your consent? How do you communicate to your partner that you consent to not wanting them to ask for your consent?

What other ways are the concepts of consent straightforward and what ways are they obscure?

Kink and Exhibitionism/Voyeurism

> "Just for the sake of exhibitionism/showing off and being a tease."

When you hear the word "exhibitionism," what image comes to your mind? Even in college-level Psychology textbooks, you may see a photo of a man wearing a long trench coat exposing his genitals to a shocked victim. And what about the word "voyeurism"? Does it conjure an image of someone peeking through your bedroom window?

The imagery in media makes for good (albeit creepy) movie plots. But, this is not what we are talking about here when we discuss exhibitionism and voyeurism. These are ideas and words that are used in the kink community and are not synonymous with clinical or criminal behaviors.

Don't believe us? Let's dig a little deeper.

The recognized authoritative guide to the diagnosis of mental disorders is a thick book titled *The Diagnostic and Statistical Manual of Mental Disorders* and abbreviated DSM-5. It states,

> The American Psychiatric Association (APA) classifies the condition of Exhibitionistic Disorder as a mental health illness that centers on a need to expose one's genitals to other people. The audience of this type of

behavior is usually unsuspecting strangers; the result is sexual satisfaction for the exhibitionist. (Alwaal et al., 2015)

So, let's clear the air. Our study and this book are not addressing any mental health illnesses. No one in our study said they had a "need" to expose their genitals. We can cross that concept of exhibitionism off the list.

When the women in our study use the word exhibitionism, they are referring to receiving sensual or erotic pleasure from being watched.

And, what about voyeurism? The DSM-5 states that "Voyeuristic Disorder brings sexual gratification on seeing other people perform private activities such as undressing, being naked and/or seeing people performing a sexual act." It also states that "Not everyone who has voyeuristic tendencies suffers from Voyeuristic Disorder" (APA, 2013).

However, here we are using the word "voyeurism" to describe any activity in which the participants receive sensual or erotic pleasure from watching or observing others.

A key element in both of our definitions is the idea of receiving sensual or erotic pleasure. The act of watching or being watched, in itself, is a neutral activity.

When we discuss exhibitionism or voyeurism with other people, we commonly get the response, "It's against the law."

We are not lawyers and cannot give legal advice, but we do have some knowledge of the matter.

If someone is exposing body parts as part of a political protest, that action in America might be protected by First Amendment rights. More importantly for our discussion, it's being done for political reasons and not for sexual or erotic pleasure, so it is not included in exhibitionism.

Sitting on your roof and using binoculars to watch a soccer game being played across the street is not illegal. However, looking through your neighbor's window might be. Legality comes into question with expectations of privacy.

Let us again stress: we are not lawyers and are not providing legal advice. We are simply pointing out that the act of watching or being watched is not in itself an illegal activity. If you have questions, please contact an attorney.

All right. Now that the definitions and legalities are out of the way, let's look at some examples and you can decide for yourself if they are exhibitionistic behaviors or voyeuristic behaviors.

- A woman attends an annual holiday party wearing a low-cut little black dress, stockings, and heels, and enjoys the attention of others.

- A man dressed in booty shorts and tank top lifts weights in an outdoor gym, his oiled muscles glistening in the sun, aware that a crowd frequently gathers to watch the powerlifters.
- A theatergoer admires the dancers as they move their bodies with grace and strength across the stage.
- A bar hopper on a night out walks slowly through a semi-lit room while wearing a black leather jacket, skinny jeans, and Doc Martens, hoping to see and be seen.

So, what do you think?

Remember the key element in our definitions is that if the activity is done "for your own sensual or erotic pleasure," then we have a match. Otherwise, it's just an activity. And only those watching or being watched can tell us if they are receiving sensual or erotic pleasure. Thus, for all these examples, the answer might be yes and it might be no.

Let's talk about our research.

When conducting our study about human sexual behavior, we researched a number of sources to acquire a comprehensive list of erotic and sexual activities. Two of the activities on the list were exhibitionism and voyeurism. In both cases, they were almost exclusively documented as clinical and criminal cases rather than as a normal and common activity. So, one of the questions included in the study asked, "Which of the following activities have you done (in front of unsuspecting people) for your own sensual or erotic pleasure?" and included behaviors that could be classified as exhibitionism, specifically showing bare breasts, showing genitals, acting out sexual fantasy/role play, being naked, and engaging in public sex.

What we found from our responses was that women do indeed get sensual or erotic enjoyment from being seen, noticed, watched, appreciated, and desired. More than half the women in this study had engaged in exhibitionism, and they enjoy far more types of these behaviors than the ones mentioned in the survey.[1]

The part of the question that got some people feeling squeamish was the caveat of "in front of unsuspecting people" (which was included to be in-line with the clinical definition of "exhibitionism" at the time of the study; see DSM-IV-TR, 2000). It seems that the concept of consent is such an important value within the kink community that some participants were upset that the survey even asked about doing these things in front of "unsuspecting people." Yet, many of the same people state that they do enjoy participating in these exhibitionistic behaviors in front of a supportive group of willing viewers.

Some people stress that their activities are never done in front of unsuspecting people or outside their kink community.

> "I have never participated in front of 'unsuspecting' people."

> "Again, don't involve the vanilla community."

> "Again, I don't blatantly impose on others my kink, who are not into kink. But the slight risks taken were primarily at the request of a male partner."

> "I don't involve unsuspecting people … It seems that too many questions referred to 'unsuspecting' people who were made part of scenes. If you're asking these questions of legitimate members of the leather/BDSM community, we don't involve people without their consent."

Yet the following women enjoy the thought of someone seeing them either naked or having sex in public spaces.

> "Just because I wanted to? walking naked in a high-rise apartment—blinds open, with lights on at night—SOMEONE might see or not—not aimed at anyone—but not hidden either."

> "Especially if said public sex is outside … and if someone starts watching …"

> "No other reason than I wanted to have sex and couldn't afford a room, plus I love to do it outside."

> "Master exposes me in his vehicle as we drive and has both pulled my skirt up to deliver a swat in a glass elevator and made me bend at the waist to pick something up for him when we are shopping … short skirt and no panties."

> "I like being seen by the group as powerful, and especially enjoyed the 'shock' value of flogging in front of a mostly non-BDSM mostly straight group."

Some women participate in kink activities in public with the intent of being discreet and not being caught.

> "Great care was taken to make sure that no minors were present. While it was in a public place, someone had to intentionally observe in order to see the activities."

> "My favorite kinks—most of which weren't listed—all involve public sex among people who want to watch and/or participate. I refuse to do these things among people who don't want to watch and/or in situations in which they are forbidden."

Perhaps the idea of consent is contained in the observer's ability to look away. For example, consent is explained here as having the ability to choose what to watch.

> "I'm finding the question about 'willingly observed' an interesting inquiry. I attend dungeon parties and events, and frequently observe role play or behavior that I find appalling. It's 'consensual' in that I've chosen to attend, but I will frequently quickly leave the room."

You can see that there are a multitude of ideas about exhibitionism. The circumstances of the event, the notions of propriety, and the motivation are as unique as the participants.

We are wired for social connection and we enjoy being observed when performing a fun activity. If that fun activity has a sensual or erotic content, what are ways of accommodating one's desire to be seen?

One solution is to attend events that have some controlled or limited access, such as invitation-only events or play parties, in order to be seen by people who would be appreciative.

> "To enjoy putting on a show at a play party."

> "I prefer public play with others in the lifestyle."

> "You asked about exposing one's body to unsuspecting people, but there's something to be said for exposure to others who are not participating in your scene but who are like-minded people."

> "I enjoy being watched by the crowd as I scene my submissives/bottoms. I like knowing that I can bring another person to a point nearly equal to a climax by my torturous ministrations."

> "You asked only about exposure to an unsuspecting public, but I enjoy exhibitionism at group parties, sex clubs, nude beaches and festivals where acting out is expected. The idea of accidentally getting caught is lost on me as the entire point is to be seen and to visually interact with willing observers."

While engaging in exhibitionism, it can be important for adults to be comfortable and surrounded by like-minded people who would enjoy watching them.

Let's encapsulate what we've discussed so far by looking at what other women say about exhibitionism as it relates to consent, eroticism, and acceptance.

> "OK ... what kinky female hasn't shown her breast to a trucker? :)"
>
> "Had sex in public, but without people noticing. The arousal came from the idea of being caught, not from shocking people."
>
> "How about an option for want to but have not yet had the courage to? Because I want to do public sex but I have not had a partner that has had the courage to do so."
>
> "I do not engage in any kinky sex play with my body or show genitals to anyone for my own pleasure, Only my partner and that is not in public. BDSM activities and sexual arousal/pleasure are not linked and never should be. Kinky sex is not the same as Lifestyle BDSM."
>
> "I do not engage in nonconsensual exhibitionism."
>
> "I am a balloon fetishist and a latex fetishist. I often wear latex in public (tastefully yet very fetish). I play a lot in public but always in an appropriate manner. I am stimulated in a variety of ways that I feel go beyond 'sensual' and 'erotic.' Isn't this stuff at the core of who we are and who we are developing ourselves to be? Your question only spoke of unsuspecting people. What about public displays in front of willing observers (on the next page? lol). I have participated in lots of scenarios where thousands of people were watching. I am very much an exhibitionist and I realized awhile back, that some of my motivation involved liberating myself from shame. I love sharing that energy!"

And this brings us to the flip side of being seen, and that is, to be the observer.

Based on the data from the survey, the majority (86%) of the participants enjoy "observing" various erotic activities for their own pleasure. People like to watch other people.

Since our survey included only women, we can categorically state that women like to watch people. So much for the myth that men are visual and women are not.

"Also go to the fetish circuit to play on equipment and watch others interact with each other."

"I am a bottom—who is a voyeur I love to watch—and member of *(Redacted)* [Sexuality-Related Organization] I can see a whole menu of things that I would never be interested in. I will watch—but that does not mean it gets me off. It just ends up proving that I was right to feel that way I did before I had all the knowledge about that kink. It does also afford me the opportunity to get more information on things that had only previously slightly interested me. I HATE snow and cold—but yet I love Ice play—go figure. I am afraid of electricity but I LOVE—***LOVE*** the violet wand on low—go figure. Mostly though it shows me the whole spectrum and I am able to narrow it down to what I really like and know why—before I try it—and if it goes ok—how to tweak it to go better next time …"

As with most of the activities we address in our survey, the women find their own individual level of comfort and enjoyment with exhibitionism and voyeurism.

We know that some people gain sensual or erotic gratification from being seen or noticed by others (whether it's nudity, sexual acts, or kink activities). And some people gain sensual or erotic gratification from watching other people in sexy scenarios. What is socially acceptable and legal will vary depending on regional and cultural differences. We're not condoning illegal behavior, and it's important to be familiar with legal regulations before participating in any behaviors that could have negative consequences.

From the women's responses, "consent" is a common topic of conversation, and, as we have discussed, "consent" is a difficult concept to define. Do we need consent for all kink activities? Remember that the most common kink activity done by the women in our survey is kissing. Do we really need to worry about who sees us kissing? If so, what does that say about the human body and sexual expression? If not, then who decides where the line is drawn as to which kink activities need consent for public display and which do not?

Is "unsuspecting" synonymous with "non-consenting"? If so, why?

It is surely easier to discuss consent when it comes to touch—we desire bodily autonomy and want to be able to choose when and how our bodies are touched. But, what about being shown something? If we are able to look away but we choose to continue to watch, does that choice imply consent?

As more food for thought, we have additional categories of "exhibitionistic behaviors" that women reported in the fill-in answers, and some of our women expanded on the forms of erotica that they enjoy.[2]

Remember that this book is meant to be a starting point for your imagination. It is a travel guide showing you where others have already ventured so you can better understand the world and yourself.

What do you think? Which of these exhibitionistic and voyeuristic behaviors have you engaged in? Which of them would you like to try if the situation allowed? Or, are there some of these behaviors that are hard-limits for you?

And, we remind you that there are no right or wrong answers.

Kink and Role Play

> "I love abduction scenarios, I think it's fun to be 'forced' and 'kidnapped,' though if it were an actual rape you can be sure I would be upset and furious. Consensual Nonconsent, I believe is the term, and it's rather freeing. Besides, when you trust someone enough to let them do such things to you, it only deepens the relationship!"

We all have fantasies. They are a benefit of having a complex mind that allows us to mentally play-out scenarios that can't be or shouldn't be.

The internet allows us to explore some fantasies safely and, if desired, anonymously. We can explore the beach of a tropical island via a webcam. We can fight in battles and help save a simulated world. We can virtually travel to foreign lands and interact erotically with other like-minded travelers or their avatars.

Many people enjoy a more hands-on fantasy experience. They work with their partners to construct a hypothetical situation, then see where that adventure takes them. The experience is called "role play," and is used to bridge the gap between imagining a fantasy and living the actual experience.

In the kink community, role play is a popular activity, and our survey listed ten common role-play scenarios to see how many women participated. Almost 90% of the women role played, with the top four scenarios being Master/slave fantasy, danger fantasy, jobs/occupation play, and animal play.

We also asked the women to tell us any other role-play activities they participate in, and which role-play scenario is their favorite; from these questions, our participants came up with 188 additional categories.[3]

That number surprised us. But, since no one had, until our survey, researched kink and role play to this extent, we could not have anticipated there would be so many additional scenarios. And if you keep in mind that these 188 additional role-play scenario categories were from only about 950 of the participants, you can appreciate how much more information might be discovered if we could survey the other billions of people on our planet!

In addition to specific activities, some role-play scenarios are set up with a distinct outcome in mind, as shown by the following "anything that" statements.

> "anything that has me controlling the sub, using CBT."
>
> "anything that involves me being handled like a pro."
>
> "anything that lets me be completely submissive."
>
> "anything that requires me to say 'yes Sir' and beg for more."

The quotations we include in this chapter are selected to provide a range of examples of role play. We do not include much analysis because, after all, they are just fantasies. However, we encourage you to contemplate each role-play experience for its creativity and execution and consider if you would enjoy such a scenario.

Another aspect to pay attention to is role play being used as a catalyst. If you've ever been in theater, "What's my motivation?" is a question every performer considers before walking on stage. Instead of just jumping straight into a flogging scene, having a reason for the flogging can add to the fun.

Role playing allows these players to extend their Master/slave relationship in new directions.

> "As far as living it as close to 24/7 as possible, Master/slave is my preference. It requires significant commitment, trust, respect, communication, and remains difficult to do well for many people. If you are asking for a 'scene' or 'one-off' situation, I prefer teacher/student as it allows for continued learning, training, and maintains the D/s structure."
>
> "Master/slave role play is my favorite, because technically i am always a slave to Master, but i enjoy when W/we get into an intense scene, where He takes FULL control of me and lets His extremely Dominant side show. Usually in everyday life He lets me have a lot of freedom, so i enjoy when he kinda snatches reality out from under me and puts me in my place."

Playing provides the opportunity for these women to find the extra comfort, security, and kindness that they sometimes crave.

> "i am Daddy's slave/baby girl. We don't do age regression, rather it's a matter of letting him take over all control of me and being allowed to be the child within that needs to be held and cuddled sometimes. He takes care of me emotionally and nurtures me."

> "Age play is my favorite type of role play because I enjoy the comfort and care that my top provides for me in that role. It's a natural extension of his personality, so it isn't confined to the bed room but in everyday life since he enjoys being watchful of me while happily giving me my own space to be me."

> "I tend to enjoy being a pet. Not necessarily going as far as not using words or actually pretending to be a specific animal, but I enjoy taking on some of the characteristics of that animal. For instance, being able to curl up in my owner's lap, having him care for me and pet me, these are all very relaxing things for me. They help me let my guard down and are ways I like to show affection."

Role playing with situations not available in everyday life is an experience these women love.

> "I love play/scenes where there is an element of fear for me. I enjoy the mix of feeling scared and perfectly safe at the same time. I love where I can play the role of victim. I generally never experience these feelings/sensations in real life, so to play with them in the roll of fantasy and play with my long-term partner is deeply erotic and a huge turn on for me."

> "I only play with other butch women like myself. My fav is when my Top is called Sir and I am Her boi as in a submissive to her. In reality I am a couple of years older than she is. I love it! I participate in Daddy/princess style of BDSM in which, while we don't necessarily participate in age play regularly, my Daddy is my protector and guardian and I am his little princess, even as an adult. My favorite scenarios include morphing that a little into age play where I am younger and bratty/slutty and must be prevented from going out with my 'boyfriends' because Daddy is jealous."

Playing allows these women to explore circumstances they may not want in real life.

"I do enjoy playing out as various cats, wild and domestic. Otherwise, sometimes I really need specific kinds of psychological degradation to get my fix in, but it isn't exactly role play, since both I and the top are just being ourselves, but he or she is saying things that they do not truly mean or believe about me."

"Rape. I love watching rape scenes in movies, like *Clockwork Orange*. I love doing them in real life (with partners I am already sexually intimate with). I arranged for a partner to break into my house and grab me out of the shower and then 'rape' me. Of course, it was consensual rape. i don't know why i'm fascinated. but i crave to be completely violated and made to feel really dirty."

"abduction. how hot is that! I fantasize I'd be walking along, wearing a white blouse, tight business skirt, stockings and heels, and pass by an alley. Of course, I don't really want a stranger abducting me, but having my husband do it, and pretend he's a dangerous stranger, throw me in his car, bound in the backseat drive me to some deserted barn to have his way with me in the hay … what a husband!!"

We remind you that role play is ingrained in our society in many ways. Job applicants may role play to prepare for interviews. Businesses train employees for customer service positions using role play. Students learning foreign languages practice talking about imaginary situations. Schools have fire drills, soldiers have war games, ER nurses rehearse life-saving techniques.

And some people create imaginary scenarios for fun and adventure. Role play provides a time and space to be anyone or anything you want to be. What if you have a domineering boss? Wouldn't you like to be the one to give the orders every once in a while, or, perhaps your partner can give you the praise you deserve? Role play can be an extension of your natural personality, or it can be the complete opposite of how you usually are.

Role play need not include exotic situations nor provide dramatic insight. It can simply be wearing high heels when you cook a meal, or, "at the restaurant, I'll order instead of you." It can be a visit to a local Renaissance Faire and assuming temporary identities or speaking with a foreign accent and acting as that character.

We've shared women's quotations and introduced ideas. We encourage you to role play what it might be like to live out a fantasy of your own.

Kink and Fetish

> "A man's arms/shoulders/chest if well-muscled and defined can have me orgasming at will. And a gorgeous eyes and smile can make me melt into a submissive puddle."

"Fetish" is an odd word. In common usage, the *Cambridge Dictionary* defines a fetish as "an activity or object that you are so interested in that you spend an unreasonable amount of time thinking about it or doing it" (*Cambridge Dictionary*, n.d.).

In science fantasy novels and some religions, a fetish is an object believed to have a spirit or magical powers. There is, of course, a clinical definition which you can find in the DSM-5 (APA, 2013) if you are so inclined.

But when we talk about fetishes in this book, we are referring to someone's personal preferences and turn-ons for things such as objects, situations, attitudes, and body parts.

Since the word "fetish" has so many meanings, and sometimes carries a negative connotation, we did not ask our participants, "What is your fetish?" but rather the following two prompts.

- "Are you sexually aroused by any of the following? (including clothing, fabrics, uniforms, specific body parts, body fluids, and other (please specify))"
- "If you answered yes to any of the categories in the previous question, please specify what kind of clothing, fabric, uniforms etc. are sexually arousing to you."

We found that 75% of our women (that's 1,192 out of 1,580 participants) are sexually aroused by various objects, situations, attitudes, and body parts, i.e., they have fetishes.[4] More than 1,000 open-ended responses to the two prompts above provided additional details about fetishes.

Like role play, fetishes can be a mechanism for eroticism. It can be a signal to oneself or to others for flirting, play, arousal, or sex.

> "Tight fitting clothing. I don't think it is a specific type of clothing, just sometimes [someone] I know and see often looks really 'oomph' just really good that day and it makes me more flirty towards them."

> "Leather, sexy revealing clothing, the kind that does not imply desire, but demands it."

"… Also, seeing my Master in certain outfits triggers the knowledge that He is preparing for a scene, thus arouses me."

"I love variety. Anything from Lady Gaga to actual military gear, the clothing gives me an outlet through which I can experiment with different identities, sexual scenarios and possibilities. That arouses me. The possibility for play that the clothing or fetish gear suggest and inspire."

"I don't have any out and out 'fetishes' for any of these things, in the sense that I do not need any of them to be aroused, nor do they necessarily enhance my arousal. But they do serve as a kind of more obvious signal of someone's openness to play or being sexual and their use or wear is something I use myself to signal that I'm looking for experiences."

Wearing certain clothing may affect how these women feel about themselves.

"Wearing any type of lingerie for my male partner arouses me, makes me feel more feminine … there are too many sexy body parts to even begin to list which ones turn me on the most. Almost all of the human form is arousing in some way."

"Clothing depends on my mood to some degree … if it's something i'm wearing, it would be something soft and sensual feeling that makes me feel attractive and sexy …"

"I love the look of clothing as well as a costume makes me feel like whatever I dressed for. I love my breasts and breasts in general and love when what I [am] wearing displays those for my and others pleasure, knowing the men and some women want them …"

"I love corsets, heels, leather skirts, and vinyl tops. I love the way they make me feel sexy, like I'm the most beautiful girl in the world. I love that my partner's eyes light up when I wear them. I love the feel of his hands as he runs them over my body enjoying the way the fabric/vinyl clings to my body. I love the curves of a woman's breasts, it's beautiful and sexy. I love feeling a hard penis push against my body."

And sometimes the fetish is more about who the experience is with.

"Dress ups of any sort when associated with my beloved … and bits of her showing seductively."

"Being dominated by a man (my DOM) is what arouses me the most. All the things He does, says to me and the things He makes me do."

"… If it was something he is wearing, it just needs to look good on him and fit well. i love to see Daddy in his suit and tie, but i feel equally aroused when he's in his sleep pants and robe. Fabrics would be the same thing … soft, sensual feeling, silks, satin (not sheets), fleece, really any fabric that holds his scent and body heat. i love his eyes and smile, his hair or the curve of his ear, neck, and jaw … his entire body really."

"I also have a client who is a professional Santa Claus. He visits me just before Christmas every year, in his complete Santa outfit. He tells me about the trials and frustrations of listening to children all day and how adolescents and young women irritate him at times. He asks about my year, wanting detailed information about what I've been doing in my work. He demands a deep-throat blow job and then gives me a hell of a spanking, followed by performing anal sex on me. It's a very hot and kinky little scene. I look forward to it!"

"I have a black see-through negligee that feels wonderful against my body and almost always gives my husband an instant erection. The bodice of the garment has holes for my nipples, and he will suck and rub them to get me warmed up. I rarely remove the negligee when it is time for sex; rather, we open it up, and he has free access to my body. He has one of those silk thongs which accentuates the size of his penis, especially when he becomes erect. Sometimes I will masturbate him through it, and sometimes I will suck him through it until we are ready for coitus."

We asked our participants to expand on the categories provided (including clothing, fabric, uniforms, etc.). The following are some of their detailed responses, including new categories of fetishism provided by the women in the survey.

Clothing:

"i love things on women that complement their figures. i love things on men that fit well (tailored). I love curves and i love someone with a good fashion sense. Uniforms generally are well cut :)"

"Lingerie—something form fitting that accentuates the attributes my partner enjoys most. I find a man's shoulders, neck, and back to be sexy as hell and there is something about a man in a suit that I find amazingly sexy. I imagine disrobing him one piece at a time."

"I'm sexually aroused by very masculine and/or dominant pieces of clothing. Like a well-dressed man in a suit, someone wearing mostly black/dark colors, and if he's wearing a strong black belt with a silver buckle, that's always a turn on. Basically, if he looks how I like to picture a 'Dominant male,' I get turned on."

"It's not just the clothing, but the combination of the clothing and the shape of the person inside it. There are plenty of divers, but once or twice I've seen someone in a wetsuit who looks particularly attractive. Same went for someone who was wearing motorcycle clothing—but again, she was just one of a number of people. I guess the commonalities are: 1) The fabric is clothing a shapely and otherwise-attractive individual 2) The fabric is tightly-fitting 3) The fabric is at least somewhat shiny—leather, rubber, etc. … This is probably not so much a requirement as something which enhances the effect …"

"I have a huge fetish for male formal wear—I particularly groove on three-piece suits worn with suspenders. For uniforms, I love the Naval dress whites and the Marine Corps dress blues. I have yet to come across an article or mode of dress for women that works the same way for me as those do. However, it should be noted that the suspenders don't work if just anyone is wearing them. They're an added kick, not an attractor in and of themselves. Three-piece suits, particularly of a conservative cut, work on anyone, as do the aforementioned military uniforms."

Uniforms:

"Men and women in uniforms are a powerful fetish … not the uniform itself, but what the uniform represents and how the uniform accents the wearer. Additionally, the uniform's fabric can play a part in the sexual arousal."

"I love a man in uniform. I think it has to do with their dominant look …"

"Mostly school uniforms, though the very idea of uniforms has a kind of sensual appeal to me. A normal piece of clothing can take on an erotic personality just be being designated as a uniform."

"I LOVE taking a military man against his will … big strong men in uniform submitting to me makes me wet!"

"… I am aroused by just about every type of uniform there is—policeman, fireman, doctor … I have had several erotic occasions with a fireman at the fire station on a firetruck—so the sound of a siren makes me very aroused. I also have had several events with a policeman that involved the use of hand cuffs and this is extremely erotic for me."

"I like women in some kinds of lingerie and or corsets. I'm a sucker for military uniforms. Particularly women in uniform. *swoon* It's the person wearing it rather than the article of clothing itself—I would not, for instance, want to masturbate with an article of clothing like that. I'm not clear if you're asking about e.g. someone who would collect panties, or shoe fetishists."

"I like a man in uniform, but I think that comes from being an army brat. There was something solid and demanding about a man in army fatigues or dress. Perhaps it's the idea that a man can kill me with his bare hands, twisted perhaps but honest. Corsets are restrictive yes, but they also take grace, balance, and poise to wear, similar to high heels with higher lifts. There is a strength in that submission I find arousing."

Body Parts:

"Large testicles, I love them, they are great for clothes pins but i love to kick them."

"I love penises."

"… As for body parts, even though I am mostly hetero, I like the look of girls naked better than boys. Penises are soooo much fun but not all that attractive. Testicles are just plain gross looking. Sorry guys."

"… There is something erotic about a naked body, both male and female. i love my own body, relish even in the lines and curves of my form. i love what it can do to others, arousing them, both men and women. i love the male form, in its strong lines, and the firm muscles. i love how a big man makes me feel so petite and fragile. The human body is the ultimate art form. and i love art."

Personality Traits:

"I do like a proud submissive attitude in a sub, I don't like doormats."

"I like strong Dominant women in almost anything they are wearing. I like masculinity in women."

"… WIT. If you're clever and we mesh well and you can keep me in puns, that does more than most other things. Demonstrating compassion, not like 'oooh look at me I'm a sensitive chap!' but the little signs of habitually caring for others (e.g. 'Oh, you don't have any allergies or dietary restrictions, do you?' or 'can't make it that night—it's my shift at the phone bank')."

BDSM Related:

"… I love to see the back of a woman's shoulders, especially if she's wearing that kind of shirt or bra that goes up the middle of the back showing off the shoulders, even a backless dress (for the femmes) … this drives me wild, cuz I just want to pat or flog those shoulders! … Oh, of course I LOVE Leather boots … very much a boot fetishist … wearing 'em and having 'em worshipped, and seeing them on others …"

"… I like broad shoulders on a man and round hips on a woman. I'm a sucker for pretty blue eyes and I'm aroused by blood WHEN I HAVE DRAWN IT. Wounds caused by anything else bring out the caregiver and I want to mend them."

"I love stockings, socks and shoes, corsets and uniforms, blood and cum. Kinksters are able to fetishise most things and it is difficult for me to put into words the feeling that I get when I see my own blood drying on my skin, or feel the constraint of a corset around my waist. It isn't just something that I can portray in a sentence or two. Seeing someone cry because I have changed their world with pain and pleasure isn't something that can easily be described."

"The power or submission expressed in a corset. The sexiness of boots or heels. The sexiness of lingerie. The slickness of rubber, the smell of leather, the power of a uniform. The scent, feel, and sight of blood. The round curve of a belly."

"… I'm not a uniform person, don't really wear them, but when I see a Dom in a police Uniform looking all official I just want to admit to a crime I did not commit … I love eyes. It tells me a lot. Not really sexually arousing to me, but when allowed eye contact gazing into a Doms eyes whom you trust, who is making you fly and can see that, whom you have turned yourself entirely over to. It's astounding, mind boggling reaction to surrender willfully. The end result is unlike [any] other."

Leather:

> "Leather is just erotic, the feel, the smell, it is just orgasmic …"

> "… I love leather because it reminds of whips, floggers, etc."

> "Love wearing corsets (love feeling beautiful, but I don't really get off on it). Love the smell and feel of leather (this has gotten me off) and admire a well-built man in a uniform (but what semi-hetero sub woman hasn't gotten a tingle from a drill sergeant?)."

> "… The smell of leather is incredible, I love when the boot blacks condition my leathers as I wear them. Feeling the tight latex on me is another, but more for sensation. Swimming in full latex is like nothing else …"

> "I love sexy shoes, leather boots, the smell and sound of leather. I once took a trip to Southern California and there (unbeknown to me) was a leather shop in the mall. As I walked past the store, the smells were somehow wafted into the main walkway and without warning or intention, I nearly had an orgasm as I walked into the cloud of leather scent. I know I visibly shuddered, felt embarrassed, and hoped no one noticed, as I walked away. I never knew the scent of leather had such an effect on me until that moment. That being said, I own no leather garments and aside from the times my partner flogs me, leather isn't generally a part of our play or lifestyle but it is enjoyed when it does cross my path."

What a list! Looking back on our definition of fetish and what has been shared by these women, we can see many variations of personal preferences and turn-ons. It appears that no two people have the exact same erotic disposition.

Even among women from the kink community, there are many opinions about what are, and who has, fetishes.

> "I think fetishes are for men only. I rarely if ever meet women with fetishes like this."

> "No, my fetishes are more about ideas (submission, etc.) than about objects."

> "I'm not aroused by any of the following in themselves as a fetish item. For me they simply can enhance the experience but are not necessary."

> "All of the above and none of the above. It depends on the mind inside the body."

"Just about everything *could* be sexually arousing in the right scenario, if you're open to it …"

"It is more about the relationship than it is about the 'surface.' In the right relationship, almost anything can be sexually arousing, but without the relationship that same thing could be almost repulsive."

"These days I'm very much into latex and heels, but I'm constantly surprised by the things I find shockingly arousing. You don't pick your fetish; your fetish picks you. Anyone who thinks they have any kind of control over this type of arousal has never really had a genuine fetish, in my opinion. *The Matrix* trilogy are the hottest movies I have EVER seen and I am continually amazed they are PG-13 or whatever. Sigh. I'm just wired differently, what can I say? Ditto that *Stigmata* movie with Patricia Arquette."

Someone may have one single fetish or a wide variety of preferences and turn-ons. Some fetishes are enhancements to eroticism, some are triggers to receptivity, and some are associated with sexual memories. Some people are fixated on their fetish for arousal, some require their fetish for fulfillment, some enjoy fetishes as embellishments to their lives, and some don't like fetishes at all. And it's all part of the umbrella of human sexual expressions.

It's all good!

What were your thoughts as you read about these women's fetishes? Did you think, "Yummy," "Yikes!", or "I don't get it"?

Here are ideas for you to consider.

If you are familiar with animal husbandry or have unneutered pets, you are well aware that a female in estrus is irresistible to males of the same species. The males are genetically predisposed to respond to the female's pheromones.

A female bird will be attracted to a male bird that sings in a particular way. If she is correct in associating the male's singing with strong reproductive qualities, her offspring will inherit her wily knack of finding mates; if not, then those genes will not be passed on. And if she is attracted to the sound of a cow mooing, she is going to be one lonely bird.

So how the heck did humans end up predisposed to being sexually aroused by so many non-sexual objects, situations, and attitudes? Think about uniforms: even if you conjecture that attraction to someone in uniform is due to the idea that soldiers are a survival mechanism, currently, more than 99.5% of our population are NOT soldiers, and they are reproducing just fine. And we are pretty sure that nylons and high heels were not around in prehistoric times.

If sexuality was only about reproduction, then all humans would have a predisposition to be aroused at opportunities to procreate only. However, as we already know, sexuality is much more complex than that of baby-making. Sexuality has social, relational, and inspirational purposes. Eroticism and passion can cultivate creativity.

Like we said, these are ideas for you to consider.

Can you remember the first time you felt erotically turned-on? What prompted that response? Is that situation or type of person or object still sexually arousing to you?

Has your idea about fetishes expanded after reading the variety of ways these women incorporate objects, situations, attitudes, and body parts into their erotic lives?

Do you consider your turn-ons a fetish? If so, is it a single item or a combination of elements?

Reading this section, maybe you have found that special something that finally makes sense for you, the final piece of the puzzle, and maybe you get to rethink what lights your fire.

Kink and Money

> "I never did anything for money that I didn't want to do which is why I lasted so long in the business."

We have explored ideas about kink as an enhancement to sexuality, a way to help to deal with pain, to expand one's mind, and to experience spirituality, among other aspects. Now we will look at the notion that some of these people also participate in kink activities for money.

This should not come as a surprise to you. Everyone must earn a living, including those who specialize in kink.

Passions, careers, and personal lives can intermingle. On the one hand, you wouldn't be shocked to learn that a professional chef loves preparing delightful meals when at home. On the other hand, when a surgeon leaves the office, she's done for the day.

Even when careers intermingle with personal lives, we have the capacity to separate the two. A professional soccer player does not demand the same level of play when coaching her daughter's fourth-grade soccer team.

We expect that people have at least some interest in their job. Waiters working their way through college probably enjoy interacting with people and appreciate customer's gratitude for their service. And actually, it's even a bit unsettling to hear someone say, "I hate my job."

We should expect nothing different from a kink professional.

You are probably wondering, "A professional what?" In our survey, the following occupations were described: fetish model, bondage model, professional dominatrix/pro-domme/professional dominant/professional domina, professional submissive, sex worker, prostitute, massage parlor worker, worker in a strip club that had sex acts, burlesque dancer, burlesque theatre manager, phone sex operator/adult phone sex service, making/selling videos, owner of adult websites, pornography actress, and webcam model.

And, we can add an additional occupation from our own experience: authors of a book about kink.

Let's look in more depth at how these professionals describe their occupations.

"... I am a pro Domme, yet I take this stuff very seriously! I could never have a vocation that was not my passion. I believe in this work. It is a much-needed service ..."

"I am a fetish model. That is why I get paid to do some of that stuff."

"For Money is for making videos for sale, I am in the business."

"I sometime[s] get paid for sex, I give workshops on sex and sexuality, I'm in a wheelchair and I do have more play partners, I've been into BDSM since I was 16."

"I am beginning a career as a professional dominatrix. At the moment, most of my experience has been online. I have had some experience with real time play with friends, as well as at dungeon parties, but not for pay."

"I'd also be open to doing some of this sort of stuff for money, so long as genitalia touching isn't allowed."

"i also worked as a stripper and while that isn't technically prostitution i was paid by men for masturbation and lap dances, even a few blow jobs in the VIP room."

"... As a sex worker, I draw a sharp divide between activities in one place and another, where money is involved, friends, so on. I find it very very difficult to experience sexual pleasure with someone and not get attached to them rather deeply, but if money has been exchanged, it's like flipping a switch where my love for them is on a timer. It's real and genuine, but it also ends when I get back in my car and fades into a simple fondness …"

Many people in the world enjoy their job, so why wouldn't that apply here? Well, it does! Some kink professionals state that they also enjoy kink activities in their personal lives.

"I do fetish modeling for money but also enjoy it and like taking and sharing sexy pictures."

"I do this for both fun and for money, i work for an adult phone sex service for money right now."

"Introduced into BDSM while stripping and found I LOVED IT! I am a Switch. Pro Domme over ten years ago. Profession does not allow me to do certain things I would like or enjoy on a personal level …"

There is a balance between work and play in any profession, and that distinction seems very clear for these women.

"I'm in a BDSM relationship and work as a Pro Domme."

"I am paid for BDSM activities, but only as a top, I am a lifestyle submissive, but I am a professional dominatrix."

"While I am completely kinky, and love to play, the reason I answered 'For Money' is because I am a Professional Dominatrix, and my last 20 or so play sessions have been with clients. It's been a couple weeks since I had a personal play experience with a non-client."

"As a Pro-Domme when doing customers, I am switched off from my emotions, so I do not feel the kicks or reactions I would normally get from playing with someone of my choice. It was my decision to play like this thus keeping the distance totally professional. I am a hard player and have many years of experience, so can safely play extremely. But will not allow myself to become emotionally involved. I have non-paying slaves that I own as well as my 24/7 partner/slave, but if they fall in Love with me then it is game over. I also keep an emotional distance from them. I have a big problem with Dominant Males, and will avoid them at all costs. If approached at a party or munch I will say hello but keep a safe distance not wishing any further contact or friendship real life. males are for Dominating, not the other way around, I do not trust a single Dominant, macho male."

"I need to make it clear that I am a professional Dominant. I am fully clothed 100% of the time in my sessions. my clients pay me for my skills and for our time together. I never strip, nor is there any sexual exchange. My clients are only heterosexual or bisexual males or couples. Women, FtM and the overall queer community are part of my personal life and the rules there are completely different but no money is ever exchanged."

"i am a pro-sub, so i do some activities with my clients that i don't usually do with my partner(s), and vice versa. foot worship and humiliation are not part of my personal repertoire, but my professional one. by the same token, golden showers, age play, and sexual service are things i only do with my husband."

Some of our respondents clarify that they no longer are kink professionals but that they once had a career in kink that has come to an end (for various reasons).

"I have been professional in the past and paid for services, but that was over a few years ago now."

"I have worked as a professional Mistress for three years. That was ten years ago. It was fun!"

"I was previously a Professional dominatrix, but now retired."

"I was a professional dominant so it was at the behest of my female clients."

"I've lived in *(Redacted)* [City] since 1968, been a sex worker from 1968 to 2005 (prostitute, massage parlor worker, burlesque dancer, burlesque theatre manager, phone sex operator, professional domina) ... I only stopped pro-domme work because of health issues."

And yet, some people are of the opinion that kink and money do not mix.

"I have worked with several bondage photographers and some of my pictures have been published in photography albums. I never took any money. I did it for sheer fun. I feel proud, when I see those pictures today."

"I have a very very full kinky AND vanilla life. I travel a good deal in the name of BDSM. I run outreach and education groups regarding BDSM. I know folks from many states, some I am pleased to know and others I am simply gracious with but don't feel I have much in common with. This said, I do not know ANYONE who has paid for sex/play/services, nor have they been paid. The truest and best defenders of bdsm in the world I know would NEVER agree to this. There is a clear and distinct line that separates those who do this for the pure sake of personal enjoyment, and those who engage in activities for financial gain. The two are … thank goodness … most often worlds apart."

Getting paid to provide kink skills and services is like any other job: it takes time and energy to build it, sustain it, and be successful. Does "financial gain" negate someone's "personal enjoyment"? As with many occupations, sometimes it does—having the pressure to perform in order to pay the bills can detract from the enjoyment of the activity. Yet, hopefully, the interest and passion that leads someone to a profession can continue even with the added ingredient of making a living at it.

Ultimately, each individual will have to find their own line between personal enjoyment and work.

What does this mean to you? What are your reactions when reading about these women's jobs?

Are there any quotations that resonate with you negatively? If so, let's try an experiment. Pretend that our survey was about surfing and the title of this section was "Surfing and Money." Go back to quotations you found unsettling and substitute "surfing" for the kink references. Do you still have the same reaction?

Consider what you do as an unpaid specialist. Perhaps you are a coach, a gardener, a blogger, a cyclist, or a quilt maker. If someone offered to pay you for your skill, would you accept their offer, or would you feel your specialty would be sullied?

Are there any of the above quotations that affect you positively or that you identified with? Do you have any special skills or services that you could market? How would you feel about your passion if it was also a source of financial profit?

What Does This Mean?

In this chapter, we discuss women's thoughts concerning kink and sex, pain, the mind, spirituality, community, safety, consent, exhibitionism, voyeurism, role play, fetishes, and money. You might be wondering why we selected these particular topics to talk about.

Well, we didn't. The women in our survey did. Remember that we asked them to tell us anything they want, and this is what they want to tell us.

How does this apply to you and your life, dreams, hopes, and ambitions? What does this mean for your relationships with your friends, your partners, and your spouses?

It is a place of beginning, of inspection and analysis. Maybe it is a conversation starter, a way to discuss things that might be. Or perhaps it is a quizzical diversion from your interesting and happy life.

At the very least, we expect you have learned more about life and the possibilities that exist in the crazy and wonderful world we have created for ourselves, and we hope you use that knowledge to shape a happier and more fulfilling life for yourself and for those you cherish.

Perhaps the most important idea we hope you learned from this chapter is that there are no right and no wrong answers. Kink is about sex and kink is not about sex. Consent is mandatory and consent is hard to define. Kink is spiritual and meditative and it's also about pain. No one should ever be paid for kink services and being paid for professional services assists the community. Safety is vital and risks should be assessed.

You might have been delighted by some of the activities described and you might have been distressed by them. That's pretty normal. We are supposed to decide what we like and what we don't like.

And it's also normal to have fantasies about things that can never be, even those you might find distasteful in real life. We know people who say they would love to be a professional football player, but they would never take on the grueling training program; it's just a fun fantasy. If you had something like a holodeck from Star Trek and could do anything you wanted with no consequences, what kind of fun and adventure would you conjure for yourself? Can you discuss those ideas with your partners and friends as a starting point and see where they lead? Because maybe just imagining the endless possibilities would still be fun.

Notes

1 A detailed list of additional exhibitionistic behaviors is in Appendix C.
2 A detailed list of additional forms of erotica is in Appendix D.
3 A detailed list of additional role-play scenarios is in Appendix E.
4 A detailed list of additional and favorite fetishes is in Appendix F.

Engagement with Kink 3

"I am a well-educated, single mom. I am active in my church and community. I'm considered by most people to be compassionate, on-task, and a problem solver. No one has any idea what I'm like in the bedroom!"

As you read our book, you are discovering that women do not fit any standardized or Hollywood notion of kink. Many women are not involved in kink aspects of pleasure and pain, and some women are more interested in the social aspect of the community than in any particular activity. And you now understand that there is so much diversity in the way people think about kink as it relates to a variety of topics.

The same holds true when examining the depth of involvement in kink activities and lifestyle, and in how kink integrates into people's lives. Each person's engagement with kink is unique, covering a broad spectrum including enjoying kink as a fantasy, being new to kink, participating in kink activities only in private, participating in kink activities without identifying as kinky, asserting that kink is an element or a core component of their identity, and treating kink as a casual indulgence.

We learn that some of the women in our study have recollections of kink from early childhood or adolescence, and that others discover this aspect of themselves later in life. Involvement with kink waxes and wanes as needs and desires change. The time, place, and intensity of engagement in kink are as varied as the women themselves.

For the sake of discussion, we are grouping engagement with kink into a number of loose categories. Join us as we explore these ideas in more detail.

Kink as (Mostly) Fantasy

> "To date, my interests have been much more in my head than things that I've done in real life."

We humans possess a wondrous gift of imagination. Our minds can take us to far-away lands where we meet interesting people, explore enchanting places, and experience fabulous sensations. Erotic fantasies can be anything, from silly and whimsical, to goal-oriented, to dark and forbidden. There is nothing wrong with any aspect of a fantasy—we don't need to pass judgment on whether it is "good" or "bad." The important part is knowing whether something should or should not be acted on. Meaning, unless you're ready to retire, maybe you shouldn't tell your boss what you really think.

For a variety of reasons, some fantasies should stay as fantasies. Here are examples of people who enjoy the excitement of their imagination without an intention to pursue the reality.

> "I have had many student/teacher fantasies, but because they typically involve a specific professor and that would be unethical and immoral on his part (the whole [fact of him] being my professor thing and he has a wife and children). I have not tried to act this fantasy out with him or a surrogate."

> "I would consider myself lightly kinky, though there are many things I have thought about but not yet done (or that I may never want to do in practice) …"

> "My favorite role play fantasy, which I have never done with another person is Daddy/little girl where Daddy gently but firmly initiates his daughter into the pleasures of sex. The taboo makes it really hot, but also, I think that the fantasy heals the wounds of a nasty introduction to sexuality at the hands of people who didn't care and the abandonment by my father figure at an early age leaving me in the custody of an abusive woman. I don't condone incest in any form, it's just an archetype my spirit has chosen to meet the needs of my damaged inner child. That's my best guess anyway!"

> "I am generally dominant but I have 1 very submissive fantasy. In my 'vanilla' day job, I am a social work supervisor for the state government. There is a very attractive male co-worker who though is not under my direct supervision, is a subordinate as he is just a social worker and I am

a supervisor. I have this fantasy that he will come into my office. I am wearing a really hot business suit and heels and he bends me over my desk, ties my wrists to the post on my desk, lifts up my skirt, pulls my panties down and starts having sex with me, spanking (not too hard nor too lightly) my ass as he is fucking me, lightly pulling my hair and caressing my neck."

The following people indicate that they haven't acted on their fantasies because they haven't had the opportunity to do so (yet?).

"I wish there was a way to indicate on this survey the things I am interested in doing, but have not yet had the opportunity to do so."

"A lot of those things are fantasies, but have not had the chance to act them out."

"I have engaged in mild self-bondage, and in that context have used clothespins *on myself*. However, I have not gotten that far with others. I am interested in trying several of the above behaviors, but need a partner to try them with—and I seem to be of a monogamistic temperament. I suspect (without having read any of the research) that there would be neural changes akin to the desire caused by having tried certain drugs. I don't want to end up craving kink but being (again) with a vanilla partner—and for me, the desire for a long-term partner is more important."

Fantasy can be a place where we delve into needs and wants that are longing to be fulfilled. Fantasies are a safe way to explore our desires without constraints of societal norms or even laws of physics.

If you take a moment to think about your favorite fantasies, are there similarities among them? Does a theme arise? Do you notice any patterns?

Perhaps you will discover something about yourself when you allow for exploration of your own fantasies.

New to Kink

"Always have had a curiosity and now come to the point in my life where I wish to move into the experience part of BDSM."

Popular media portrays people involved with kink as being experienced and knowledgeable, with an insider's grasp of the complex nuances of their arcane world. In the real world, there's a range of ability; everyone starts somewhere and acquires knowledge at their own rate.

> "Thus far, my experiences have been mostly vanilla. I am very interested in branching out into more bdsm, starting as a sub (I'm a switch). Am now investigating my options."

> "... I'm pretty inexperienced overall, but would like to indulge a little bit more."

> "While my actively engaging in these activities is only within the last two years, the desire to do so has been in me a lot longer."

The next group of women have only recently put these ideas into action and consider themselves new to kink.

> "Still new to BDSM, and only to spice up our love life."

> "I'm still in the early learning stages of BDSM, so my experience is extremely limited."

> "i am a relative newcomer to this lifestyle; it has only been a year since i discovered my submissive nature."

> "I am new [to] the BDSM lifestyle. I have an amazing Mistress that is guiding me. If I were to answer this survey in 6 months the answers may be completely different."

> "... I have one Dom and that is Sir and he has his slave whom he is married to and me realtime ... He is my second Ds relationship and i have been involved in bdsm for 12 months, but spent 4 years reaching this stage. My hubby knows about my bdsm activities and is supportive of me, and has met Sir ..."

This section is brief, but important. When you decide to act on your dreams and desires, there are those first tentative, difficult changes that upset your routine and promote introspection. Transitions can be quick or can take years. There is no formula; we each find our own path.

If you are just beginning to explore this side of you, now you know that you are not alone.

Spend a moment to remember the times when you began a new phase in your life. Perhaps you joined a book club or a travel club; maybe you started playing golf or took dance lessons. Did it become a life-long passion, or did you lose interest after a short while? Did you find new friends, or did you never quite fit in? What did you learn about yourself from these experiences? If you decide to venture into the world of kink, what lessons can you take with you to ensure a happy adventure?

Kink as Private

> "BDSM in the bedroom."

Some people are regular patrons at restaurants because they enjoy being attended to by professional waiters. They may appreciate the opportunity to get dressed up and be noticed by other people and the chance of interacting with someone new. They may also like the convenience of having someone else cook for them, without the obligation to clean the kitchen afterward.

Other people do not frequent restaurants, finding that the noisy, exposed tables do not provide the intimate ambiance they seek. They would prefer to share the experience of creating and enjoying a meal in the comfort of their own home, without anyone else knowing what they ate, how they cooked it, or having anyone watch them eat it.

We use this example to show that people might make decisions about dining out based on personal preferences that have nothing to do with the restaurant's menu.

In the same way, people make choices about keeping their kink activities private that might have nothing to do with privacy itself. We may not know the ultimate reason they seek privacy, only that they do and that they feel it was worth telling us.

For some people, kink activities are best enjoyed in the privacy of their home. They do not want to meet other people, to join a community, to go to a dungeon, or even to attend a munch. Kink is something only done between them and their partner and they prefer not to share these experiences with outside people.

> "I'm in a BDSM relationship which concentrates solely in the bedroom meaning no 24/7."

> "It's a great thing to do but I don't want it to rule my life. My private life should never mix with my public life."

> "Our kink occurs almost exclusively in the bedroom. I consider me a bottom and him a top. I have found myself over the past year or so doing

things just because he asked me to. Before BDSM came into our lives, I would have argued and probably not agreed to do these things, but now our relationship dynamic has changed so I will do things just because he asks me to."

"… I have several friends in the local kink community and hope to soon be brave enough to go to a social event or munch with them! :)"

"I tend to prefer to do my bdsm activities behind closed doors, although I enjoy the energy of a play party, I have only actually played at a party a few times since I've been involved in the local scenes (about 10 years)."

There are many aspects of our lives we keep confidential for personal, social, or professional reasons, and kink activities, for some people, are included in that discretion.

"I have a boyfriend that does not know this side of me."

"It is private, it is not something trashy to be shared with everyone. It is not a joke. It is a serious lifetime commitment just like any other relationship."

"… I've never been to an in-person 'kink community' event, like a munch or fair or party, and am a bit leery about going to one—from what I can gather online, it seems like a lot of those have the expectation that if you show up you will play at least a bit, and that doesn't sound like much fun to me. Anonymously or pseudonymously online? Sure! In person? Sorry, but I might run into you while getting my groceries and that's a bit more private/public overlap than I'm comfortable with."

"I am a Master's degreed, professional, Caucasian female, and I enjoy my sexuality—however I do tend towards a more conservative side when interacting with those I do not know to be accepting of my lifestyle."

"… while I do not advertise that I participate in a BDSM lifestyle, I do not deny it. If someone I know asks me a question, I do not shy away from my truth. It is not a secret what I enjoy. I just know that there is a time and a place to properly express it."

Which of these quotations did you agree with, and which did you find strange? Where do you draw the line between your personal and private life? Are there parts of your life you never share with anyone? How about with only your doctor, or your best friend? Are there aspects of other people's lives that you'd prefer that they keep to themselves?

We are not advocating any change to your ideas about privacy. We are instead inviting you to consider why and where you have set your boundaries around privacy to learn more about yourself and how you choose to experience your life.

Remember, keeping something private doesn't have to be a guilty secret—unless, of course, doing so is titillating for you!

I'm Not Kinky!

> "I don't really identify as kinky, but I guess I am in some limited way."

Just because you go grocery shopping every week does not (necessarily) mean you describe yourself as a "shopper" to your friends. You shop and you enjoy it, but in no way would you consider shopping to be a core value or identity. One does not necessarily internalize an identity based on their desires or activities, or, to put it less clinically, "what you do" is not always "who you are."

This section looks at those women who are involved in kink activities, yet do not identify with kink as an aspect of their relationship or themselves.

> "I am a pathetically straight, monogamous, vanilla girl joyfully corrupted by my professional polyamorous pansexual DaddyDom."

> "I find BDSM is a facet of my life and relationship but doesn't define it. I am a girlfriend first and a submissive secondary."

> "I don't feel as though I'm remotely kinky but I've found that many of the things I enjoy are described as such, so I accept that I must be. A rose by any other name, etc. I feel perfectly normal and open minded. Quite conservative in fact. It just seems that a lot of people are narrow minded, uptight and infatuated with knowing about and controlling other people's sexual habits. However, I accept that I'm not. This also seems to be the way I feel about myself generally but I have a cousin who is a Psychologist and she tells me that I'm a bit extreme compared with most people. For example, I scuba dive and find it relaxing and have parachuted and love it. Perhaps there's a correlation there. Also, I grew up swinging on chains in my father's engineering workshop, used ropes in scouts (I'm a Queen's Scout), am familiar with neoprene suits from scuba diving and used to

volunteer for a helicopter rescue outfit, so I've jumped from a helicopter into the sea in training a few times. None of those things seem anything but normal to me, not sexually exciting at all."

We included this short section to reassure our readers. You might feel good about the kink activities you enjoy and at the same time, the label doesn't suit you. You might even cringe at the notion of calling yourself kinky (or any other label pertaining to these desires). That's okay; we are not presuming to apply labels to anyone or anything except as it helps us to understand and learn. Enjoy what you do and be who you are. As we said at the beginning of this section, what you do is not necessarily who you are, and we leave it for you to decide for yourself and about yourself.

Kink is beyond Novelty

"My master/slave relationship is for more than sexual, it is part of our lifestyle."

Up until this point in the chapter, people have referred to kink generally in terms of fantasies, role plays, just a bit of fun ... and for some people, that is all it is or ever will be. However, for others, kink helps define who they are as individuals or how they structure their relationships. The range is wide, from kink being one element of a complex series of a person's characteristics to kink being a substantial part of their lifestyle.

"I was a collared kajira (slave) for two years, so the slave role is a little less fantasy for me, and a little more real life. I'm not that anymore. As I'm coming into my own, I switch with most play partners. I sub/slave for my primary."

"... My sexual lifestyle is a part of who I am and not a role I play or an action that I am doing. It is more comprehensive and complicated than that ..."

"It's not a lifestyle, it's a sexual series of likes, dislikes, and choices. Lifestyle generally refers to the 24/7 TPE people."

"I've done a lot of sexual acts & activities over the years. My sexual POV has also changed/evolved over the years—from submissive to Dominant; from overtly sexual to celibate by choice ..."

> "... After years of my adult life spent not feeling totally fulfilled by previous sexual relationships (regardless of orgasm), our leathersex Daddi/boi relationship to us feels like we are both able to express our true selves in our relationship. It is a much deeper connection than we have had previously in non-kinked relationships and a deeper connection than other kinked relationships without that Daddi/boi element, and has taken a number of years to develop fully into a relationship that feels to me (us) totally natural and fulfilling both mentally and sexually."

In the section of the survey that asks about various forms of role play, many respondents clarify that the activities and relationships they participate in are important elements of themselves, and that they are not "playing" a role.

> "I don't 'role play' per se ... I've been a 24/7 slave for 16 years, so it [is] more of just my normal daily life :)"

> "I am serious about this. I find it a tad bit offensive when people just treat Master/slave bdsm as a hobby or a bit of fun."

> "I am a submissive woman/little girl. It's not really role play, it's who I am. However, if picking a favorite role that would definitely be the one."

> "That it's incredibly offensive to determine that the Master/slave relationship dynamic is a 'fantasy' or 'role play.' I teach in adult sexuality/kink classes and it is such a difficulty to have to show people that these are real people in real lifestyles. There are deep, meaningful connections and reasons for doing this. Are you going to call homosexuality a 'fantasy'? What about transgendered people? Tell them they're 'role playing'?"

> "I am not a fan of any role play. I might be strange in this, but what I like about BDSM ... mostly D/s ... is that I can be myself, be accepted for who i am, what i like, and the secret part of myself most people don't know. Authenticity is integral to the experience for me. If I had to choose ... boss/secretary would be my choice, however it would really work for me best if it was a real boss and I was a real secretary."

From those who start to identify kink as a part of who they are, to those who specify that it's not "just a role play," these women show how kink becomes more important to their character, sense of self, and relationships.

As a clarification, it's necessary to point out that the same activity can be both a fantasy and an identity. In the same way that a medical doctor and registered nurse can also role play a Doctor/Nurse fantasy, a Master and slave can fantasize about their relationship and engage in Master/slave role play.

What have you internalized? What words do you use to describe yourself, something that, if taken away, would change who you are? For what activities or knowledge do you call yourself an aficionado?

Ask your loved ones about themselves and what words they use to describe their character, sense of self, and relationships. Listen and consider what they say; perhaps you'll better understand why you love them as you do.

Self-Identity Includes Kink

> "It's who I am."

Some of the women in our study express that kink is satisfying for them in ways that nothing else can be. Kink is described as both mentally and physically fulfilling, helping to "make sense" of life, or feeling balanced. Kink is an integral part of these women's lives and a key component of their core identity, and without the ability to express their kink identities, they may feel incomplete.

> "Many people in the community and outside the community look towards a lifestyler's past to figure out why they enjoy these activities. i had a perfectly 'normal' childhood with no abuse of any kind and yet i am drawn to this lifestyle because being submissive comes naturally to me and because i am simply a masochist. there was nothing traumatic in my life that brought me to where i am today."

> "It is my life, part of me, it is who I am. I am a Mistress—Not requested by someone. I am this person all of the time, I need to hide parts of me from regular society."

> "As i mentioned, this is about who i am not what i do. For me, my life is about being with a man to serve as he wishes and loving him, living life as he lays it out for me as my protector and guide. i am a highly intelligent woman, and i have passions and things that drive me, so this is not about anything less than that. i have never been abused, sexually or otherwise, this is simply what makes my life make sense."

> "My sexual discovery has been a long journey and I don't intend for it to stop anytime soon. BDSM in particular has not only helped me develop as a sexual being but as a human. I don't get to be weak or fragile in my

everyday life. I do not feel powerless or helpless. I do not get to feel lesser. It just doesn't happen. Only in the confines of submission, in giving up the choice to defend my physical safety, do I find that emotional and sexual spark that comes with vulnerability. On the reverse side, I am somewhat a sadist. I enjoy inflicting pain on other consenting adults. Without the BDSM scene and activities it would not be possible. My sexuality allows me to be a whole and complete person. It creates balance and stability in my life."

For these women, being involved in kink goes well beyond the activities they enjoy; kink becomes an essence of how they see themselves, an expression of who they are as a person. It's like someone who goes from dancing occasionally for fun and fitness to the person who says, "I am a dancer."

Take note in the following section where "I am a …" or "I identify as …" is often a prelude to the woman's identifying word or phrase.

Dominant/sadist:

"I identify as Domme."

"Dominatrix."

"I am a sadist because I enjoy it and my partners consent and get off on it."

"I am sadistic and giggle when a masochist enjoys being hurt."

Switch:

"I am a switch, currently in more of a top mode."

"I am a switch who is submissive in my D/s relationships with men but I enjoy topping women."

"I'm a switch—mistress to one man, my secondary partner, and slave to another, my husband. (Note: I hate the word slave for its appropriation of historical and contemporary oppression, but it's the most accurate term as used by the community for my relationship.)"

Submissive/masochist:

"I really am an adult/little girl. While I do take care of adult responsibilities and I certainly do not let my little out when I am with people that don't understand, it is a great joy in my life to have this and some of the other outlets."

"I identify first as a masochist and second as a submissive. My involvement with BDSM related activities started as a result of my wanting to explore pain as pleasure and the simple act of submission. It has simply become a part of my life, now. My sexuality, though viewed as abnormal by many, feels completely normal and common to me."

"… In general, I participate b/c I am a submissive (in the same way one is straight or gay, I've known and engaged in such activity since puberty at 11 years of age). As a sub, fulfilling the request of my partner (which has been M, F, and TS on differing occasions) pleases them, which is pleasing for me …"

"i am a submissive, down to my very core … and i have no doubt what i will become with the right One. i'm also an old-fashioned kinky girl … whereas … i am monogamous … One Master/one sub … and straight … i am not into this 'poly' business … and i'm not bisexual or bicurious … maybe that's why it has been difficult to find the right One. A great many in this lifestyle are just in it for the kicks … great kinky sex … they have no idea what this lifestyle is truly about. It used to be … before the internet … that you had to meet the right people … train … learn … now, with the internet … anyone can get in the 'club' … including those that are not true to themselves … or anyone else … they just want to play."

Exhibitionist:

"I am an exhibitionist."

"To fulfill a fantasy, and because I'm an exhibitionist."

"i am very much of an exhibitionist, but i don't have a lot of opportunity to act on those desires."

Intersections of identities:

"I'm a queer dyke boi switch with an amazing partner."

"I consider myself a Top leather poly dyke."

"i am a slave, a bit of a brat, kitsune, sometimes a babygirl, though not in terms of ageplay. Usually in terms of taking innocent pleasure out of experiences. i am learning more about myself every day. :) "

"i am service oriented. Next i am a masochist. Then comes my high sex drive and i also enjoy topping willing victims and using the skills Master has taught me. i do not think many folks only fit in one section of the box, but tend to flow and ebb across many of them."

Lifestyle:

"My lifestyle is very focused around being a boi and D/s. I am a butch who likes other butches as well."

"Age play was part of our 24/7 lives, so it felt normal to me to continue it on the subway as we traveled around town, although we did, of course, try to tone it down. Plus, it was *(Redacted)* [City], so I wasn't too worried about shocking anyone. :)"

"I identify myself as a lifestyle Domme … and enjoy the company of 2 wonderful subs … and always keep an eye out for more."

"It's our way of life we both like, but we don't really have the need to public play except in our club."

Acknowledging the importance of kink in their identities helps these women realize that they are fulfilled only in relationships that are aligned with their kinky selves.

"I would Never even consider dating someone who is not kinky. Sex is a dime a dozen. If I am not being fulfilled in my kink (the pain and/or the service), I will not waste my time."

"Too old now to pretend to be anything else besides who I am regarding the BDSM Lifestyle. I have dated 'straight lesbian women' and sure the sex is good, but it lacks the fire that makes an LTR …"

"I am enjoying how free it feels to be totally open about what I want and need with a partner. There is a level of honesty in my M/s relationship that never existed in my vanilla ones due to the fact that communication is really key to playing in a way that makes us all happy."

"I only go out with bi guys anymore. I ask pretty early when I'm interested in a guy if he's ever entertained the idea of being with another guy. Sometimes I'll present it as a precondition to getting with me."

"I find that it creates a stronger connection (and does so more quickly) than my vanilla relationships. Since embracing my submissive and masochistic sides, I find that I am more centered, more self-confident, and more outgoing. I have tried kinky/vanilla relationships since and have come to the realization that I will not be content unless there is an aspect of D/s present. It has not diminished my desire for the more romantic and emotional types of sex in the least. I simply must see my partner as a Dominant male."

"There is a freedom in the Scene that i can't find anywhere else. All past relationships outside the scene have failed because of the lack of play and the lack of understanding. i am a sub, i don't like having the control in the relationship, i enjoy making my partner happy by doing as he wants. In non-Scene relationships, it gets difficult, because the man doesn't really understand where i'm coming from, and it didn't help that i was unsure of how to tell him just what i needed."

"I identified as a lesbian until recently, now identify as queer. I have only recently started playing with men, and now being open to sexual relationships with men. I am finding I am more open to individuals, chemistry being the criteria, do not want to be put in a category by anyone. I want my freedom to see who I want when I want without being bound to one person. Could not have a vanilla relationship. Need to have freedom to play with others. I have different levels of relationships with different people …"

And sometimes, being connected with the kink community and living authentically is as important as staying in a marriage.

"BDSM is something my husband does, but it is something I AM. This nearly broke us up a couple of years ago. It is important enough to me that I would have walked away from my marriage before I walked away from the community and my participation in it. For me, it wasn't a choice between my husband and some other man, it was a choice between my husband and being true to myself. But, we do not live the lifestyle 24/7. In many ways, we are a typical couple. I am content, now, with my life, and don't feel a need to live the lifestyle 24/7, but it is also not something I will or can ever give up."

For the women whose quotations we included in this section, kink is an integral, inseparable part of who they are. Take a moment to review some of the quotations above and ask yourself what beliefs you have that could be expressed in the same way as "because it is my identity and fulfils me."

And if you are feeling particularly introspective, consider why you have such passion for your beliefs, how that passion has influenced your life's choices, and what you have learned about the world and about yourself due to those passions and how you express them.

Some of the responses might seem harsh or uncomfortable to you. "I would Never even consider dating someone who is not kinky," might seem unkind, but if you substitute "involved in similar political interests" or "from the same religious background" for "kinky," perhaps you can better understand that woman's passion.

Kink over Time

> "… Also, what you test on today may be different two years from now. Sexuality is fluid, and those of us who participate in the scene on a regular basis have to continue exploring in order to satisfy our sexual urges, so they continue escalating to be more taboo."

Our relationship with our own kink is personal and unique. Some people recognize their desires for kink in childhood, while others discover them later in life. The specifics of those desires can change and evolve: roles can reverse, preferences may broaden or become more focused, situations and relationships can vary, and simply aging can require modifications. Along with all of this change is the opportunity to acknowledge certain things about yourself—from "I've always known" to "How did I not know until now?" to "I can't believe I used to find that fun," and everything in between.

So, we start with these women who recognize that the discovery of kink goes way back to some of their earliest memories.

> "Just that I've known I craved being spanked & had fantasies as early as I can remember (3–4 years old), way before I knew what sexuality is. Also, that in my real life, I'm an aggressive, dominant woman LOL."

> "My desire for being bound and being taken down has been with me since a child. I would get aroused when watching cartoons where the female is tied. My first recollection was with Olive Oyl being tied in Popeye cartoons."

> "I'm a switch, which means I'm dominant sometimes and submissive sometimes. I'm also bisexual. I've been bi and into kink as far back as I

can remember, even fantasizing about kink and same-sex related activities while masturbating when I was young."

"I fantasized about being tied up and fondled by a line of strangers before I understood what sex was (like age 5 or 6). I have literally always been kinky. Since I have become an adult, my parents have actually discovered their own kinks and become involved in the kink scene, but they definitely were NOT kinky when i was growing up and did not influence me to become that way (We've discussed it)."

"I've always had fantasies of kidnapping, imprisonment, being owned and used by a male for sexual pleasure. These fantasies began around age 7 or so and childhood games often included those themes as well, without my prodding or bringing it up. I'm a strong-willed woman and often hold positions of decision making outside of the home, but in my home, I like my husband to be in charge, most especially in regards to sex."

"I started realizing I was into D/s when I was about 12 yo. I have been exploring my sexuality ever since."

Other women share how kink has been an aspect of their personal development throughout their life.

"I have known I was kinky since I was 16 (I am currently 34) when I was given my first pair of handcuffs by a boyfriend. I have known I was submissive since I was 21 and figured out what the term was and I have been involve[d] online in the community starting around 20 and offline starting around 24 …"

"As I get older and older, I feel more and more comfortable exploring various sexual activities. Part because of experience, but mostly because I feel more confident and secure in exploring these things and consider them to be on the spectrum of sex but not freaky. I definitely have more of an open mind."

"At the point where I am at, having withdrawn temporarily from the kink lifestyle but now just returning to it afresh, there are things I now know that I would like to try but which I have not yet done. I am more focused in a certain sense, and more able to head forward. I have many fantasies that I now acknowledge and try out with others."

> "I would like to say that once we began engaging in more 'rough sex,' then the more the BDSM components began to emerge. We've begun to engage in more intense play patterns during our interactions. If we were able to see each other more often I believe things would have gone much much further than they have at this moment."

For many responses in this study, the word "evolving" is used to describe how exploring the world of kink is filled with change, growth, and insight. How someone feels about a certain activity, characteristic, or idea can change in both small and significant ways over time, due to personal changes and choices and to outside influences.

> "i have slowed down my activities in the past 3 years due to having 2 children, tho i & partner still have [a] fulfilling lifestyle …"

> "When I get a little older I have every intention of becoming a 'cougar.'"

> "I have a wide array of interests and they all are related to my mood. If I'm in the mood for my submissive male to be my little girl, then that's my favorite at the time. If it's that I feel the mood to tie him up and flog him, then that's my favorite. All the things I do are totally dependent on my mood."

> "As I get older I feel that many things take too much energy, and the economy and increased work load to get by has really put a damper on my lifestyle. I am not as active as I once was. My primary partner is also vanilla, so that is an impediment to getting my kink needs met …"

There is no ideal age to uncover a propensity for kink. Some of our women explained that they hadn't realized these desires until "later" in life.

> "i did not discover this lifestyle until i was 54, until then i hated sex and had been celibate for 18 years."

> "Late bloomer. Didn't get into the BDSM lifestyle until age 49. I enjoy being nude in the dungeon/play party setting. I enjoy watching a good scene."

> "An interesting side note might be to find out the differences from before entering the lifestyle to how it was afterwards. Before, I was in a monogamous relationship for 31 years that did not include sex for the last 8 years due to [the] health of my partner. Our sex life was pretty 'standard.' Since

learning about the lifestyle and experimenting, my sexual experiences have grown by leaps and bounds!"

"Recognized that I would never truly be happy in vanilla relationship at age 53!!! Although it was something I had known deep down inside my whole life. And something that had tried to surface many times before. And had surfaced before, only to be pushed back down. This final recognition of my true nature and my decision to express it brought about the end of a 12-year marriage. And I was supporting my husband the whole time!! LOL And he STILL left me for being kinky. And he was totally unwilling to participate. Thought that story was worth telling as I am quite the late bloomer, but no longer ashamed anymore. Good luck with your work … I think research on sexuality is important."

You might have noticed that the topic "kink over time" included many quotations. Numerous women in our survey recognize and acknowledge that their involvement with and attitudes toward kink change as they change. Kink is not a destination, but a journey, as are many aspects of our lives. Desires change, friends change, relationships change, what you want in your 20s might not be what you want in your 60s. These women accept and embrace these changes, even when the changes take them places they never imagined.

There is a saying, written in various forms, that goes like this: when the student is ready, the teacher appears. It's never too early or too late to begin or continue learning; what matters more is a readiness to do so.

What changes are you ready for? If you start down that path, where might it lead?

What Does This Mean?

Kink is a lifestyle, not a lifestyle, and a misunderstood lifestyle. "My master/slave relationship is for more than sexual; it is part of our lifestyle." "It's not a lifestyle, it's a sexual series of likes, dislikes, and choices." "A great many in this lifestyle are just in it for the kicks … great kinky sex … they have no idea what this lifestyle is truly about."

Kink is roleplay and not roleplay. "I was a collared *kajira* (slave) for two years, so the slave role is a little less fantasy for me, and a little more real life." "It's not really role play, it's who I am."

Kink is a fun pastime and kink is an identity. "It's a great thing to do but I don't want it to rule my life." "… this is about who i am not what i do."

Kink is for the young and kink is for the not-so-young. "Just that I've known I craved being spanked & had fantasies as early as I can remember (3–4 years old), way before I knew what sexuality is." "i did not discover this lifestyle until i was 54."

Kink is forthright and kink is private. "It is not a secret what I enjoy." "My private life should never mix with my public life."

Yes, we should acknowledge a social aspect to kink in which forbidden activities are more enticing because they are socially or personally taboo. "I need to hide parts of me from regular society." "No one has any idea what I'm like in the bedroom!" "Sexuality is fluid, and those of us who participate in the scene on a regular basis have to continue exploring in order to satisfy our sexual urges, so they continue escalating to be more taboo."

There is a vast spectrum of the importance of kink in these women's lives, from being fun and frivolous to characterizing aspects of themselves to embodying a core identity. The women in our study show us that this is not a linear progression and that everyone finds their own place and path. There is no right or wrong amount of kink, not an optimal time in your life, no perfect balance among fantasy, privacy, novelty, and lifestyle. It's a matter of figuring out what is important to you, what your preferences are, what you desire, who you are, and, in some cases, finding a partner you are compatible with.

Your involvement with your kink might be too intense to discuss even with close friends, or it might be a casual topic of conversation. Your involvement might change regularly or it may be so hard-coded in your desires that it sets your future. Your kinky side might be your sexy side or it could be completely separated from your sexuality. In any case, allow yourself to accept yourself as kinky (if you are so inclined), even if you have not yet begun writing your own story.

Relationship Status 4

> "The one thing I appreciate most about this 'lifestyle' is the range of choices. We tend to grow up learning the 'official script,' you know, house, fence 2 1/3 kids, dog, cat, one man, one woman. If I'd known there were more ways to build a family, relationship, or a life when I was a young woman I might have been able to skip two bad marriages. I was in my early 40's when I finally started building a Family that suited me …"

Why are we including a whole chapter about relationships in a book about kink?

When we asked women about kink, we also asked them to tell us anything they wanted to. They told us about their relationships—they told us A LOT about their relationships. It was obvious that their relationships were intimately entwined with kink. So, if we are going to talk about women and kink, we must talk about women and relationships.

The women describe many types of relationships beyond the standard categories of single, married, divorced, or widowed. They are in casual relationships, long-distance relationships, monogamous and non-monogamous relationships, and more. Their relationships are in flux, transitional, very long, and very short.

It's complicated.

> "Monogamous by nature/when in love, unsure whether I want to commit to my current main partner to that extent, in [an] open relationship. Can only ever be in love with one person at once—monoamorous, if not

solely monogamous. When in love with one person, would be happy to negotiate fidelity or otherwise according to their preference."

"I would not mind being in an open relationship, but my husband would not approve of this lifestyle. Love him too much to make the sacrifice."

"In addition, we are polyamorous and that greatly affects what we do in our BDSM relationship because we do not participate in any kind of kink with our primary partners."

"I have a dear lover right now who is also into many of the same things I am and we are exploring together."

"I'm in a rather complicated situation with my former boyfriend and dominant. We lived together for two years in a D/s relationship, although we were never engaged or married. We split up around a year ago but have still continued to be BDSM play partners. We no longer fuck, but we occasionally have oral sex."

"Just that I met my primary partner at a sex club that he and I are members of. Thank goodness we don't have to explain our lifestyle to each other!"

"The most exciting type of relationship (for myself) is one you don't mention and that is a Dom/Domme relationship. Both are powerful individuals expecting their own way at all times. It becomes edge play, always on the razor edge, who will force the other and achieve the top position … for now … mentally and physically. It heightens senses and responses. Intensity seems elevated over a D/s type encounter."

Did they throw away the rulebook? Do people really live like this? What does this mean for us?

Well, let's see, let's imagine a housewife in a typical American TV family, courtesy of the 1950s.

She is connected to her three children, loving each fully. Her connection with her husband is intense and is certainly different than that with her children. There is a special place in her heart for her parents and brothers and sisters, one that stretches back to her earliest memories. Less strong but just as important is her connection with her in-laws, whom she loves but wishes they wouldn't visit so often.

Okay, you get the picture.

Fast-forward to the present, modern-day woman and she's got an ex-husband who is the father of one of her children, three former lovers who are

Facebook friends, the guy in the office who flirts with her over coffee, and her current wife whose adult children still live with her.

What do you notice about these two hypothetical examples?

On the surface, they seem quite different. But look a little closer—in both cases, the "main character" is surrounded by people she is connected with to varying degrees and with varying purposes.

The world has always been an exotic place full of wonder, crying out for exploration and discovery. Yet many of those places are too distant, dark, mysterious, strangers living in strange lands, a vast terra incognita, treacherous to the novice and to the timid.

Then the world changed, suddenly and for the better. Today we can easily make new friends or chat with anyone on the internet, anywhere in the world. We can talk with friendly folks who will tell us the stories of their lives without fear of reprisal or censorship, who will describe their forays into uncharted waters where *hic sunt dracones*.

The women in our survey candidly describe the intricacies of their relationships, their desires for family and friendship, and the simplicity and complexity of their past and present lives. We have a great opportunity to learn about the world and how people live, in intimate detail, including relationships without formal commitments, power-dynamic relationships, relationships with more than two partners, marriage, and other chosen families. Perhaps, by considering these new ideas, we can examine ourselves and get closer to being who we really want to be.

Relationships without Formal Commitments

New Relationships

> "I am dating and there are currently several guys that are possibilities (less than 3 dates each). Once one stands out, I will become monogamous with him."

Have you ever been in a relationship where you aren't really sure what to call each other? Are they your girlfriend, your lover, your significant other, your boy toy, your friend with benefits? Perhaps you've talked about commitments, lifestyles, responsibilities, hopes, and dreams, but not everything has solidified yet.

Well, that's not surprising; our world is always changing and we, too, are growing, shrinking, exploring, experimenting, and reconsidering. We are complex creatures, so it's no wonder that we sometimes don't have the words to describe how we relate to other people.

Here, we discuss relationships that are new, that are filled with promise and focused more on potential than on certainty.

> "I have recently entered into my first BDSM relationship, which is also my first relationship period."

> "D/s 1990–2005. M/s relationship from 2005–2009. Took a year off (well … 18 months) from relationships. (4/2009–09/2010). Attended bdsm events and parties during the last 18 months, but didn't engage in casual dating or bdsm play. (had to take some time to re-center and heal.) JUST started seeing someone as a 'friend/Top/play partner' but it has only been one play-date so far, plus 'vanilla-hiking-hanging out' dates. So … I had to answer this 'other.' 'Dating someone' maybe? But guardedly and without heavy expectations."

> "I am in a new relationship which is still developing. Hard to say long term since it has been 2 months. He is new to the bdsm lifestyle but I consider myself either monogamous or someone who is sexual monogamous but may also have some play partners. That isn't clear to me yet."

The period of new connections can bring a sense of hope and dreams of what the future might hold and what new things we may discover about ourselves and each other. This may be a time to evaluate whether you have similar life goals, compatibilities, and values. And sometimes, it's a time to just enjoy the moment and not worry about the future at all.

There are times in new relationships when it's too early to know whether or not the potential of a committed relationship will come to fruition. But at what point does a relationship move from something new to being more clearly defined? What event signals this transition? The answers to these questions are not universal, and may depend on several factors, including the culture and personalities of the people involved.

Casual Relationships

Casual relationships tend to have no timeline or end goal; the people involved have few expectations and are not looking for a firm commitment. Not every connection requires both parties to step onto the relationship escalator—meaning specific milestones such as moving in together, getting married, or having children. Although each of the following relationships is unique, the common element here is the use of the descriptor "casual."

> "I have never had a relationship beyond casual play partners."

> "I have some people I might play with casually but I would not consider them play partners at this point in time."

> "Met a man online, we play once a week; he introduced me to the BDSM community this year (at 60). I have a play partner that is a woman in the BDSM community, play and sex, not as intimate as the man. Both casual, no long term in sight, no time, no inclination."

What have we learned about casual relationships from these women?

Casual relationships can be for sex, for some level of emotional connection, for friendship and companionship, for intellectual pursuits, or any combination of these.

Some people enjoy relationships without expectations and commitments. A relationship doesn't necessarily need to shift into one with more specific roles, titles, future plans, or even have a timeline.

What relationships do you have in your life that are not tied to milestones, timelines, or defined expectations? Can you imagine the same model being applied to intimate relationships, too?

Single-Plus

When filling out demographic information, there is usually a section related to describing marital status by checking one of the boxes labeled single, married, divorced, or widowed. If those are the only choices, then single has to mean "is not and never has been married." This is important if you are filing your taxes, but not so much in real life.

What does being single really mean? Is it a permanent condition or a transitional stage? Can someone be single for sexual or romantic reasons? Is being single synonymous with being alone, with being lonely? Should it even be called a "relationship style"?

In fact, "single" describes so many different relationship styles that we coined the term "single-plus" to describe myriad variations. Some single-plus women identify as single, and they maintain stable kink relationships. Some are dating, which may mean that they are pursuing first dates or that they are in non-committed romantic relationships. Some single-plus women are looking for long-term relationships, some are in multiple relationships, and some are a non-primary partner to other relationships.

> "Single at this time, but don't like to just casually play ... would like to find my Master."

> "Actively seeking an LTR, but playing to take care of my needs in the interim. I am also seeking out an ANR relationship."

> "i am single, but i am in a long-term BDSM relationship (age play—Mommy/little-me being the little)."

> "'casual' is a little too vague—I have several play partners who are also good friends. I think of myself as single and poly."

> "I am an out lesbian who is presently single. I am involved with several play partners, but I do not consider these relationships to be moving towards an emotional relationship outside of kink."

> "I am surprised dating wasn't on the previous question. I am currently dating a married woman with the consent of her husband and it's working out pretty well so far."

> "I currently have no primary relationship but am dating a man and a woman who both have poly relationships (separately, not together). I also play with people at kink events I would not consider myself as being in a relationship with."

> "I'm involved in two serious dating/bdsm relationships. One is with someone who has a live-in primary partner and is polyamorous; we see each other one evening a week and one weekend every 2 months; we've been dating for about 9 months. The other relationship is with someone I've been dating since June; we live in different cities but see each other for at least a few overnight visits per month and often attend weekend-long bdsm events and play parties together."

Isn't that interesting? This is not the "single" we typically think of, especially the one that we check when being asked our marital status. When reading about these single women, we can see that they are engaging with others, playing with others, and creating different relationships that suit them and their needs while also maintaining a status of being single.

Someone can be single and simultaneously have meaningful connections with other people.

What does being single mean to you? How do these examples open your eyes to new possibilities of being single? If you're single now, how would you like to rethink ways of being single?

Power-Dynamic Relationships

> "Lately, I've been playing with a married couple. It's been a fantastic way to discover more about myself as well as the dynamic of a young, professional, educated, married couple and how they incorporate me into their relationship. It's very flattering. It's also been great to submit to two people, as opposed to just one."

While some of the examples throughout this chapter include elements of kink, here we are focusing on relationships in which kink is a central and core component of the connection. Bear in mind that there are a wide variety of other kink-specific relationships that exist, well beyond what is covered here. Truly, the combinations and types of relationships are legion.

The examples in this section help illustrate the variety of ways a relationship can be centered around power dynamics—that is, having deliberate assignment of responsibilities. Included in power dynamics are the subcategories of Dominant/submissive, slavery, collared, total power exchange (TPE), and closed kink relationships (those who specified that their kink relationship is with one partner only).

But before we get started, we should take a moment to discuss the topic of ownership and slavery, submission, and service.

"Slavery" (and the words associated with it) can be a trigger word for many people, and with good reason. However, in the kink community, a slave is one way to describe a person who willingly enters a relationship to serve others in that relationship. Slaves, and their Masters, are treated with care, trust, and value, just as you would expect of anyone in a relationship.

It can be difficult to wrap your mind around the idea of ownership and servitude, especially when we place such a high premium on individual rights and freedoms. But when we consider these notions, are the concepts of owning people and voluntary servitude really that foreign to modern society and everyday life?

Let's look at the most obvious example of owning people: parenting. If you are a parent, then you decide where your child goes to school, whether they get vaccinated, and what foods are served for breakfast. Parents make all those decisions, and the tiny, helpless person must comply. Parents have anxiety because they never really know if they are meeting all the physical, mental, and emotional needs of their child. Owning someone is a serious responsibility.

Another way to envision what it is like to be a 24/7 servant and submitting unconditionally to someone is military service. In America today, people serving in the military do so voluntarily. However, once they join, these servants are not allowed to quit. There is no safe word. There will always be someone whose orders they must obey. Despite this, or because of it, there are about 1.3 million people serving in the US military, and military personnel feel a sense of honor for serving their country.

Maybe a less extreme example of the pleasure of providing service is in the responsibilities and obligations that are tied to volunteering. There is often a pleasure and fulfillment by serving your local community or a cause that you strongly believe in. The organization will require dedication and a commitment from you for as long as you are able and willing to provide them with your time and resources.

Okay, now that we better understand the relationship dynamics described here are consensual and deliberate, let's get started with our examples of kink-related relationships.

Dominant/submissive (D/s) relationships are those in which the Dominant person willingly accepts responsibility for some or all elements of the submissive person's life, and the submissive person willfully surrenders control and decision-making for those elements. These relationships can range from very casual to 24/7 (full time).

> "To clarify: i'm in a long-term committed 24/7 D/s relationship and we are also swingers. We live together and i have never been married."

> "Non 24/7 but non-casual BDSM relationship. I have a dom, but we are not 24/7."

> "I worship an adored Dom and give myself to him. He spanks me and fucks me, and many other things besides. He is very strict and he thinks I am special. I try very hard, but there's always room for improvement. He may motivate me with a caning to pay more attention to detail. But he will console and fuck me afterwards as I abjectly apologize for my mistake. And then he will show me his fierce love, by penetration. He knows how to fuck slowly and make me come over and over. I am completely under his power."

> "One manifestation of a D/s relationship is one of 'Daddy/little girl' (and Daddi/boi with alternative spellings of 'Daddy' and of 'boy,' each with various meanings). These relationship styles tend to have nurturing and service elements to them."
>
> "Committed Daddy/little girl relationship to become long-term."
>
> "I enjoy a full time Daddi/boi relationship with my partner of 8 years. We both enjoy this for the nurturing/protective element on my part, and the service/caring for her Daddi aspect and the being cared for aspect on my boi's part …"
>
> "It's not whips-and-chains BDSM, but our dynamic is more than enough to brand us as freaks in the vanilla world. Even within the scene, it's not unusual to find people who assume that Daddy/girl relationships are about incest or are otherwise sick and wrong."

Those who are in service to another may have very specific protocols, roles, and expectations. Typically, "in service" refers to doing physical tasks and manual labor such as household chores, taking care of day-to-day tasks, service of a sexual nature or kink nature, various sensual acts (like giving a massage, grooming, bathing), among other service-oriented activities.

However, the types of service mentioned in the following quotations were not specified.

> "In service to another woman outside my married relationship."
>
> "In service to a dominant couple but live by myself."
>
> "I have had my Daddy/Master for 5 years. We are poly and looking for at least one more gal to join us. In addition, I have a boy (submissive) that is mine, and I am 'In Service' to a Mistress and take care of her and her home."

Someone who owns a slave is typically referred to as a Master or Mistress; note that a male or female could choose either title, and the title could be another word denoting authority, such as "Lady," "Lord," "Ma'am," or "Sir."

> "We also own a slave."
>
> "My slave moved in with my husband and me. It's a closed triad."

"Master/slave but we do not live together. I have a live-in boyfriend who also, at times, dominates my slave."

"I have several Long-term BDSM play partners and a Live-in collared slave/boyfriend open relationship."

On the other side of ownership is the slave, the one who surrenders to another.

"i am an owned slave, real life, living with my Master 24/7."

"Because it's who I am. I am always his slave in public and private. It's not overt in public and appears more like a strict male head of household type of relationship."

"Enslaved to a Master and Mistress in a polyfidelitous household with two other slaves (one male, one female)."

"The total exchange of power between Master and i was an unexpected occurrence. Never had i expected to derive such pleasure/freedom in being a slave. More surprising since i'm considered to have an extremely strong personality among my peers."

"I am a slave with a master for all intents and purposes. Yes, I realize that slavery is illegal and that I could walk away but I have committed to do as my Sir says and unless he turns into a sociopath who wants to put me in danger (he takes very good care of me) I will continue to do as he says."

Some people described their relationship as "collared." A collar can be a physical collar, a symbolic necklace, or a frame of mind. Wearing a collar can be as simple as a fashion statement, it might be a symbolic representation of the beginning or end of an event (such as a kink scene), or it might refer to a serious relationship commitment.

Since there is no authoritative definition of what it means to be collared, we remind you that we cannot be certain of what it implies to these women.

"i am in a relationship as a submissive and have been collared to him for the past 4 years."

"I checked polyamorous but not because we have an open relationship. I am an owned, collared pet and my Owner and I may or may not choose to add a third or fourth to our relationship. We have in the past and enjoyed it. It doesn't make our relationship open, but it isn't all the way closed to possibility."

"I am polyamorous, bisexual and submissive. My legal husband of 11 years is not really into the kinky lifestyle. My non-legal partner (bisexual, Dominant male) and I have been together for 3 years. Most of that time has included a BDSM relationship which gradually evolved into a 24/7 Master/slave relationship—I wear a locked collar and cuff. The 3 of us live together right now, though we will most likely eventually end up living in separate housing close to one another."

There is a relationship status called "TPE," which stands for total power exchange. We don't know the details of the specific agreements in our examples, except that they consider themselves in TPE relationships.

"My main interest is in a 24/7 TPE relationship with my husband. All the activities listed are mere tools to that way of life."

"I am in a TPE (Total Power Exchange) Relationship. When we live together it will be 24/7 D/s."

"My lifestyle is a 24/7 TPE (Total Power Exchange). My spouse and I live in a 50's style relationship where I have sole responsibility of taking care of the home and children (we do not share chores) and I also work outside of the home in a very successful professional career."

Closed kink relationships are those in which a couple explores and participates in kink behaviors exclusively with each other (without additional play partners).

"I am currently in a long-term monogamous relationship with a man, who also happens to be my Dominant."

"I am a monogamous person. I do not like to play with multiple partners, much preferring the intimacy and trust levels between myself and my Master. The act of the play is purely a symbol of the trust and care we have for each other."

"I only play within my lesbian relationship. It's a loving, caring relationship in which we both enjoy the D/s lifestyle."

"I live apart from my Master but stay with him every other week. W/we have been together for over 2 years. He was my first long-term D/s relationship and possibly my only One."

"I have my lifestyle as it pleases me to do these things. The specific activities are fantastic and I am willing to try pretty much most things. However, I will only do these things with my Master. I choose to hand the control of my sex life and many decisions of my vanilla [life] over to Him. There are natural limits imposed on this such as the rearing of my children, what I do with my finances, and basic day to day decisions. He asks for my opinion and input but the final decision is up to Him in other matters."

These women emphasize marriage within their kink dynamics.

"To specify: I'm married with my Master and we live monogamous. So: married and BDSM is ONE person."

"Have been with DomSpouse for 38 years (34 married)."

This next group of women provide even more details outlining how and why their kink dynamics work for them within one committed relationship.

"I have been in the BDSM lifestyle for 10 years and have been now in a monogamous M/s relationship for the past 2 years, i have finally found my soulmate in life. this is the first time in 10 years that i have actually been able to let go and experience what i have always dreamed about with a partner that i love with all my heart ... life is wonderful."

"For the most part, my Master and I live a BDSM lifestyle 24/7, excluding work and family time of course. We live together, sleep together, eat together, and are monogamous in our relationship. We're as 24/7 BDSM as we can be without shoving it in other people's faces."

These relationships illustrate ways that two people will incorporate kink together, without any additional partners or relationships. Some people prefer to have one—and only one—partner and explore kink within that relationship.

What other examples can you think of that have Master and slave or Dominant and submissive aspects to them? Were there any kink-specific configurations that resonated with you, or that you did not know were even possible?

Non-Monogamy: Relationships with More Than One Partner

> "I am in a committed open poly relationship for over 9 years. We are mostly monogamous but the option is there for sex and play with others as long as it is all as agreed to by the three involved."

Consensual non-monogamy (CNM) is a sexual or romantic relationship in which participants have multiple partners with the willing agreement of everyone involved. A basis for CNM is that your partner or partners are informed of your activities so there is honesty and transparency on all sides.

A large number of women in our survey describe relationships in which they have a primary partner plus other participants, or that they are in a stable relationship with more than one person. These extra partners are for sex, romance, kink, or other reasons not explained.

Just as we coined "single-plus" to handle the complexities of being single, we will use "primary-plus" to categorize relationships in which there is an established couple who have a relationship agreement that is:

- Open for sex
- Open for relationships
- Open for kink
- Open for a combination of the above, or for other reasons

Sometimes the women label their relationships as polyamory and sometimes not, even when their relationship styles are similar. Swingers and non-swingers can also have similar relationship styles. Some of the women are married. Some women are sexually or emotionally exclusive with one person. Some are mostly monogamous and some are in committed groups.

We will also discuss the phenomenon of non-consensual non-monogamy, in which some participants in one of the relationships are unaware of all of the relationships or activities. Some of the women in our survey speak about being in relationships where either their primary partner, or their partner's partner, are unaware of their relations, and we would be remiss to exclude these stories.

Keep in mind there are entire books dedicated to non-monogamy. We recognize that the following examples are not an exhaustive list of the ways in which non-monogamous relationships can be structured, but are simply based on examples from our survey.

One reason to form a primary-plus relationship is for sexual expression without an emotional connection. In other words, "you can have sex with other people, but don't fall in love with them."

> "I would describe myself as monogamous, but my partner and I have 'dirty fun' with another couple we know very well. We would not call ourselves polyamorous and we do not swing with anyone else."

> "Primarily monogamous for the past few years (married for 11, together for 20), but out of convenience/laziness rather than idealism. Not what I would call an 'open' marriage—more like we keep a key hidden in the garden, and will occasionally let a third party know where it is so they can join in for a while."

> "Summary = I am in a long-term relationship with a live-in partner (except we are temporarily living apart while I finish my Master's Degree). We have been together 5 years. It is a 24/7 D/s relationship. We do not consider ourselves poly. Rather, we consider ourselves non-monogamous; meaning, we engage in sexual activities with others only after explaining we are in a committed relationship and only seeking encounters with 'friends' and not offering any sort of love relationship or deeper psychological bond … with others it's a 'friends with benefits' category."

> "I am in a primary relationship, living with my long-term male partner. We are 'open' in that we engage in sexual activity with people outside of our relationship, but we are not 'swingers.'"

> "By 'Swingers,' I mean we would have sex with another couple or group sex, but without male-on-male sex (I am bisexual, my spouse is straight)."

One woman shares an example of how boundaries can look different for many couples with open relationships.

> "I have had sex several times with my brother-in-law, as my husband and I have an open relationship. Just to add a kinky thing there for you."

Primary-plus relationships can have the extra partner specifically or exclusively for kink activities.

"My Mistress and I have been together 12 years. Our relationship is exclusive in real life but not always on line where she has other submissives. With her permission I am sometimes allowed to play on line."

"Basically, a bisexual, nudist, poly, spanko, who occasionally tops men and/or women, bottoms in social parties, submissive only to one Man, who I am in an LTR with."

"I could never date a vanilla guy … We are in a committed long-term relationship, but since we don't share the same kinks, we 'outsource'—we have BDSM partners outside our primary relationship that meet our specific needs. I have veto power over his partners and vice versa, and it all works out fine. It's often an advantage in trying to find play partners, actually, since they don't have to worry about us trying to pursue a more serious relationship with them in light of our monogamous relationship status. I adore our arrangement!"

"… I do not play without my primary partner present. It is only with his permission that others play with me and there is no intercourse …"

"I am in a long-standing vanilla marriage. My spouse is aware of my BDSM activities. I do not have sex with anyone other than my spouse. I enjoy the power exchange as well as the aforementioned activities."

"My husband and I are Monogamous; however, we do play with others at play parties and sometimes in our home. We do not have sex with others! We are both Dominants and have subs whom we enjoy playing and watching one another with at times. We are (sort of) looking for a girl to live with us, in a Poly Triad as a family in a closed relationship. In the meantime … we enjoy our friends and the local BDSM community. We are active in the local community in town, as well as in a near-by larger community. We go to Leather events and support Gay's rights, as we have many friends affected by this issue."

Occasionally a primary-plus relationship is very specific as to the reason for the "plus."

"I personally enjoy some sadomasochistic play that involves some pain, but, my partner is not a pain-giver, so I defer that part of myself. We do own floggers and he will occasionally give me the pleasure of flogging me. It is never to a point of inflicting deep pain or leaving marks. It is definitely more of a sensuous activity. Occasionally he will allow a close friend of ours, who is a pro-domme, to play with me and flog me. She knows what my/his limits are when we play and 'No marks' is a hard limit."

"My husband and I are in an open relationship; however, he is not into the fetish scene as I am and tends to be relatively vanilla and lifeless in the bed which means we have a limited sex life with each other. Without my 'lifestyle' choices I would be cranky and hard to live with. The outlets I use give me the freedom to be who I really am inside without having my mood swings and fantasies impact on my family's lives."

We describe the types of primary-plus relationships for clarity, but obviously there is overlap.

"One committed long-term relationship with my best friend, male partner, but I'm allowed female lovers, and most forms of BDSM play with other partners. Defined detailed list of what is play and what is cheating is yet to be found out."

"One main long-term primary relationship 10 years and counting, never married. Also play partners and friends with benefits on the side for the kinkier stuff. This is all open and honest."

"Involved with a primary partner and until recently with a secondary partner. Also, very occasional and extremely casual long-distance cyber-play with a dear MTF friend who is married and has a domme of her own locally. Considering possibly adding casual play partners sometime within the next year, but unsure as to the logistics of this, and need to discuss with primary partner."

"I am bisexual, married to a man. We have always had the understanding that I don't need to deny myself when it comes to meeting my desires for women. We are not technically polyamorous, but we do have flexibility when it comes to my bisexuality. Also, I am submissive only to my husband, but being a Switch, I have the freedom to dominate female partners when I feel the need/desire to do so. It's a unique arrangement, but it works well for us."

"My husband and I consider ourselves Kinky Swingers. We are emotionally monogamous but physically casual using extremely safe sex practices."

"I don't consider myself poly, but I am married to a vanilla man, have 1 primary BDSM partner (long term) & occasionally play with others."

Some people engage in multiple partnerships and call it "polyamory."

> "Bisexual, poly, switch but mostly bottom. Separated but dating husband. Currently have the aforementioned husband, three boyfriends, and a girlfriend. One boyfriend is long distance. All my partners have other partners."

> "I'm married & we are both open & poly—that is we are free to be with others casually, both together or separately, AND we have long-term relationships outside our marriage. Currently I have a husband, a boyfriend & a girlfriend (they are also an open/poly married couple) and I occasionally play with a casual partner at a BDSM event, play party or sex party."

And some people engage in multiple partnerships without calling it "polyamory."

> "I've been with my primary partner for 5+ years and have another serious girlfriend. I'm also open to finding casual play partners."

> "My partner is also married to another woman and is bisexual. My husband generally does not have other partners, though he has permission to do so."

Sometimes, one person identifies as being polyamorous while their partner identifies as monogamous. And they find a way to make it work.

> "I'm not really polyamorous but my boyfriend/Master is, and I accept it".

> "Master/slave—I'm monogamous to him, he's poly."

> "Partner is more monogamous; I am more poly; we are in an open dialogue about how to give me the openness I want and have him still trust the security of the relationship."

When three people create a primary-plus relationship, it can be called a triad or a trio (among other names).

> "Poly faithful triad: one woman; one man; one transgendered MtF."

> "I am polyamorous and in a committed triad with a man and a woman. Most scenarios involved both of them."

"Open trio with 2 bi fems and a straight man for 5 years."

We again remind you that words have usage, not meaning.

"Long-term, Monogamous, Poly Triad."

Another example of words having usage is with the term "cuckold." According to the *Cambridge Dictionary*: "If a man is cuckolded, his wife has a sexual relationship with another man" (*Cambridge Dictionary*, n.d.). The synonyms list includes verbs such as "adulterous," "affair," "cheat," "faithless," and "infidelity." Yet, the examples below show that cuckolding is not only with their partner's approval, it is with their involvement.

> "Although my partner and I are currently monogamous, we are exploring the possibility of adding cuckolding to our D/s repertoire."
>
> "Though my husband and I are monogamous at heart, I am currently exploring cuckolding and forced-bi activities with both my husband and another male submissive. The three of us are in a closed polyfidelitous 'v' with me at the center."
>
> "More recently I've met a new play partner who is a cuckold and asked me to top him. I have been doing that and seeing a whole new side of me blossom. I'm exploring light CBT and more precise use of impact implements."

Some of the women in our survey spoke about being in relationships where their partner or their partner's partner was unaware. This can be described as non-consensual non-monogamy because not all parties involved (in sexual and/or romantic connections) have knowledge of everyone else's involvement, and therefore are unable to make informed decisions about the relationship structure.

> "My husband is disabled and unable to function sexually in any manner. After 18 years of celibacy due to this, I've elected to *carefully* indulge in safe sex with a few, discrete partners."
>
> "I am in two long-term relationships. One with my husband, one with my lover. My marriage is not open. My lover is a secret from my husband. My husband is not a secret to my lover. I have a sexual and emotional relationship with both partners. My sexual relationship with my husband

is vanilla or non-kinky activities. My sexual relationship with my lover is both vanilla and kinky in nature."

"i identify myself as a submissive; i am not formally collared. i do not live the lifestyle 24/7, but whenever i can. my Master is married to another woman who has no idea about our relationship."

"In a secret (His wife does not know, my family doesn't know) BDSM affair with a married man … He is my DOM … I am His sub. We see each other weekly. He is poly in the fact that He is still with His wife. I have to remain monogamous. Have I? noooooooo."

"I am in a Dom/sub relationship with a married man. His wife is not aware. I am owned by Him. His orders are that no other person can 'play' with me or can have 'sex' with me … I am in a relationship with a Daddy/Dom. He found me. I give Him respect, pleasure, and do what He asks of me in all my actions, thoughts, and words. I enjoy being submissive to Him. Our time together is amazing. He does not share me except under certain circumstance, except He would consider swapping. He is teaching me, protecting me, controlling me, adoring me, molding me, training me, conditioning me, and much more. In turn I receive so much pleasure and have lots of fun, too. I am very grateful to Him. I will never be the same. This is all done in the context of the bedroom or any room. After play and sex, we have a normal relationship with conversation, sharing meals, and normal activities. He is married so we have to keep our relationship secret and discrete."

On the other hand, some people will not consider interacting with those who engage in non-consensual non-monogamy.

"Both I and my bdsm play partner have (a) permanent life partner(s) who is/are aware of the situation, but choosing not to participate although being on good terms with everyone involved. I wouldn't play with someone who was cheating on their unsuspecting partner!"

All these variations of non-monogamous relationships are a lot to digest, aren't they? There are so very many ways for people to create relationships; you can see why we had to put them in one category rather than attempting to find a label for each one.

Yet each relationship is unique and each deserves its own label. These people create their own happiness outside of social norms, and we are fortunate they shared their stories with us.

Do any of these relationships delight you or disturb you? Are you pushed out of your comfort zone when reading of these women's lifestyle and choices?

Is the idea of juggling multiple relationships enticing? If you were to modify your current relationship to include a "plus," what would your plus be for? And what would be your first steps toward making it a reality?

Of course, we are not advocating for opening a relationship. And understand that some people are wired for monogamy and will not be comfortable with the idea of a relationship with more than two people.

On the Topic of Marriage

> "I am monogamous, but my Boyfriend is married and in an open marriage."

When we think of marriage, we probably think of the legal union between two people who share love for one another. What has not been widely discussed are the spaces in between dating and marriage (engagement), various ways of being legally married, and platonic marriages, let alone unions between Masters and slaves, Dom/Dommes and their submissives, polyamorous marriages, and other types of arrangements that are not necessarily legal but are considered marriages by their participants. These marriages illustrate the many options available to those who cannot find their place in traditional marriages.

Engaged to be Married

Before we begin looking at the different types of marriages, we feel we should explore "engagement," the time when a couple has committed to marriage, but are not yet married—a limbo that few people seem to recognize as a relationship style, yet important enough that some of the women highlight this part of their relationship status.

> "My fiancé and I are currently monogamous, with occasional bouts of 'extra-curricular activities.' We are currently meeting other people with the possibility of becoming polyamorous, we just haven't met the right people yet. We have been together for 5 years and are engaged to be married next fall."

> "In a long-term relationship (soon to be wed) with another submissive girl. We allow each other to have casual (or long term) play partners on the side, but I do not currently have one."
>
> "I am a collared submissive to my Master who is a[n] FtM (Female to Male). We have been engaged for over 2 years but since he understands I have female needs, he allows me to have sex with other men as long as he knows about it."
>
> "My fiancé is also my Dom. We are not exclusive, but we are each other's primary partner. I exercise the option more often than he does. I have casual BDSM play partners w/ whom I am not sexually active, I have a few female friends with benefits. I currently have no 'relationship' outside my primary relationship, but that is an option that we are open to, should a[n] fwb or a play partner should turn into a more romantic relationship."

Even though a couple has a formal intention to marry each other, it is not necessarily indicative that they will be "exclusive" with each other, whether sexually, relationally, or in regard to kink. And, some people already know at this stage in their relationship that they have a shared interest in cultivating a kink dynamic as part of their upcoming marriage structure.

Do these descriptions above pique your curiosity? When you think about what it means to be engaged, do the ideas about multiple partners, collared submissives, and other non-mainstream possibilities come to mind? Can you imagine the possibilities for how these engagement parties could look? Does a non-traditional celebration intrigue you?

Legal Marriage

The *Cambridge Dictionary* states that marriage is "a legally accepted relationship between two people" (*Cambridge Dictionary*, n.d.). The key aspect is "legally accepted." The legal aspect may only be between two people, but that doesn't necessarily limit the configuration of relationships with other people; this relationship style can mean a commitment to one person, BDSM relationships, polyamorous relationships, and more.

> "I am married in a monogamous relationship. He was my first partner ever and that was on our wedding night."
>
> "I'm married to my Master."

"I have both a vanilla wife as well as a BDSM Owner, and we all live together."

"I think that my experience is a little unusual in that I have only ever done BDSM things with my husband and we have only been in the lifestyle about 2–3 years but have been together for 15. We developed BDSM into our existing relationship."

"I am married for 31 years to [a] man that is not kinky. My husband granted me the liberty to satisfy my kinky nature elsewhere. My Master and i are in a 24/7, poly relationship. Master and i have been together now 16 months."

"Polyfidelity is the actual term, and it should be listed far separately from 'open relationship' or 'polyamory' which would include a large amount of random partners. Polyfidelity is a closed group with no outside random partners. My polyfidelity status includes a legal marriage and a 24/7 BDSM partner under the same roof with no outside partners …"

"We are a legally married Lesbian couple (one of the 18,000) here in *(Redacted)* [State]. We do have a Daddy/boi relationship, but are mostly equal in everyday life. She is monogamous to me, and I am supposedly polyamorous, but haven't acted on that in ages, even if I want to (well last year at *(Redacted)* [Kink Event]). We are a fully committed couple. We used to co-top others in the past, but that was a long while ago."

"I met my husband online 8 years ago. He lives in *(Redacted)* [State A] and I live in *(Redacted)* [State B] so I fly back and forth monthly to see him. He introduced me to the BDSM lifestyle as it was always a fantasy of his. We started trying it out together and have enjoyed it. Our relationship evolved into a Master/slave one and we married a few years ago. We have participated in BDSM activities in [State A] and [State B]. Neither of us can see ourselves participating in 'vanilla' sex as kinky sex is so much more fulfilling. He has a sex buddy that he sees once a week or so in my absence. As soon as I am able, I plan to relocate to [State A] full time."

The commonality of each of the marriages is that there are qualifiers to the "I am married" statement. That certainly describes a great many marriages in today's world; however, these "ands" and "buts" don't show up on the census form.

In the following examples, not only will we see how kink can be incorporated into marriages, but how marriage can extend beyond two people.

Notice that the woman's legal marriage is the first relationship specified. However, these women simultaneously enjoy a complex network of connections with other people.

> "I am married to my owner, and I own a man who lives with his wife."

> "I am married, but I also have a Dom and a girlfriend I regularly have sex with."

> "Married to a man, also have a male Dominant. Husband is aware of Dominant and we have all played together."

> "I am married, poly/swinger with DH and in play partners with a female."

> "Current relationships: Married to a man for 25 years; in long-term BDSM relationship with another male (he is Dom, I am submissive); I am dating a transsexual MtF (we both switch); I am sometimes sexual with their other partners and our friends (friends with benefits) … Most of my sexual and BDSM activities are 1:1, but I very much enjoy 3somes and moresomes when there is a heart connection and there is opportunity. I do not identify as a swinger or have anonymous sex. I have always been pansexual and polyamorous all my dating/romantic/sexual life."

There is a tendency to think of marriage as the goal of adult relationships and the de facto state of couples. Yet, we can see that the legal arrangement does not address the ways couples express their desires within the marriage and does not necessarily imply exclusivity.

Platonic Marriage

Platonic marriages are those in which the married couple is not having sex with each other. That does not mean that they do not get along; they can be best friends, sharing intimacy and affection. Platonic simply describes the couples' (lack of) sexual activities within the marriage, and does not address the emotional connection.

In the following quotations, people in platonic relationships describe having shared interests with their spouse and having no shared interests with their spouse, living together and not living together, being involved in kink and not mentioning kink at all.

"I am separated from my husband, but we were not married out of love. Just convenience as we are both interested in the same sex."

"I am platonically married to a bisexual male, but we live separately. He has his partners and I have mine. I am queer and date women and transmen who have kinks in their tails."

"I have a platonic husband who I live separately from, a boyfriend who I am fluid-bonded with who is not in the lifestyle but understands my being queer and need for that energy in my life, so I have a hall pass for queer folk in my life and BDSM play partners."

"I am married to a guy, but we are just friends, platonic. I have a boy that belongs to both my hubby and me. He is not a sub, just a bottom. I have a Mistress who i serve. I also have a trainer who i answer to. I also have two sons that know about my lifestyle and they are ok with that. I am female but live my life as a boi. I like to serve High femme and Daddy's and Butches too :)"

When you hear the expression "sex-less marriage," you might have imagery of sad, neglected couples dealing with anxiety or sexual dysfunction. Instead, these women do not disparage their spouse or marriage, and treat that relationship as normal and perhaps even desired.

A platonic marriage can assist couples with meeting certain needs (such as friendship, companionship, medical insurance, tax benefits, financial concerns, and business endeavors) while providing each partner the freedom to explore romance and sexuality with other partners.

Consider Themselves to be Married

The Indian philosopher Osho wrote, "A marriage is only a real marriage when it grows out of love. Legal, illegal, does not matter. The real thing that matters is love." Some people have taken that lesson to heart.

"Married legally to one non-trans husband and married non-legally to one trans husband. :-)."

"I am in a polyamorous, committed quad. Two men, two women, all considered to be married even if not legally. Legally married to one of the males."

These women expand the definition of marriage; they don't necessarily need a proper license to feel love, connection, and happiness from one or many husbands and wives. Parties in the relationship may have a verbal or written agreement that clarifies their roles, expectations, and responsibilities. Note that these agreements are not uncommon in many other relationship styles, too.

We remind you that we do not advocate or oppose marriage and all its variations. We merely present quotations of women who call themselves married.

What are your thoughts on the types of marriage these people have built for themselves? Which marriage styles appeal to you and which might you find unsettling?

When you think, "they lived happily ever after," what do you imagine? Is marriage a journey or a destination?

Divorced

> "I don't really understand (and have never understood) how you can ask for a CURRENT relationship status and list 'Divorced' or 'Widowed.' That's not asking about a CURRENT relationship's status. That's asking about PREVIOUS relationship(s) status, which isn't ever really applicable to almost anyone asking about relationship status."

Why do we become unmarried? Maybe we married for the wrong reasons, maybe we believed the other person would change, maybe we were seduced by the romance of a wedding without regard to the realities of marriage. There is probably a different answer for each divorced person, but, in general, it's because we grow apart, in different directions, at different rates, toward different dreams.

Is "divorce" a moment in time, an ending and a beginning, not too dissimilar from a wedding? Or, is it a relationship style with its own benefits, different from being single?

Divorce marks the end of a relationship that (hopefully) began with love, trust, commitment, desire, hopes, and dreams. It's good to remember that divorce is also a beginning, encouraging the possibilities of new relationships with romantic pursuits, sexual partners, kink participants, Doms, submissives, and more. These women are rebirthing, creating, and exploring new hopes and new dreams.

> "I am currently seeking divorce because I have felt that I had to hide my real sexual wants for 12 years."
>
> "I am getting divorced from one man and in [the] process found my dominant self and met a man who worships my dominant self. Submissive and I are celebrating our one-year anniversary."
>
> "Previously in a long-term open marriage with elements of BDSM. Separation not related to issues of polyamory or open relationship! :)"
>
> "Separated—heading to divorce—in an Open Relationship with my top of 1yr designated as his primary—so more than casual—still top/bottom and in a solid relationship."
>
> "I am about to divorce and then I will be able to be monogamous to Daddy. We are in a long-term cyber relationship that will become physical and hopefully lead to a permanent real time 'together' relationship. Daddy is a teacher and I am taking college courses, so when I do well in my studies, I get rewarded for it."

And while we don't know why this woman is divorced, we do appreciate that she has kept her sense of humor about it.

> "Marriage: won't get fooled again! Hehehe."

The next group of women disclose how they divorced and have started relationships with new partners.

> "I am divorcing my vanilla husband; I am a collared slave in a polyamorous relationship with my Master."
>
> "Divorced, in LTR with male partner, I am monogamous, he plays and does sexual things with other women, and we occasionally engage in sexual and BDSM play with other women together."
>
> "I am divorced and in a new long-term relationship (5 years). I have one bdsm play couple and one other female play partner. All with consent and in full knowledge of my partner."
>
> "Domme living with my sub. Vanilla and BDSM, divorced with children."
>
> "I have been divorced and am living with my owner in a BDSM 24/7 relationship."

> "Both of my marriages have strictly been for the benefits, but I don't think my first husband believed that. I had told him that I didn't believe in traditional marriage & still wanted to explore three-somes. He said he was uncomfortable with that, but would work on his feelings of jealousy. After 2 1/2 years together, we ended up fucking 4 women (only one of whom I was actually remotely attracted to), but no men. This didn't seem fair to me, & I was starting to realize that I am not built for monogamy. We separated for several months before officially divorcing, in which time I moved to the city & began really exploring my sexuality. My current marriage is to my submissive partner. I allow him to play with some friends (male & female) when he behaves. I personally have several top play partners & lovers, one local, several scattered all over the country & world. I also have casual fuck buddies & clients spread equally wide."

A pattern emerges: "divorce" simply means previously married.

Upon divorcing, many of these women discover something new or renewed something old. Importantly, they continue to find new ways to connect with others and to get their needs met. They do not stop when their marriages end but instead, learn the importance of knowing oneself and being able to state needs firmly within their new relationships.

We have some ideas for you to consider.

Why is "divorced" a marital status?

You can undo a marriage with a divorce, but divorce is forever. Even if you remarry, you are still divorced from the person in that earlier marriage. When does "divorced" become "single" or "married," and why?

Why do you suppose the women in the section describe themselves as divorced rather than single? Perhaps there was something important in that marriage that still warrants a connection. Perhaps it is just their way of speaking, and we shouldn't read anything substantive into it.

Notice that some women *are* divorced and some women *have been* divorced. If you were once married but now are not, which of those verbs would you use to describe yourself?

Widowed

> "Four long-term partners 3 of whom are sexual partners. One casual partner. Two previous spouses one dead one divorced."

Many people cannot imagine what it is like for a spouse to die, and don't even want to think about it. How does someone endure something so devastating?

A spouse cannot be replaced, and learning how to live without them can be a painful process. Grief can become an opportunity to explore one's own goals, values, beliefs about relationships, and priorities in life. This does not mean that the loved one, their memory, and their death, are absent—they are a part of the journey.

One way to help cope with grief is to get support from others. Eventually the sharp edges of the pain may dull and space opens for friendships and new experiences because ultimately, we are all searching for connection.

> "I am a submissive woman. Whilst I am currently not in a relationship I have friends I play with and am looking for something more permanent but to be honest I am not holding my breath. I am a widow with 2 small children after all but then my vanilla friends have similar problems. Sometimes I think we make issues for ourselves to feel special when really things are just about human beings interacting no matter how they have sex."

> "I was a swinger with my first husband but divorced him when I became disillusioned because he only wanted to have sex with me after we were with others, he called all the shots, and fell in love with my best friend who was not in the lifestyle. My second husband and I were happily monogamous for 12 years; he died 6 years ago. I've enjoyed about 100 partners while searching for my next monogamous relationship/marriage over the past 6 years, but I've lately been wondering if polyamory might work better for me. In the past 2 months, I'm currently seeing a 52yo fella who's polyamorous for 3 years, a 47yo who I'm bareback with (he's into monogamy but is leaving the state to live—in several months), a 34yo MTF trans, a 33yo friend-with-benefits, and a 20yo. None provide exactly what I'm looking for in a mate or BDSM-wise, but I'm enjoying each for their own merits."

After the death of a spouse, some people set about to discover many facets of themselves and of relationships that were previously unavailable. These new experiences may allow them to focus on their own needs and explore the world anew.

Perhaps being widowed, like divorced, describes a moment in time—a time of transition, change, and discovery.

> "Was married vanilla for 25 years, with a spattering of random affairs. After husbands' suicide, I decided to fly my kink flag and not get roped

into a monogamous relationship as I have a very high sexual appetite and men have a hard time keeping up."

A relationship status of "widowed" has some of the same difficulties as "divorced." It happens at a point in time yet lasts forever, and it is probably better described as a marital status than a relationship status. We include these women's quotations because we hope that they will offer inspiration and promise to others who have similar experiences.

Additional Chosen Families

"I am queer identified, who is in a loving bdsm family as the girl to a lesbian Daddy, Girl to my Mamma."

"Chosen families" are groups of individuals who cultivate connections with people who they consider family even if they are not biologically related. One common example of creating a chosen family is to marry your partner—who then becomes family.

Additional chosen families described in our study include the following titles: polyamorous families, BDSM families, leather families, and leather households, among others. Note that other relationship styles could also be considered families, even if they aren't described as such. The relationships of the people involved in chosen families might be platonic, romantic, sexual, or kink in nature.

Polyamorous families are composed of multiple relationships with individuals, couples, triads, or more. The structure of some polyamorous families includes the tasks of raising children, and the roles of co-parenting may vary among the adult family members.

"I found a male partner who understands my needs, soon we formed a polyamorous family with as many as 4 men & 5 women (with 3 small children) …"

BDSM families can be non-sexual and individuals within families can be involved in relationships outside of their family dynamics.

"We are also forming a BDSM family and exploring poly."

"I myself am single and have never been married. But I am in a long-term relationship with a married man who is in an open relationship with his wife. We are also all in what we call our BDSM family, and it is 24/7 for us. I also am allowed casual play partners when my schedule permits."

"I am under the protection of a BDSM family, though not sexually involved with any of them. They guide me and provide wisdom/advice. i am under consideration and in a new relationship with a Dominant man who i adore. We are exclusive, but consider the addition of a third for casual play/sex later on. We also play with people that are pre-approved in things that we don't yet have skills in, but not in a sexual fashion."

In the following leather families, the members have power dynamics and a hierarchal arrangement within the family.

"I actually have a Leather Family, which is not, IMO the same as BDSM family. Also, I have been in 24/7 power/authority exchange relationships in the past."

"Leather Family, 24/7 Master/slave relationship."

"Married with two husbands and one wife. One husband is a slave. All are part of a leather family."

"Three Dominant Leather Household with Male Head of Household (my Master), Myself (Dominant masochist Female), and my boyfriend (another Dominant male, though not my Dom). We have a few specific 'casual' partners, but we are open to longer-term relationships with the right people."

There are other types of chosen families that involve power dynamics besides BDSM families and leather families.

"I have a female partner I have been with for 13 years, and a submissive who has been living with us for 3 years. We are a committed family."

"24/7 D/s relationship with Male as HOH and poly with another female who is not submissive, but bottoms to both me and the male."

"MY life is now as I wish it, I have a Loving Family of slaves and Sisters, FemDomme style 24/7. After years of abuse from Dominant men who think they rule the world I can finally relax and enjoy my life. (I have been the victim of abuse since I was a small child). I kept finding the wrong men until now."

"(clarification, rather than 'other'): I am single but am in a family with a D/s couple. The 's' is actually more of a switch and I submit to both of them. They provide protection and we celebrate holidays, etc. together. We are just as likely to get together for chatter and a meal as we are for play. They do allow me to 'date' or have other 'play partners,' which I do on occasion. I also have an LTR (~7years) with a friend who was my first Master but who is now long distance. It's more mentorship than a partnership though so I still generally classify myself as single. My ideal situation would be a long-term, 24/7, monogamous (or possibly open with very specific boundaries) relationship."

There is not an authoritative definition of these family types, nor a clear idea of roles and relationships involved, except as chosen by the members of the family. Recognize that these women made deliberate decisions to create or join a group of people (which could be just two) who want to accept the roles, responsibilities, and benefits of family life.

Consider for a moment if you have a chosen family. Who are the people in your life who you are closely connected to, with whom you have a sense of caring and trust? It could be as simple as "every Thanksgiving, I prepare a meal for these friends" or "I'm elderly, and my neighbor checks in on me every morning." It could be the extended family provided by marriage. It might be someone you rarely see in person but with whom you've maintained a bond through regular correspondence.

If you don't have a chosen family, does the idea seem interesting to you? As you read the quotations above, did any of them appeal to you? How would you find others with whom you could discuss creating your own version of a chosen family?

What Does This Mean?

Relationships refer to our associations with other people and our relationship styles. Commonly called "marital status," relationships have historically been reduced to selecting one of only four options: single, married, divorced, or widowed.

However, even within this conventional framework, each relationship and relationship style is unique. Imagine the various ways one couple can be different from another:

- The way the partners met each other
- Shared memories, overcoming challenges together
- Division of labor, roles, responsibilities, and expectations
- Financial and economic considerations
- Living arrangements
- Unique personalities of each partner: preferences, habits, quirks, pet-names, inside jokes, rituals, goals, plans, and dreams
- Sexual preferences and compatibilities
- Communication styles
- The way each partner shows and receives love and affection
- Parenting experiences: whether they struggle with fertility issues, want children in the future, don't know if they want children, already have children or step-children, or choose to be child-free
- Cultural, religious, and/or age considerations

With so few examples in media about what people are actually doing, the default narrative is the one that makes for good storylines in books, movies, and television: if you are attracted to or have a physical/sexual encounter with someone outside of your relationship, then it automatically means that you love your partner less, that your marriage is in trouble, that you will leave your partner for this other person, or that your partner should leave you.

Remember our opening quotation for this chapter? It included, "… If I'd known there were more ways to build a family, relationship, or a life when I was a young woman I might have been able to skip two bad marriages …"

There is not only more than one way to build a family; there are infinite ways, each as unique as the people involved! Maybe you don't know anyone who has veered from the social expectations of the "'official script,' you know, house, fence 2 1/3 kids, dog, cat, one man, one woman." But now that you read this chapter, you have all of these examples from your new friends on how they have formed their families, relationships, and lives.

And even if you don't fit in any of our categories, that's okay!

The purpose of categories is to organize. It is easier when the organized parts are easily distinguishable, and the fewer the options, the easier it is to categorize. But, when there are overlaps, to varying degrees, of many things … well, those categories that are meant to organize become messy. And messy categories are real life.

People are creative and imaginative about how their life or love should be. We aren't always able to fit into the boxes of categories in a survey when none of them accurately describe our actual situation (even when categories are expanded beyond the basics). And isn't that wonderful?

Reasons for Participating in Kink   5

"In my humble opinion, it makes little sense to categorize along activities. It is much more interesting, [to ask] what are the driving forces behind the activity, i.e. which desire does the person wish to satisfy. If e.g. a woman likes to be gagged, she may do this, because:

- she seeks liberation from an urge to control others through words,
- she likes the incisive pain in the corners of her mouth,
- she loves to have an orifice (mouth) penetrated,
- she likes the taste of latex,
- she seeks the humiliation of drooling in front of others,
- she likes to obey her master who asks her to,
- and a million other reasons."

Do you ever ask yourself "why" you enjoy certain activities?

Why do you enjoy riding your bike with your friends on the weekend, love hiking through the forest on a fall day, or find happiness in backyard gardening? Why do you love the taste of rigatoni, the smell of pine needles, or the sound of a cooing pigeon?

If you research "Why people like what they like," you'll find that the best assumption is that it's a combination of predisposition and life's experiences. In other words, you like what you like. You can delve deeply into your psyche, but when you follow the thread long enough, it still comes down to the simple statement, "It makes me happy."

Kink is different, isn't it?

We know from our research that kink includes activities such as being urinated on, being punished, humiliated, and objectified, using painful clamps on labia and scrotum, being choked, anal stretching, and acts using menstrual blood. And we know that kink also includes activities such as cuddling, massaging, kissing, and licking, hand jobs, playing with breasts, and oral sex.

It's a strange combination of activities, don't you think? "Kink" includes common behaviors that are wholesome and unique practices we didn't even know exist. And now you should be asking yourself, "Which of those activities do they mean are 'common behaviors' and which are 'unique practices'?"

Some people jog for 30 minutes on a weekend as exercise, and some run dozens of miles daily until their feet bleed. Some families vacation by journeying to a foreign land and living with the locals, and others spend a week on a cruise ship, scarcely leaving their cabin. Some folks dine at fine restaurants to enjoy the subtle flavors of each dish, while others snack quickly just to not be hungry. And each person considers what they do as normal and what the others do as a bit odd or even incomprehensible—yet we are all the same, all finding our place in the world, seeing what works for us and what doesn't.

In fact, kink is *not* different. It's no different than preferring coffee to tea, being an early bird or a night owl, or listening to heavy metal music versus smooth jazz. It's just another aspect of ourselves that we discover and accept, whether that aspect is cuddling or clamping.

Let's take a step back and explore these ideas at a higher level. While we should accept ourselves and our likes and dislikes, we can't answer every "Why do you like that?" question with "It makes me happy," or we'd never learn anything about ourselves or connect with other people.

For example:

- I like the smell of pipe smoke *because* it reminds me of my grandfather
- I like cooking *because* I take bits and pieces and create a dish irresistible to my appetite
- I like talking about fashion with my friends *because* we all have such different ideas and I always learn something new

It is important to know, at some level, why we like what we like. Being able to clarify, "I like that *because* ..." is what allows us to understand other people and find the shared commonality we have with everyone on the planet.

That is what this chapter is about: the reasons women participate in kink activities, the *"because"* part of what they like.

Let's begin.

The most common reason these women participate in kink should not surprise anyone: "for self-discovery/personal pleasure." This is basically why we do just about everything, right? However, we found that many women in the survey elaborate even further about motivations for engaging in kink.

> "It is a part of my being; it isn't something which can be turned off. It is who I am as a person."

> "I could and should write a book but to summarize, I consider myself as a therapist, opening up other worlds and moods for everyone."

> "The scene has been a tremendously positive influence for me and I can't imagine living without it. It's a healthy way for people to express themselves in a safe environment and I am honored to have had so many truly amazing BDSM experiences throughout my life. :)"

> "As I said before there are healthy ways to enjoy and express oneself sexually. No one should ever try something that they aren't comfortable with and they should never feel pressured to. This life isn't for everyone, and anyone thinking of experimenting should do so safely and intelligently."

The reasons these women participate in kink activities can be categorized into three themes:

- Personal
- Relational
- Sexual (which is both personal and relational)

Naturally, there is overlap between these themes and this discussion isn't meant to pigeonhole people's reasons unnaturally. Rather, it is a mechanism to allow us to better understand by classifying the reasons into categories we can all relate to. We hope that these women's motivations for doing what they do will both inspire you and resonate with your own reasons for doing what you do.

Personal Reasons

> "BDSM allows for extensive personal reflection, responsibility, and growth. It encompasses numerous dynamics, all of which require

continued education and intelligent, intuitive, communication as individuals and smaller groups as well as within the community at large."

Sometimes, the reasons we participate in activities are personal, meaning, "it gives *me* pleasure." For example, "I like the feel of the sun on my face," "I love luxuriating in warm baths," or "I enjoy listening to my favorite music." We don't associate those feelings with relationships or sexual activities, but rather with a warm fuzzy happiness inside.

This is also true when it comes to kink activities. Words such as "fun," "enjoy," "love," and "want" are regularly used to explain reasons to engage in these behaviors. To drill down a bit further, we can divide personal reasons into sub-categories including enjoyment, self-discovery, and resilience. Let's explore each of these categories.

Enjoyment

"I do them because I enjoy them. They feel good and allow me to express my sexuality the way I want to."

Enjoyment simply means to take pleasure or satisfaction from something. That doesn't really help much, we know, but it's very difficult to find words to describe an emotion; we are all supposed to understand it from our own experiences. So, remind yourself of something you enjoy, and think about that feeling as you read these women's reasons for engaging in kink behaviors.

"I only enjoy giving up control to my husband. I enjoy topping from time to time with women or cross dressers."

"They are all for my pleasure. I am a bottom but not a submissive, so I only do things that I enjoy."

"My sexual lifestyle is complicated, but very interesting. I enjoy having the freedom to participate in activities that I enjoy, as long as they do not hurt others and are consensual."

"Most of what i enjoy falls into the category of submissive behavior … i enjoy being tied up and 'abused' and 'used,' taken violently, to follow orders. it is incredibly hot to think of yourself in this way … that you're so irresistible that your partner must have you then and there. if it is 'against your will' … which of course it's not. :) *(Redacted)* [American Author] once said that bdsm sex is just cops and robbers for grown-ups with no pants. i think that's true! it's fun to play out these scenarios … and i get an orgasm at the end, even better!"

Now there's an interesting idea! That kink behaviors we enjoy as adults are simply our childhood games taken to a different level—allowing for more lightheartedness and playfulness. Is that true for you? Think back to your childhood and all the activities you did and the games you played with your friends. How many of those do you still do in a modified form now?

Kink is not always so serious. Each of the following women thinks that "fun" or "silly" is the perfect reason to engage in kink behaviors.

"It's all fun and games; a stress reliever; would live it 24/7 if I could with my existing partner. He feels the same way."

"Just to be, and was with friends. I am a bit of a Betty Boop type, so they expect silly like sexual things as such."

"For fun, for a desirable physical sensation, for a challenge, and as a key aspect of my sexuality and my relationships."

"There's so much more to learn and discover and new partners to learn them with! It seems the more I learn/try, the more fun and free I feel with my sexuality."

"It's fun. Really, really fun. Puts a smile on my face and a song in my heart, and I'm more than fine with covering a bit more skin to hide marks so long as everyone goes home happy. Know what's the best? When things are going so well that they're laughing and cursing and straining to kiss you, or vice versa. Love it!"

You can't go wrong when the reason you engage in an activity is simply because it makes you happy.

"Very, very happy as a slave."

"Please don't make me click so many buttons next time. Have a 'check all.' I am an adventurous woman and have sought to try out anything in any combination that could still be considered 'happy and safe.'"

Even when you are involved in kink for personal enjoyment, it's wonderful when you find someone who helps make it even more enjoyable.

> "Another lover wasn't kinky at all but told me she was glad to make me happy. She also happened to naturally have just the right level of dominance that I want from a partner when I'm in a submissive mood."

> "When something is hot to my partner it becomes far more attractive to me. I have gone further in the moment and not been able to reconcile how much I enjoyed it and was into it when no longer in that moment."

Sometimes we do something simply because we are bored—the antidotes to boredom are stimulation, activity, and creativity.

> "Bored."

> "because i could."

> "TO AMUSE MYSELF."

When your activities are in spaces that allow for play and creative expression, you can feel imaginative, ignited, and inventive, which provides an opportunity to find your inner artist or create something unexpected.
We see this artistic expression in the following three women.

> "For Art."

> "Fun, sensual, connected, creative, intimate, expressive, deep, emotional, healing, joyful, luscious—just a few words to describe how I feel about BDSM and/or how I feel when I participate in it."

> "Also enjoy doing the unexpected, i.e. a dominant with a lot of fancy torture and pain tools gave me permission to do whatever I wanted while he was naked and blindfolded and expected me to use his tools/gear to inflict severe pain. Instead I finger-painted him with various foods …"

We have shown how personal enjoyment of kink activities can be fun, playful, happy, and creative, and this enjoyment can be intensely felt.

> "I'm still learning a lot about myself in this lifestyle but I find everything I have done extremely erotic and wonderfully fulfilling."

> "My sexuality is blossoming, and I find more and more about myself the more I let go and allow myself to try things and let my fantasies rule."

> "These activities are physically and emotionally fulfilling to me. They add to sexual excitement and they aid in the building of close relationships.

My participation in them is grounded in the ideology of freedom of personal choice and self-expression, not in as a physical or moral necessity based on gender roles, religion or custom."

Some women share what they enjoy during certain circumstances and scenes, and briefly explain the meanings behind the activities.

"Love to have a switch fight … meaning with another person who is 'switchy' and wrestling/fighting and loser gets fucked or winner gets fucked … FUN!"

"My favorite activity is actually adult nursing relationship/adult breastfeeding (ANR/ABF) and lactation. NOT as a mommy but as a submissive woman providing for those she cares for by having them suckling from my lactating breasts."

"I don't remember there being anything listed about fire, though maybe it was listed with fire cupping. Something else I like to combine is cutting and fire cupping. It's beautiful when you cup someone's skin after a cut and have the privilege of watching their blood being drawn out of their body and into the cup."

"The other scenario that was not on the list was fisting … i have tried and succeeded in vaginal fisting! it was AMAZING! by far the best treatment and most intimate experience ever! i have wanted to try anal fisting but i am sure that would be just as intimate if not more so that vaginal. the fullness to the breaking point but not going over the edge is amazing! it's definitely intense."

Additional descriptors used by the participants to describe what they meant by "enjoyment" are as follows: feel good, expression, stress-relief, smile, delight, desirable, adventurous, artistic, connected, healing, luscious, satisfaction, emotionally fulfilling, grounded, beautifully complex, and wonderful.

How would you describe the imagery and pleasure that come to your mind when you think about "enjoyment"?

We offer another idea for you to consider.

As you read statements such as "I enjoy," "I love," "I really like," "very, very happy," were you able to ignore the specific activity they enjoyed and, instead, relate to them as individuals and share their feeling of happiness? Try it now: go back to the previous quotations and just focus on the feelings described rather than the specific activities. We can't tell you what to think, of course.

Self-Discovery

> "The more I learn about these activities, the more I learn about myself and my limits and what is important to me (and not just within the 'confines' of this arena, I am learning a lot about respect and how to demand it)."

The *Cambridge Dictionary* states that self-discovery is "the process of learning about yourself and your beliefs" (*Cambridge Dictionary*, n.d.). What a curious notion! I've been me since I was born, and I already know what I believe. What else is there, right?

Wrong!

The world never stops changing; every day brings something new. Fortunately, we all have a fascinating ability to continue to change ourselves and our beliefs and to adapt to new situations throughout our lives. And this gives us the opportunity to discover novel aspects of ourselves, to reexamine and rearrange our beliefs and perhaps our whole belief system, and to find new and exciting ways to express ourselves and to *be* ourselves.

Notice in the quotations below all the times these women use the word "new" and how cathartic it is to say, "I am new."

> "I'm new to the 'scene,' and am just getting started! :)"

> "My partner and i are fairly new to the community, but we like to try new things."

> "I love to continually learn new skills, have new experiences and continue to grow through the path I am on."

> "I'm new to the whole BDSM scene, so, haven't experienced much. But what I have experienced/experimented with, has been a great eye-opener to who I am."

These women state that there are parts of themselves they wish to explore, develop, and grow. So, they actively look for new experiences in the kink realm and are motivated by these adventures as a path to self-discovery.

> "The discovery of these avenues of freedom in sexuality have given me an intense and overwhelming positive experience."

> "Not everything I tried ended up being pleasurable, and one or two were really bad experiences, but on the flip side, some things I thought I'd hate (e.g. cupping, fireplay) ended up being my favorites."

> "… Learning to exercise surrender and vulnerability has been instrumental in my development as a human being and positively affected my life outside of the kink world."

> "There is so much to do in the context of a BDSM lifestyle that I don't think even the lifetime practitioner could figure out everything they like to do or everyone they are attracted to. It's a fascinating and ever-evolving part of sexuality that I am glad to have discovered and be a part of."

Several women express that their personal pleasure co-exists with self-discovery, and in some cases, necessarily so.

> "I think all sexual activities should be done for the purposes of personal pleasure and self-discovery, whether you are with your partner or not."

> "My male partner's requests tend to fall in line with my self-discovery/personal pleasure. When they don't I say no."

> "I feel that all good sexual activity should be pleasurable and provides room for self-discovery. I'm a huge proponent of continued growth/learning throughout life."

These women remind us that discovery begins with exploration.

> "Exploring has given me better insight into who i am and why."

> "Everything has been done with a loving partner who understands my limits and helps me explore myself and our relationship."

For some people, personal growth is not a passive activity; it comes from purposefully moving out of the comfort zone and striving to surmount challenges.

> "To push the edges of personal limits, to assess how 'real' the ideas in my head are :-}"

> "Most talk about limits and such. Luckily W/we've been together long enough that i don't worry about that. He pushes my limits but not any further than i can handle."

> "Wonderfully freeing activity, exciting, relaxing after, sense of accomplishment if difficult torture, great sexual releases."
>
> "To me BDSM is about growing and experiencing emotions. It is a way to get in touch with myself. To me it is a kind of therapy. It is about being with people who have an open mind. It is about self-expression."

It's pretty obvious, isn't it? When we experience something new, we learn something new about ourselves. One of the goals of new experiences is to delve deeper and consider what you can do with your new knowledge. How can you expand this self-discovery to encourage self-growth? How do you develop new feelings and ideas into concepts that actually improve your life?

The answer lies in the definition of self-discovery we examined at the beginning of this section: "the process of learning about yourself and your beliefs." It's the *process* of learning. It is a cyclical series of steps involving new ideas and activities that then further influence and educate you.

You certainly are involved with self-discovery every day, but perhaps you don't give it the acknowledgment it is due. Find time to identify what new experiences you've recently had, both subtle and substantial, and consider how they changed you and, even more, how they might continue to change you.

Resilience

> "I'm a depressive, and the impact play, flogging and whippings seem to help me deal with the disease a lot more than just meds alone."

Resilience is "the ability to be happy, successful, etc. again after something difficult or bad has happened," according to the *Cambridge Dictionary* (n.d.). People find that, sometimes, participating in kink activities can help to overcome circumstances, like negative past experiences, stress, medical issues, shame, and grief. Life is full of challenges, and kink is one way to cope with those challenges.

The women in this section share their experiences with resilience, illustrating how kink helped them grow and work through personal struggles.

> "To deal with past issues."
>
> "This lifestyle offers me a mental and physical type of therapy. Helps me to release myself and be accepted for who I am. I am a lesbian but will

play with men but no intercourse on my side. I will perform intercourse on their side."

"I see kink as only a small part of a relationship. I also find there are times in my life—particularly during highly stressful periods—that I am drawn to being bound or beaten (even if the desire is not actualized), whereas at other times I have either minimal interest or am even somewhat repelled. If I do end up in a non-vanilla relationship, kink would be the spice in an otherwise normal life."

As we've learned, kink activities cover a spectrum of human behaviors in terms of intensity. To build resilience, some people seek out the more intense activities, those that require an inward focus. This helps them to see themselves through a different lens or as a different person than they usually are allowed to be.

Some women employ kink activities as a method of dealing with mental and physical health concerns and disabilities. In our survey, several respondents discuss how they've adjusted their kink dynamics and behaviors due to aging or physical disabilities. Each person brings a different perspective to how kink can be integrated and used in various forms depending on their life circumstances.

"Just for the record, I am legally Blind (NOt Totally) and I am an amputee ... I use an electric and a manual wheelchair, but that sure as hell doesn't stop me from having partners and getting my needs met and meeting the needs of my partners."

"I am a bottoms bottom with sensory integration disorder—I don't feel things the same as everyone else. I need total silence and darkness to feel my own skin—to concentrate on the feelings being brought out of me. if the scale was bottom, bottom/switch, switch, switch/top, top ... I would be under bottom—I need 90% of the interest and desire focused on me for a long while before I can reach back—and participate—not want—but can't reach back. then I get nippy—bitey—grab the hair hot and bothered and let them know—the rest of the time I chirp, cooo, hum, whinny, giggle, and make all kinds of enduringly cute noises—but I don't reach out."

Kink play can help replace a fear of needles (and, let's be honest, needles are designed to puncture skin. Ouch!) with a focus on pleasure, and in some cases, enough pleasure to happily return to the healthcare system.

> "I was someone who was so terrified of needles i did not go to a Doctor or Hospital for 10 years. Then i lay and relaxed, and prepared my brain to accept needles as play, and i found i love them, i now focus on the endorphin rush instead of the perceived fear. I went from Freak Out no way to Yes, Yes, i love them."

Some women discuss how they lived either in denial or shame for their sexuality, and that through kink play, they overcome these thoughts and feelings to find self-acceptance.

> "I was always ashamed of the 'out of the ordinary' things I was interested in until I found the internet. I now feel a lot better about myself and my sexuality and have learned a lot more. Sex should be less of a hang-up …"

> "There are almost none of these activities that I enjoy at all if dominance or submission are absent. I don't enjoy pain much if there isn't at least a little role play. It helps me set aside sexual shame if I'm pretending to be someone else."

> "At 44 I have been doing this for about 2 years: it was something that I recognized very early in myself (4/5 possibly younger) but was taught by family and early lovers to be ashamed of. That lead to years of an abusive marriage (very common story btw) until divorce and finally through FetLife recognition and acceptance for who I am."

Someone who is experiencing grief will feel a range of emotions—of sadness, shock, denial, disbelief, anger, rage, disappointment, pain, guilt, and more. All of these emotions during a time of mourning are valid, can come and go in various levels of intensity, and are not experienced in any particular order. We all have to find our own way to process loss; there is no single answer.

The woman below finds value in the kink community during periods of grief. The community can provide additional support networks through creating and building connections with others. At a time of grief, these connections can help us realize that we are not entirely alone in the world.

> "My late husband introduced me to this many years ago. It was this that brought me out of mourning to be able to find someone to dominate me and bring me back to life. Since then, I have made a lot of good friends through local groups, the local dungeon, and online. Through some grief support, I met someone else that helped me through my

grieving process. He also went through a death. We became friends, then we played once in a while, then we found we were very alike and started a D/s relationship. While I used to switch roles of dominant and submissive with my late husband, with this relationship I am the dominate. While I didn't think I would like that all the time, I have found it very rewarding. We moved in together 8 months ago and live D/s 24/7 and life just couldn't get any better."

There are many tools available to build resilience and you must spend time investigating to decide which are right for you. You now know that kink activities and communities have the potential to be of service as well.

Kink activities range from simple, silly fun, filled with giggles and laughter, to a profound source of personal growth, eye-opening, filled with revelations about the world. Cathartic releases, filled with tears and, yes, even screams, may be needed in order to push through a challenge and get to a place of processing pain and emotional wounds.

There is no prescribed way to be involved with kink. It's a personal choice, something you alone get to decide the purpose of. We hope that, whatever you decide for yourself, you have a warm fuzzy happiness inside you.

Relational Reasons

"For me it is more than a way to 'have sex.' This is a way to authentically connect with people who enjoy expanding the boundaries of what is possible and pleasurable in an intimate relationship."

Let's refocus for a moment on the theme of this chapter: reasons for participating in kink. Besides participating for personal reasons, women stated they participated for relational reasons.

Relational? Yup. It refers to the way in which two or more people are connected.

Visualize a diagram showing your connection to all the people close to you, joined with lines thick or thin depending on the strength of the bond. Now consider that each of those people will have a slightly different diagram with lines of different thickness than yours. How can we manage such complexity to create relationships we can cherish and nurture?

For some people, participating in kink activities and community is a way to do just that, to feel closer, more connected, and more closely bonded with their partner or partners.

What are the points of connectivity that are unique for those involved in kink? Let's examine some of them.

> "We've had a wonderful, amazing, long, and HOT monogamous and very fulfilling marriage."

> "Everything I've done has brought me intense pleasure and satisfaction. My relationship with my partner feels like something more beautifully complex than a vanilla relationship could ever be. Long live BDSM!"

> "Where else can you manipulate another person's naked body and you both regard it as fun?? What a delightful level of intimacy is provided by BDSM!"

> "I have found the BDSM arena to be a higher level of interest for me. It's not simple sexual intercourse, touching, masturbation that I would have had in a vanilla relationship. It's so much more fulfilling."

Let's look further into some of the relational reasons these women participate in kink: how experiencing pleasure can be bonding, how defined roles and structures help to create a foundation for their relationship, and how trust is an important factor in forming secure attachments.

Giving and Receiving Pleasure

> "I never do anything except for personal pleasure. If my Master asks me to do something, this very fact already gives me pleasure."

Sometimes, we participate in activities because it's something we know that our partner will enjoy. We may not consider going to a theme park of our own accord, but when we know how much a loved one is enthusiastic about amusement park rides, we can't help but feel happy to oblige. The same may sometimes be true with kink behaviors. We may feel pleasure and connectedness in knowing that a partner's desires are being fulfilled.

> "I use these activities to please a partner who in turn pleases me. Variety has kept sex interesting for over twenty years of marriage."

> "As i said before, i am a slave, so His desires are my desires."

> "I like to be forced to fuck other men for my partner's pleasure."

"90% of my exploration and fun are self-driven, though occasionally I will participate in activities that may interest my partner when I am neutral. I will not participate in something I do not feel comfortable with for someone else's whim."

"There are things I have engaged in for the pleasure of others that I don't personally enjoy but do willingly for them. The main one is water sports, more specifically being urinated on. It's not something I enjoy, but I was willing to do it for that specific partner because I wanted to do something special for them. I wouldn't consider it something that I find pleasure from."

"… The first man that I found to scene with is not very dominant (he has a beautiful dungeon, lots of toys and skills but is not dom in his nature, way too nice) and not into pain. After many sessions of pleasure torture with a Hitachi and electrical play, he finally gave me some pain. To my surprise I didn't enjoy it. I realized I only enjoy it if the dom gets off on it, otherwise he's doing something that makes him uncomfortable just to please me, which I find boring and vanilla (I have had a number of vanilla boyfriends in the past that only wanted to do what I wanted to do etc. which is why the relationships ended) …"

This leads to the topic of mutual pleasure, where both partners are interested in the activity for reasons that complement each other. Depending on the activity, partners can either be doing the same thing (say, kissing or cuddling), or one person can be doing an activity to another (think of massaging—one person gives a massage and the other receives a massage). In both examples, each person is finding pleasure in the same activity.

The following are examples of women who participate in kink activities for the purpose of mutual pleasure.

"For fun and mutual enjoyment."

"I am fond of a puppy and enjoy playing with her and owning a puppy."

"For the pleasure of myself and my male partner. Because I need it and he gives it because he loves me."

"I have a boy submissive I play with regularly. He does request we play occasionally and I am more than glad to do so when he wants or is able to. We live in separate towns, so it is on his schedule many times and I am fine with that since we both get enjoyment out of it!"

Pleasure and delight that is derived from participating in a shared activity that both partners enjoy can bring people closer.

> "Owned a pet and enjoyed sadistic play he enjoyed."
>
> "I love my partner, and these activities make us both happy."
>
> "i have a very open sexually relationship with husband. we both explore our fantasies with the help of each other."
>
> "Because my husband and I (grandparents, with very good jobs, and college degrees) love hot, kinky sex with each other."
>
> "I enjoy participating in BDSM-activities, which is the primary reason I do it. My boyfriend feels the same, so we engage in these activities together."

Then, there is the pleasure from giving pleasure. To enjoy the moments of focusing on your partner's experiences and find joy in their excitement and fulfillment is gratifying in its own way. And some people can gain pleasure only from pleasing their partners.

> "i would rather please the Dominant Woman with whom i'm with than experience an orgasm."
>
> "I gain pleasure from giving pleasure, and the satisfaction of my partner. If they are happy, then so am I. If they are unfulfilled, then I feel that lack and feel diminished by it."
>
> "To fulfill [my] own need to serve :) ... the only thing i found when i answered your questions, in reference to self for erotic/sensual pleasure, [for] most of my activities (although give me pleasure in serving) the abundance of my own pleasure comes from actually serving and fulfilling the other partner's needs ..."
>
> "... To sum up my sexual activity preference, however, I am most motivated by my partner's satisfaction. I do identify as a submissive and can very rarely instigate any sort of 'play time' with my partner though I may want it. I enjoy having someone else in more control, especially over my sexual practices."

Some of these ideas may be, on the surface, foreign. Are "If they are happy, then so am I," or "His desires are my desires" concepts you can relate to?

Consider how you feel watching someone open a birthday present, a puppy playing in the grass, or a bride and groom running under a cloud of rice. We are designed to derive enjoyment from the pleasure of others, and for some people, it is a significant portion of their life and of their love.

Defined Roles and Structures: Creating a Foundation

> "And a slave does what she's told, you know?"

Kink relations differ from most other relations in that there are no rules other than those agreed upon. If you say, "I'm married," we know the rules: there is a legal bond between you and another person. If you say, "I'm in a kink relationship," we know … nothing. Your kink relationship could be your marriage or it could be anything. You are able to establish your own ad hoc rules, roles, and expectations.

You might be thinking, "Rules? Why do I need more rules?"

Good question! You may already have plenty of rules with your partner that you've never discussed. Think about all the small tasks that happen regularly which seem to always be your job or always your partner's job.

Did you just fall into these roles without much discussion?

When you have a kink relationship, you may still fall into some roles, but others are more defined and explicitly discussed, which can be helpful in avoiding misunderstandings, meeting expectations, setting boundaries, and minimizing disappointments. When you work together to create boundaries and limits, it can give you the freedom to be more of what you want to be, i.e., yourself.

Can you see the way defined roles and structures can help create harmony within relationships in the examples below?

> "My partners have input into our activities, but I decide what we do."
>
> "I enjoy being in charge of what happens between myself and the partner. I am somewhat sadistic, so I enjoy CBT quite a bit."
>
> "I have a little protocol, behavioural rules, in my D/s relationship. Since recent[ly], I have to call my partner the Dutch equivalent of Master and the polite, formal form of 'you' in Dutch. These rules are in order at all times. We have a love relationship."

"I am also a 'service bottom' ... serving/being a body servant (butler type duties) are VERY rewarding and pleasurable to me. I usually 'top' more often when I am single and reserve 'bottoming' to a primary relationship. I have been a kinky woman for 33 years. In the early days I bottomed to numerous people (women only) regardless of whether or not we were dating. In the past 15 years I have become more selective about bottoming and limit it to 'serious dating' or to a committed partner."

"As i have said, i am a sexual submissive who knows [my] role in life is to be used for sex. Lucky for me, i have always loved sex. i am lucky to have found a partner that finds joy from making certain i am used often and in using me himself. i do what i am told as long as it is within my limits—no pee, no poop, no blood, no animals, no children—these have always been my limits and my partner agrees. my partner is always nearby during my use to protect me as well as direct the play (if need be). he has worked hard to set-up marvelous playdates with great people. some are nice and easy... some are rough use ... i love them all."

Of course, there are other roles and structures that can be helpful to discuss. Do you remember the list of the top 20 erotic stimuli/behaviors participated in by the women in the survey? The number one activity was touching: caressing, cuddling, massaging, and tickling. So, rather than just allowing your partner to cuddle with you, discuss each of your roles and structure and find common ground before beginning.

We know you are probably thinking, "Jeez! Really! Now we have to negotiate cuddling?"

And here is your agreement: "We agree to turn off our phones for the next 30 minutes."

Yup, that's it. That's all it needs to be. You have just used one of the fundamental aspects of kink philosophy: mutual consent.

And as you grow to understand the usefulness of discussing roles and structure, you will be better able to communicate your own preferences, boundaries, and limits, and to better understand your partner's. This can be as simple as "I want you to pull my hair, but only if you grab it at the base of the scalp so that you aren't pulling individual hairs out," and "You need to tell me each time when you are ready to be kissed, because I can never figure it out."

See? Rather than becoming irritated when it doesn't happen, you've expressly communicated when it should happen. You have defined structure for your cuddling and are happier for it.

Being deliberate in defining and agreeing to each other's roles can help reduce misunderstandings and allow for experiences that might not be available otherwise, which, we hope, will help strengthen your relational bonds.

Trust and Vulnerability

> "The best part of my BDSM play is having no control at all. I love to submit to another whom I trust enough to hand over all control to and let them do whatever they like. I can open up my body and mind to a range of new experiences and feelings I could never otherwise have."

Trust is having confidence in something or believing in someone. It's a quality some people search for in a partner, hoping to find someone who is trustworthy and trusting. Because kink relationships have ad hoc rules (see previous topic), some people are able to develop connections that allow them to experience trust to a far more intense level than they otherwise would.

> "It's mostly about trusting the 'top' so much that you can be immobilized, blindfolded, whipped, choked etc. with absolute certainty that he loves me and will stop the second I say the safe word. I get a lot of pleasure in being dominated sexually. I feel relaxed and excited, I am not making any decisions, just experiencing everything."

> "It is a matter of Psychology. I've had so much happen to me, that i can not relax unless i am around people i trust. In order to fully relax and let my guard down, i must be with a man whom i trust and respect such that i let him tie me up. The better a job he does of securing me (proving he is taking responsibility for caring for me) the more i am able to let go and de-stress."

> "I'm mainly interested in the discovery of 'the Other' in a relationship of any kind and duration. My approach includes a strong mental and/or spiritual connection prior to any physical contact and what happens is not the result of a rational, predetermined intention, but occurs as a direct result of that connection. It's the result of connecting to another person on the intuitive level, and it's entirely based on the concepts of shared trust and responsibility."

And for some, the level of play with certain partners varies depending on the level of trust they have for those partners.

> "Each top/partner is different. That being said, I can stay in light play or move to deeper play. It depends, not only on their preferences but the level of trust I share with the individual."

> "I also love breath play and choking … but all these activities I would only participate with a man I trusted explicitly. Therefore, I do not engage in play too often, thus I am pretty unsatisfied sexually most all of my adult life."

> "I am a switch, as I like to be a Top or a Bottom. I rarely if ever submit to a man though, as I find it difficult to trust one as much as is needed. I also rarely participate in a strictly bdsm relationship. I like to have a lot of vanilla mixed in to my everyday life. I do not have casual sex partners either. But I like to have the option of participating in some kink, rather than date someone who is strictly vanilla."

Some of those descriptions are pretty intense, aren't they? Yet the women here are able to enjoy relinquishing control and freedom only because they have someone they can trust, feeling safe and secure while also being vulnerable.

Vulnerable is defined (by the same dictionary) as "able to be easily hurt, influenced, or attacked" (*Cambridge Dictionary*, n.d.).

Think about that for a moment. The ability to be easily hurt is a quality, a quality that some people possess and strive to develop more fully. As with trust, there are those who seek to develop their ability to be more vulnerable and those who search for such a partner.

> "i prefer to be very vulnerable with someone i trust. i like mental bondage as well as physical bondage, and i am quite eager to please. Erotic humiliation is quite arousing to me, but i dislike degradation of the kind that would cause emotional harm, such as to my self-esteem. i don't play with many on the level that would make me vulnerable, because of the huge amount of trust that it takes. However, i WILL participate in demos as a bottom in order to facilitate teaching."

> "I find that it's not the actual skill-based play that does it for me (caning, flogging, etc.) … it's the power exchange and/or energy exchange. For example, if I scene with someone for a caning and it's just about the caning … [it's] not going to turn me on. But, if the person dominates me by taking my hair, making me lay over the bench, telling me not to move and then caning me … OR even doing it in a sensual way, making sure to keep contact and realizing I'm a whole person not just an ass. Either

> way, I'm surrendering in the scenario. I'm dropping my walls and allowing myself to be vulnerable to this other person. Without that, I'd rather not play."

When we are in a situation where we choose to relinquish control to a trusted person, we can surrender ourselves to the outcome; this is an example of the delicate relationship between trust and vulnerability.

A word of caution: we are not advocating kink as a way to explore trust or vulnerability, any more than we would advocate ballroom dancing or white water rafting to do the same. We are only illustrating that some women who are already involved in the kink community or kink activities have found an opportunity to explore those qualities, and those women shared their stories. Ultimately, you must decide for yourself if you desire to explore those parts of your life and if kink might offer a viable and reasonable mechanism.

Since past behaviors are a good indicator of future behaviors, when we have been able to be vulnerable with a partner and have experienced their responsiveness and care, we can build a foundation of trust. Knowing we are with a safe partner provides the freedom to explore more of our inner desires, fantasies, and aspects of ourselves, and can create close bonds with those we share our life with.

And perhaps those lines connecting you with the people in your life might become just a little bit thicker.

Sexual Reasons

> "Because I enjoy sex and the thrill of the adventure, of course."

In a chapter titled, "Reasons for Participating in Kink," sexual response should be obvious, right? Popular books and films highlight this aspect of kink, and rightly so. Many people get involved with kink activities and the kink community only for the sexual and erotic aspects.

Let's take some time to discuss sexual response. It might get a bit complicated, but hey, it's sex. What did you expect?

You can find various definitions, but we are going to use this one: sexual response encompasses various phases of physical changes in our bodies and emotional states during sexual activity. Okay, good. Now, what is sexual activity?

Well, nobody knows. In the past, researchers defined sexual activity as "intercourse." However, "In recent years, broader definitions of sexual activity have been formulated, to include 'any activity that is sexually arousing, including masturbation'" (Addis et al., 2006). See the problem? You can't include a word in its own definition. "Sexual activity is when you do sexually arousing activities" does not provide any information.

So, we are just going to go with the idea that, like an emotion, sex cannot adequately be explained but must be subjectively experienced.

William Masters and Virginia Johnson (remember them?) in their 1966 book *Human Sexual Response* described a linear progression of sexual response thusly:

Desire → Arousal → Orgasm → Resolution

This model was groundbreaking in its time and has served as a basis for many other sexuality studies (Masters & Johnson, 1966).

However, there is some lack of clarity concerning the order of desire and arousal. If you don't drink enough water, you get thirsty. It's automatic. If you don't get enough sex, well, nothing. That desire does not necessarily just spring into your head uninvited.

Rather, that feeling of desire sometimes does not happen until you are aroused. That arousal can be a kiss, a racy image from the internet, a memory of an erotic moment, or anticipation of a future erotic experience. It could be the moment you finally relax in your hotel room in the Bahamas or have your first glass of wine after work on Friday. It could be anything—we are all wired differently—but it is most often *something* that sparks arousal that triggers desire.

For most people, there are relationship factors, cultural attitudes, and many other external contributors involved in a sexual response. Add to that the fact that some people do not always have orgasm and still reach the resolution stage, and some people have many orgasms before reaching the resolution stage. Additionally, orgasm is not necessarily the focus or "end goal" of sexual activity.

As a further note, none of the women in the survey talked about a "resolution" phase (which is when your body no longer responds to sexual stimulation and needs a break), but some of them did mention what is known as "aftercare." We will discuss aftercare at the end of this section.

Okay, now you know the basics of sexual response. The most important takeaway is that there is no order of the sexual response cycle that is true for everyone.

So, let's start with arousal.

Arousal

"Because it turns me on."

Arousal is the physical state of being "turned-on," evidenced by blood flow to the genitals, typically resulting in vaginal wetness in women and expansion of erectile tissue (which is found in penises AND vulvas). And, arousal is the subjective feeling of being "turned-on." Arousal is a result of erotic stimulation and/or sexual contact, and may happen before or after desire.

In other words, you are horny.

But, let's back up for a moment. "Penis and vulva"? Why not "penis and vagina"? A vulva, or pudendum, is a collective term for the external female genital organs that are visible in the perineal area. The vulva consists of the mons pubis, the labia majora, the labia minora, hymen, the clitoris, the vestibule of the vagina, the urethral orifice, Skene's glands, Bartholin's glands, and the vestibular bulbs. The vagina is the neuromuscular vault connecting to the cervix of the uterus that unsheathes the penis during sexual intercourse and allows passage of the newborn infant during birth.

Of course, you do not need to know all of this to be aroused, but we have a responsibility to ensure the correct information is available. And now it is.

Okay, back to being horny. Remember that there is not always a direct connection between arousal and sexual activity. You might feel sexually aroused when you get a big raise at work, when your favorite baseball team wins the game, or simply by being outside on a warm summer morning.

In the same way, someone may enjoy kink activities, and they may become sexually aroused, but the activity may or may not include overt sexual activity or orgasm.

"My partner and I decided to do so together, because it turned both of us on."

"i got into bdsm with some sex partners & found it to be arousing."

For some, arousal comes from the exchange of power. Knowing that a partner is aroused by the sense of power gifted to them can be its own source of arousal.

"Consensual power exchange between partners can be very erotic."

"The turn on for me is to sense, experience, feel someone aroused by the sense of power using me provides."

So, the reason some people participate in kink activities is to feel turned-on, which can lead to a feeling of desire, which can circle back to feeling arousal. It is not a linear progression but rather a circular one, and there is no right or wrong way to feel arousal or desire.

Desire

> "There's nothing in your questionnaire about one-night stands. i like just grabbing a man once in a while, because i need a fuck and need someone new on my list. i like my lovers as well, but sometimes i want a taste of something new."

Desire is that strong feeling of wanting something, and sexual desire is that strong feeling of wanting sex—whatever "sex" means to you. We can describe desire as organic internal feelings, but, as with other emotions, you must experience it to understand it, and we all have slightly different experiences.

We are sorry we can't give simple definitions of these concepts. Like we said, it's sex. What did you expect?

The following women allude to their sexual desires as their reasons for engaging in kink activities.

> "I've always enjoyed a very high sex drive."

> "He'd been deployed for a long time and we were both very horny. We both equally wanted to do that."

> "I'm 57 years old, not yet menopausal, and more interested in sex than I was at 20 or 30. I think 'kink' amplifies the excitement and gratification of sexuality, and keeps us wanting to stay sexual far later in life, than your average 'vanilla' person."

Of course, your sexual desire might be unrelated to kink, and your kink activities might be unrelated to what you desire sexually. But be cognizant that there are people for whom kink and desire are deeply enmeshed, and consider how such intertwining might resonate with your own sexuality.

Orgasm

> "To cum."

Orgasm! Do we really need to define it?

There are women who state that they have never had an orgasm. There are men who ejaculate without feeling an orgasm. The *Cambridge Dictionary* states orgasm is "the moment of greatest pleasure and excitement in sexual activity" (*Cambridge Dictionary*, n.d.).

Obviously, we need some clarity. Let's see what we can find in the US National Library of Medicine.

One of the first bits of information we found was this: "There is no standard definition of orgasm" (Alwaal et al., 2015).

However, for a man, "orgasm is generally associated with ejaculation, although the two processes are physiologically different. Certain physiological features are associated with orgasm, including hyperventilation up to 40 breaths/min, tachycardia, and high blood pressure. Orgasm is also associated with powerful and highly pleasurable pelvic muscle contractions (especially ischiocavernosus and bulbocavernosus), along with rectal sphincter contractions and facial grimacing" (Alwaal et al., 2015).

A different article in that same publication states that "an orgasm in the human female is a variable, transient peak sensation of intense pleasure, creating an altered state of consciousness, usually with an initiation accompanied by involuntary, rhythmic contractions of the pelvic striated circumvaginal musculature, often with concomitant uterine and anal contractions, and myotonia that resolves the sexually induced vasocongestion and myotonia, generally with an induction of well-being and contentment" (Meston et al., 2004).

In all those words, the ones that are probably most important to each of us are "highly pleasurable" and "intense pleasure." So, although we are fine with the "no standard definition," we will assert that intense pleasure is why most of us enjoy orgasms.

Orgasms can be elusive, absent, multiple, or requiring specific circumstances; for example, some people only orgasm through self-stimulation but not through partnered experiences. For any one person, orgasms can all feel the same or each be different, and the way people experience and describe orgasms can vary from person to person, and over a person's lifetime. Orgasms do not need to be the "end goal" of sexual encounters—sex can be fulfilling without them.

Let's explore the association of kink with orgasms. In our survey, participants were asked "Can you ONLY attain an orgasm only by participating in the activities you checked in the previous section?" And that previous section was a list of BDSM-related activities. Of the 1,464 responses to this question, 113 of these women (nearly 8%) reported that kink activities were necessary for orgasm.

Additionally, some women list orgasm as a reason they engage in kink.

"It makes me orgasm."

"We also enjoy pain, giving and receiving to induce sexual orgasm. This is in no way related to abuse in childhood or in previous relationships. The receiving of pain to induce orgasm can be learnt by conditioning, i.e., by learning to associate pain with pleasure ..."

In some cases, kink helps to facilitate orgasms.

"It's not that I can only come with these kinky fantasies, but it really helps a lot. I've had many times more orgasms in the past year (since I know my current kinky boyfriend), than in all the vanilla years & relationships before."

"While I can have an orgasm without participating in any of the activities listed, it would be difficult for me to if I could not at least fantasize about them during the sex. And regardless I don't find 'vanilla' orgasms as fulfilling even if I fantasize about kink activities while participating in it."

"There was an item asking whether I could orgasm without kinky things—I answered that I need kink to orgasm, but I wanted to clarify that I'm including kinky thoughts in there. So, when I masturbate without toys or anything else kinky to 'assist' I *am* able to orgasm, but my fantasies I use for mental stimulation are always kinky. So, in that way, kink is a 'true' fetish for me. If that's what the item was meant to measure."

Some women orgasm through the sensations pain supplies.

"i seem to be one of the few (no documentational proof just what i've heard) that orgasm in a session without any penetration but from pain."

"I cannot experience orgasm without some pain. (I am a moderate masochist. I have been kinky for about 18 years.)"

"After a good beating i like to be placed on a bed and played with, with dildos, vibes, fingers, until i have reached multiple orgasms and am too exhausted to move."

As you recall from Chapter 2, pain can contribute to and enhance sexual arousal, desire, and orgasm.

Kink may help facilitate orgasm but is not a requirement for some people, while others need some aspect of kink in order to climax. What does this mean for you?

Simply this: kink activities can be a mechanism to accent sexual response, as it has for these women.

Your mileage may vary.

Aftercare

> "Into: aftercare (receiving) …"

Respondents to the survey did not mention a "resolution" or "refractory" period, which is the post-orgasmic period where your body does not respond to sexual stimulation.

However, some of them did discuss a process known in the kink community as "aftercare."

There is no definitive definition of "aftercare" as it pertains to kink. In general terms, aftercare is the process of alleviating symptoms that arose due to the activity or event that had taken place, in order for the individual to get back to their original state and to experience comfort and safety if needed.

Of course, we're not saying that arousal, desire, and orgasm are symptoms that need alleviation. But if arousal is a physical and subjective state of being "turned-on," desire is a strong feeling for wanting sex, and orgasm is intense pleasure, then aftercare is the period when the activity has come to an end and the people involved will transition back to their "original state."

Aftercare can look different from person to person. Some examples of aftercare activities can include being wrapped in a blanket, cuddling, eating or making food, providing water, talking about the scene and how much you appreciate your partner, and checking-in on any physical and safety issues.

> "… I also only seriously play with people that I trust to give me very good aftercare when I come out of my subspace or domspace (a headspace you go into while performing bdsm activities) …"

> "Love the seduction, foreplay and all that leads to the actualization of the activity involved …. also like to be watched …talked dirty to ….and then the after care!"

> "I find the build-up to be just as important as [the] after care. I get to work out my sexual desires without being seen as a bad or weak person. I never mind working for position because the feedback I get from my Top/Partner builds up my self-esteem. For me much of BDSM is about the building up of, breaking down of and rebuilding of one's ego and

self-esteem to find a more liberating experience. To be a real participant in a scene and feel the exchange of power between the two partners. It's more than the physical act of sex."

Aftercare is a way for participants to express that they are accessible, responsive, and engaged. It's a way of letting others know, "I'm here for you." It can be the time when participants tend to each other's needs, checking-in and making sure everyone is okay with what occurred.

Yes, we used the word "participants." It's an ugly word as compared to "lovers," but we are making a point. You don't need to be lovers to provide or require aftercare, nor do you need to be involved in sexual activities.

Have you ever thought about what you need for aftercare after an emotional situation?

What do you provide as aftercare to others?

We have a general idea of what constitutes a kink activity and a vague idea of what prompts a sexual response, and the acknowledgment that the enjoyment of either are subjective qualities. Combine the two, and you realize that what is magical about kink and sex is precisely what you yourself bring to it. Simply, there are people who incorporate elements of kink behavior into some phase of the desire—arousal—orgasm—resolution model of sexual response in order to enhance their pleasure.

For some people, kink is a special spice that adds flavor but isn't a requirement for a fulfilling sex life. For others, kink is a necessary ingredient for their sexual satisfaction. It can be the appetizer leading up to the main event, or it can be the main course. Sometimes kink is the dessert—not necessary to enjoy every time, but a nice treat once in a while. And for others still, kink is a completely different meal altogether from sex.

We are not condoning or censuring kink activities or sex activities or their combination. We are instead exposing you to the possibility and potential, and inviting you to investigate if you have the desire.

What Does This Mean?

These women *want* to participate in kink. They want to for simple enjoyment, for self-discovery, for self-resilience, to build and reinforce relationships, for sexuality and eroticism, and more, each reason slightly different than the others.

They are unabashed: they do not offer excuses, and they do not look for verification that what they are doing is okay.

There is no guidebook nor official set of rules. If they need help, they look to friends, family, and community, knowing that kink, like life, is an uncharted journey.

These women have accepted the truth that, for them, following their heart and doing what they want, although sometimes challenging, ultimately leads to fulfillment.

What does this mean to you?

Find a quiet time and place to think about what you want. Let your imagination roam, indulge yourself, visualize, and fantasize. Think about travel, romance, freedom, music, love, home—let your mind take you where it wants to go.

It doesn't matter if you include kink in your dreams.

What does matter is that you allow yourself to dream of what might be and you accept yourself for wanting what you desire. You now have many role models who did just that, including those who took the step of turning their desires into actions.

A small child once said to us, "I don't have to because I don't want to!" Let's turn it around and say, "I have to because I want to." And perhaps that's all the reason you need.

Stories 6

In the previous chapters, we organized the women's responses to the open-ended questions into common themes and showed how there are varying perspectives even within those themes. This was to help all of us better understand our complex and wonderful world and our complex and wonderful selves.

In this chapter, we share with you stories that don't quite belong in the previous chapters. The stories are enchanting, riveting, sad, happy, tender, and fierce, and comprise very intimate accounts of ordinary, yet very special, women discovering themselves and their place in our world. So, rather than examine how the stories are alike or different, we present them simply as a window into each woman's life.

We will suggest interpretations that you can imagine, deliberate, accept, or discard. We will help identify interesting ideas and ask questions that have no answers but your own.

Each of the following ten stories is written by one woman per section (as answers to different questions). As you read these stories, consider each woman's message and how it might pertain to your own life, loves, and desires. Allow yourself to feel the emotions of the stories. Make room for reflection on how your thoughts, ideas, and beliefs influence your activities and behaviors as you move through the world.

Some reflective questions after each section reference "your partner"—if you are not partnered at the moment, you can read them as "if you imagined a partner." If you have more than one partner, imagine the question applying to each of your partners.

Hopefully, by the end of this chapter, you will be able to write your own stories.

Story #1

Kink is deep, emotional, intimate feelings for more than one person at the same time.

"i was a virgin until I was 23 years old. I had this wonderful bf who did not pressure me about sex. He was 26. Together we discovered magazines and films about power exchange/bdsm ... between a man and women. He seemed to get excited over the idea that I could control him. This was before the internet so we did a lot of sneaking around in *(Redacted)* [Location A] looking at adult bookstores to get our information. It has been 21 years now and we are still 'mistress and slave' and we have not ever had vaginal or oral sex. I am also married so everyone who knows me ... thinks I am still having this affair with my old bf. He is simply part of my life that I am unwilling to let go. My slave is accepted by my husband and even with my vanilla hubby he understands my need to be with my 'slave.'

I am secure in knowing that both men love me but in different ways. I am very blessed and amazed that I have these two wonderful men in my life. An amazing example of how this works is when I was sick my hubby had spoken to my slave about coming 'home' ... (slave lives in *(Redacted)* [Location B] ... hub and I in *(Redacted)* [Location C]). Slave agreed it was best for him to come 'home' so he could take care of me while I recovered from surgery. (nothing major but bed rest for a few days). While slave was home his mother passed away unexpectedly also in [Location C]. Slave was unable to care for me so the roles were quickly reversed. It was not unusual for me and hubby to take care of slave and be there for him during this very difficult time in his life. It seems to work for all of us and I might also add we have no children to muddy the waters.

... I have had the same 'slave' for 21 years. I am also married to a vanilla hubby who understands and supports my domme side. My hubby does not get the whole attraction to the lifestyle and we have set rules between what can and cannot happen when I play with my slave. Slave and hubby know each other and have a great deal of respect for each other. I have been with my hubby for almost 14 years. We have no children so I also think that is an advantage. Rules include ... no sex ... no vaginal sex. no oral, also if I am out at a party ... event ... dungeon ... etc. I must text when I arrive to the hubby to let him know I am safe and I also text when I leave. I am unique as I am American but live in a border town so I go [to] [Location A] to play. I must cross an international border

... clear customs and I never carry my toys or anything to raise interest in my travels."

How do *you* develop intimacy in your relationships?

Can you imagine having very intimate, even possibly erotic, experiences with someone and refrain from being overtly sexual with them?

Could you have love for two people, describing your feelings as something like, "both men love me but in different ways"?

Does this inspire you to talk openly with your partner or partners about a desire or a wish you haven't felt ready to ask for?

Story #2

Kink is pain, both giving and receiving.

"My 'role,' 'title,' or whatever you want to call it on here has gone from submissive to masochist to dominant to switch. However, I think I've finally found the title that fits me the best out of all the options given. Sadomasochist. I've realized that I love pain. I adore it. I love being in both physical and emotional pain and love putting others in that pain because I know how wonderful it can be. The clarity it gives me is something that I can find no other way.

When you are in pain, you can't worry about whether or not you'll have time to do laundry on Wednesday or if you remembered to turn off the stove. In a world where everyone is going a mile a minute and my thoughts are sometimes two or three steps ahead of me, pain forces me to slow down. I have to focus on my breathing. I can hear my heartbeat in my ears. It makes me remember that I'm human, not some machine that needs to keep running and running and running in order to keep up with everyone else.

Pain, most notably emotional pain, can also break me, which is something that I crave like nothing else on this earth. I love being shattered into a million pieces, watching the shards of the emotional walls that I have built ever since I was a kid fall to the ground. The funny thing is that we build walls to keep others out, but don't realize that at the same time, we aren't allowing anything out either. Every fear, every worry, every self-doubt gets caught up behind those walls and it grows and grows to the point that you just want to fall to your knees and cry. By allowing myself to be broken, it gives all those destructive emotions a way out and I find that after each time a wall is shattered, I'm finding fewer and fewer pieces to build them back up. Being that vulnerable in any other situation could be absolutely devastating, but the unconditional love and support I feel around my gorgeous partner and all my kinky brothers and sisters allows me to feel safe.

I also love watching others in pain and love watching others inflict pain. Each time I watch a scene, I learn something that I didn't know before. It could be something as little as making sure to wear shoes when shocking someone with the violet wand so you don't get feedback to something as profound as realizing that when we have been pushed to our limits and are broken, there will always be someone there to pick us up."

Is your relationship with pain casual or intimate? Have you ever exercised without regard to pain just to experience euphoria?

Could you hurt someone if they needed it to feel happy and to feel close to you? How much trust would you need to allow someone to hurt you?

We all have walls to keep others at a distance. How solid are your walls? Are they there to protect you or to set you free?

Have you ever allowed yourself to be pushed to your limit and broken, just to discover something new? If you wanted to push someone until they broke, how would you know when they actually broke? And would you know how to put them back together?

Story #3

Kink is life integrated intimately into the life of another.

"He was my Husband for 10 years before we got kinky—didn't need to find partners, don't want them now. I had the best, don't need the rest!

My kink behavior was oddly non-sexual in most ways as my late Master was impotent at the time i was collared; however, with vibrators for me and oral sex for Him—which when the sexual tension became too much was relieved in harmless wet dreams. So, if it had not been for embracing the Kink lifestyle, i'm afraid we'd not have much at all sexually.

Our play was limited to a very strict hetero-monogamy by 3 things:

1. He was (is?) [involved in a Church] that is very super-strict about sex of any kind outside of marriage.
2. He felt that with His [medical] condition (*redacted*) and His being disabled by the condition, that He neither had the emotional or sexual/physical or financial resources to try to deal with a 2d woman in virtually any way and
3. He felt—and was right about it—that i was too immature and insecure to deal with it. Much of that is as a result of being molested by 3 people—once at 13 years old, once by an alcoholic ex-'boyfriend' (celibate) of my female parent's and once by a stranger on a long (about 22 hours) bus trip, where i was still too emotionally distraught from a recent break-up and other things, to even know how to handle it or stop it. As a result, it took a long time—ten years—for me to be through the PTSD of this to be able to 'play' in the M/s way—slave role—because any attempts before that put me in flashback mode and totally screwed with my mind long-term, days or weeks.

We were also an odd couple. Master was a gentle Dom and a 'Daddy' Dom. Most of the ways He controlled me was by pleasure, praise and hypnotism. Not much punishment as i would put myself through enough hell when i knew i'd done even the most minor thing to screw up. Also, our relationship did not involve me doing 'normal' slave things like cooking, cleaning, dishes, etc. He loved to cook and liked other things done in certain very specific ways, which i could not do due to my severe visual loss or 'legal blindness' (not total by a long shot). So, He did those types of 'female' thing—like a Dad with a kid. But He did them 'His way or the highway'—in a Dom attitude. i think He also took them over as being disabled and at home He was bored silly.

On the other hand, i did all legal, bureaucratic, (like for His pension and social security or anything of that nature) and political stuff—helped Him to learn to keep His check book balanced, etc.—in other words anything that involved what we, who grew up in the 60's, early 70's, called the 'establishment.' i also went with Him to doctor's appts., which were myriad in number, because He couldn't do med-speak, despite having 2 PhDs, He just didn't know the jargon. And me, having had a lot of health problems that were critical, was able to do this for Him.

So, it was definitely NOT the 'typical' M/s relationship—but from the time of my collaring from the 10th anniversary of our marriage to 4 1/2 years later were the happiest time in our marriage, which had had a lot of problems before that. i definitely had been in the 'whips and chains closet' for a long time. But it worked for us. In fact, the first 10 years of our marriage had been quite difficult—including a 14-month separation. That until i gave myself to Him for a tenth anniversary present, so to speak and was immediately collared—i think He was afraid i'd change my mind. His [medical conditions] and trouble communicating to the max and the baggage of 2 failed marriages and 1 ending in His being a widower as well as my 3 ex-husbands and abusive mom, all 4 of those people being alkies and/or junkies and abusive to the max, esp. verbally and some violence—it's why i am 'legally blind,' was a lot of our problems as well as my having untreated, then misdiagnosed as depression and then over treated to toxicity and near-death with bipolar disorder was also part of the problem.

The clearer definition of roles in M/s play helped us get past these things, to happily ever after—or at least for 4 1/2 years until He passed away, which will be 3 years ago in 13 days. it is also an odd situation since i am collared for my life— i.e. i have pledged to Him not to remarry or be involved in any relationships of sexual/romantic type for the remainder of my life. i guess i should also add that He was [more than 10 years], older than i am. i hope that helps. Having been a counselor for addicts and all, i relate to having to do research papers and such-like, good luck!

… if i were a betting person, i'd bet this was one of the 'tamest' responses to this survey you'll get from us FetLife folks—ROTFLOL. It's strange but true and worked for us. Except that for the last 3 years since He got sick and died i've been basically a little lost lamb—have trouble getting out of bed, getting myself to do personal hygiene, health has failed until i ended up in a wheelchair and i now have UTERINE cancer, i don't think that this last is a coincidence. Since His death my sex-drive has also been virtually non-existent, which i guess is good since i swore to Him not to get into any other romantic/sexual relationships of any kind for the rest of my life."

What does love, intimacy, and devotion mean to you?

When you give yourself to your partner, how much of "you" do you give? At what point does the line between the two of you blur?

When you make a promise, do you make it to yourself or to someone else? Would you keep a promise to someone after they died? Would you expect your partner to keep such a promise?

Story #4

Kink is multifaceted roles.

> "You could call me a Top/Switch, I play the roles mostly of Daddy/Sir/Master, but everyday life, I'm the Husband, she's the Wife, as she's domestic, I'm not, she's in social services, I'm in construction, I'm rough and tumble and she's a very particular faggy boi. I do like switching from time to time, as I'm pretty masochistic, sometimes more than her. She's more service oriented, less masochistic. While I'm a Dominant DaddyBear type, she's a pretty dominant Wife, but that's fairly nonsexual, more domestic.
>
> As far as me personally, I do like to flirt and in general I've been polyamorous/non-monogamous, or as I'd say most accurately: 'semi-monogamous,' meaning I'm about 75–90% monogamous, but I need an escape hatch, that is, the ability to play with others with permission now and then … to sow my oats so to speak. She prefers to watch or is monogamous, or occasionally co-top. If polyamorous implies a committed relationship beyond one, my model has primarily been: Primary partner/secondary more casual play partners. We both had separately before we met a trinary relationship that was committed and ongoing. Mine blew up and I lost both partners in a nasty double breakup … she had one that ended far more gently, when the two partners decided to have an exclusive commitment to one another.
>
> I don't know if I could have a true polyamorous relationship again, with more than one partner, beyond casual play partners/friends. That would take extraordinary negotiating.
>
> I am 100% exclusively Lesbian and only relate to bio-female women who are preferably Lesbian. Though I like Butch on Butch, there are Femmes who do indeed turn me on. I'm also 100% Leather, in that I couldn't date a vanilla dyke, it just wouldn't work for me …"

In your current relationship, what roles do you play, and under what circumstances?

If monogamous means "having a sexual relationship with one partner at a time," do you think someone can be partially monogamous? Perhaps our language is too limited, or perhaps our concepts are too limited.

Does polyamory imply committed relationships with multiple partners, or can it include casual relationships?

Story #5

Kink is passionately following your instincts.

> "It is clear to me, that the internet has had a major impact on human society and has a significant impact on our sexuality/sexual psychology. I have been a pro Domme for almost a decade. I have been self-aware sexually from a very young age, before it became physical. I enjoyed fantasies involving kidnapping, objectification and bondage, as well as texture fetishes such as plastic, nylon and rubber. I was force cross dressing teenage boys when I was a teenager. I also put myself in masculine drag (I am not transgender only andro). My father found me tied up and naked when I was 13. I was never sexually abused. I am bisexual and have been so (and unashamed of it) since my teens. I have always been a dominant personality. I am poly. I was 15 years old when I orchestrated my first threesome with my boyfriend and best friend. We did not know what to do, so I told them to fuck and went to sleep. I enjoyed this feeling!
>
> … I am not ashamed and I am proud to be alive in a time where we are seeing hopefully the birth of SEXUAL FREEDOM!!!!!!! I am also active in fighting for the decriminalization of prostitution. We should be able to do with our bodies as we see fit! SMILE!!!"

Long before puberty, did you fantasize about the sexual person who you grew up to be?

Do you think your erotic expressions are hard-wired or the influence of your environment, or both, and to what extent?

Has the internet impacted your sexuality and sexual psychology?

What does sexual freedom mean to you? Did you SMILE when you read this story???

Story #6

Kink is experiencing and longing for more intimacy.

"100% Butch Dyke. Prefer primarily Butch on Butch and it works best in my personal relationship. We understand each other, have similar desires, and only another Butch can do for me what I need done, she feels similarly. When we have played with others though, it worked best us playing with Femmes. A third Butch sometimes got too competitive. Femmes on the other hand reveled in the attention of not one but two Butches!

I will occasionally play casually with others. I don't know if we'd ever open it up to having a third party in the relationship (polyamory), unless they completely understood their junior status to serve us both … it's hard enough keeping a two-person relationship going! It's something we've discussed but not acted upon, or found the right person nor are we pursuing it actively.

But sometimes I want to play with others so I can let out my more severe hardcore Top desires … and that part of me that is a Hunter as a Top out … but not anything that would jeopardize my primary relationship … on more a casual/friendship/fuck buddy basis.

Sexually we are completely committed to each other, as far as receiving … I would fuck another woman if I felt some level of connection, even a one-night scene where it felt right. Anything outside the primary relationship, 100% Safe Sex. I'm surprised you didn't ask any questions about Safe Sex. Honesty is one of the strongest ingredients of our relationship.

I've been in the Scene for 30 years so I have A LOT of herstory around it as a LeatherDyke. I've played with so many women over the years and loved a few … and had several long-term relationships. The most long-term relationship is with my current boi, we are going on 10 years together. Part of that is because we have a good D/s dynamic, but I'd like more S/M involved … it's hard because we're getting older and she has physical disability issues as part of that that are progressive.

I've gone through being a pretty hardcore Top, occasional Switch to primarily a Dominant Daddy and we do switch. As far as formal Scenes mostly we only do those in the dungeon. Not so much at home anymore. But we have a lot of affection. I guess you could [say] we're an old married couple, and we ARE Legally married when there were same sex marriages in *(Redacted)* [State] … our hottest fantasies are around prison type scenes … like Ward and trustee … or trustee and the new boi on the cellblock! We both enjoy leather and uniforms and love our Butch on Butch dynamic, and we're both proud to be fully Female and revel in each other's Female bodies! This is rare these days and one reason we don't play too much with others anymore. Ours has become a rare breed … and our commitment is important to both of us, though occasionally with negotiation I'll play with others.

I've done a lot, and if I haven't done it, I've seen it … but some of it I no longer care to see, cuz sometimes LeatherSex at its best is spiritual for me, and I don't want to share that energy or get vulnerable in any way, and neither does she, if there are bad vibes … and the energies in the dungeons are so chaotic and mixed these days that we don't attend play parties much anymore … and there are no born female or even women only primarily Lesbian centered play parties anymore … everything accommodates trans and that's not our community or a community either of us feel comfortable in.

Beyond that, I don't want to see people literally beating each other to a pulp, if I want that, I go to my karate dojo on Sundays and put on the gloves where others can fight back, in a controlled manner. I don't want to hear a bottom screaming and screaming their bloody head off completely disrupting the energy of the entire dungeon. I'm not into blood and guts and gore … I'm into aesthetic SM that takes talent and skill … like a good piercing, flogging, singletailing, fireplay, artistic cutting, candlewax, dominant/submissive roleplay scene … whether watching or participating in some of those activities … skill intrigues me and gets me hot … not the brutality that passes for so called SM these days.

I guess I've been around too long and I miss the really hot days of some of the fantastic *(Redacted)* [City] women's play parties … where early in the night all the bottoms would be moaning and groaning from what their Tops were doing to them, and then later in the night they'd all be moaning and orgasming at the same time from fucking and fisting! It was pure women's play party Sex Magic, and I haven't seen it in years, which each Scene played off all the others energy wise, we all pretty much knew each other and there was a LEVEL OF INTIMACY in the dungeon which is sorely lacking these days … the parties were smaller and more intimate and so was the community, and it was much more Female to Female focused and that includes anybody from Hardcore Butch Tops/Daddies/Masters to High Femme Tops/Mistresses and submissives … and all female in-between … including Butch bottoms/bois/submissives and hardcore Masochists as well … there was some real artistry and THAT I miss, as well as mentorship, and even sharing between scenes at times!

I loved when I could do more than one scene a night, and there was a fluidity between players. I don't see that as much anymore. People come in with their big entourages and stick to their own, and it doesn't go too much farther than that … and there's too much mixed energy for my tastes, and much less Lesbian/Dyke specific energy, which is what I live and THRIVE for and sorely miss."

Have you ever been a part of a community that has changed over time and you no longer felt like you belong? How can you create new connections when this happens?

Sometimes more inclusivity means less familiarity and more people means less intimacy. Do you agree with these ideas?

Which sexual or erotic behaviors have you changed due to aging, disability, illness, or other circumstances? How do you accommodate these changes and still feel fulfilled and connected?

Story #7

Kink is service-oriented.

> "I am a professional courtesan and I offer submissive escort services as well. Potential clients contact me to discuss their interests and arrange meetings. However, I also play with others as a personal, non-income producing activity.
>
> … I enjoy discipline scenes that require a lot of focus, under some kind of duress. Predicament scenes where I have to choose between punishments or consequences, or where I have to do something perfectly and quickly under the threat of physical pain. A recent example would be being required to write lines—repeating a sentence a certain number of times. Making a mistake in spelling, writing or the number of repetitions earns so many strokes of the tawse, etc.
>
> … Most of what I do these days occurs in scenes with clients, most of whom I don't know very well or at least have not played with them very often. I am not a dungeon submissive: I don't work with a Master or Mistress who will look after me or protect me. I work alone, including BDSM activities into my erotic repertoire which includes sexual intercourse (which is not the case with most professional submissives). For my safety—and the client's, too—I am always topping from the bottom. The scenes are heavily negotiated and rarely challenge me or my limits. I don't feel that I am genuinely submitting or surrendering to my client. However, I am willing to experience discomfort and pain for them in part because I think that many dominant men need to be able to inflict pain or express their dominance as much as many submissives need to be able to submit.
>
> … I'd like to say that, while I enjoy a wide range of sexual activities, I find that doing this as a way to earn a living is very different, to me, from doing it with an ongoing intimate companion who is not paying me for my time and expertise. I arouse easily and have no difficulty having orgasms, and so I function well with clients. But I notice that, over time, it's increasingly difficult for me to know what I want to do or have done to me. Maybe this is because I have had to be very service-oriented. I focus on my partner's needs and interests almost exclusively, attempting to give him what he wants and/or has contracted with me to perform. I hope that, when I retire from this business, my sense of personal desire will re-establish itself.

> These days, I find that what I want is terribly vanilla. Mind, done well, vanilla sex can be profoundly intimate and personally revealing. That said, I find that it is much harder for me to know what to do or how to initiate sexual acts. I'm struggling with this at the moment. I don't want to be a passive submissive. I don't see what my partner does as being all about me, at all, but I feel that I need permission to initiate things with him. Perhaps I have become over-sensitive to being rejected or turned down. More likely, I think I have been focused too much on only doing what he wants because then I will know that it is what he wants, and not something I'm imposing on him."

If you negotiated a scene with a professional submissive, what would you ask for?

If you agreed to submit to someone for a fee, what would you allow?

Do you wonder if you are slowly losing your own sexual expression to the needs of your partner? On the other hand, have you wondered if you are dominating your partner's sexuality?

Do you ever find yourself being better at caring for the needs of others than knowing what your own wants and needs are? If so, what is one thing that you can do for yourself, in order to start to create more balance between your partner's needs and your own needs?

Story #8

Kink is love.

> "I identify as BBGBC: Born Bi, Gay By Choice. Simpler version: Lipstick lezzie, who also occasionally fucks men. Past: Married and divorced from a man, monogamous, hetero, right after college, dismal failure. Have always 'felt bi,' always had sex with both men and women, attracted to both, like some men but LOVE women—most of my serious romantic/emotional relationships have been with other women. Present: In a deeply committed long-term relationship for life with two women—my Mistress and my slave. Also: We 3 are part of a deeply committed polyfidelitous BDSM family of 12 (10 women, 2 men, all bi/queer). Never been so happy in all my life. I'm 29, others are 20 to 29.
>
> … I have almost never in my life done 'something kinky' just for the sake of doing a kinky thing. (Okay, all right, I was a teenager once too, and I did lots of shit just for the hell of it. But I'm 29 now.) I and my friends and lovers and partners 'do kink' to explore ourselves and each other, to give each other pleasure and peak experiences and wild adventures, and most of all to give each other love in every way we can possibly think of to give love. Doing something kinky just to be kinky or dirty or more *out there*, dude, than someone else is stupidly pointless.
>
> … My life is/has always been very very very sexual, and will continue to be! I love sex, live for sex, every imaginable kind of sex, think about sex all the time and HAVE sex all the time, I've been a model and a call girl and an unabashed sex object and I am now and will always be a sex slave, but my life is not really at all about sex, you know? It's about love.
>
> Sex/kink/fetish/BDSM/TPE/consensual sexual slavery/ownership/etc. etc. etc., those are all just ways to give and take more love and share more of your life and body and soul and heart (and pussy) with the ones you love. Without love (and I have done most of these things both with and without having love in my life)—without love nothing means anything. So. Love rules, dudes, and rock on …"

How strong is the connection between kink and sex and love for you?

What are all the ways you can express your love for friends, lovers, partners, and family?

How unabashed is your sexual nature?

What would you think about trying to give your partner "pleasure and peak experiences and wild adventures"?

Would you ever consider creating a different kind of family, one focused on sexual expressions of love? Could you change your existing relationship to include this concept? Would you want to?

Story #9

Kink is a love language.

> "Dominance & submission are how I show affection, caring and love. The physical aspects give me a chance to be skillful and efficacious—but they are only instruments and tools to the end result, which is the interaction and the trust and love it creates.
>
> … Some of my underlying motivations in what I love about BDSM: Beyond the physical pleasures—and they are multifold!—there is an underlying motivation to it; something beyond sex is satisfied when I undertake these activities. **NOTE** The 'you' in the below is directed at my partner, not at the survey readers.
>
> 'I want to pull you through the full range of sensation, from deepest pleasure to the edges of intolerable pain. I want to see your expression change and know that I am causing each sensation, and causing the attending emotions—to know that I'm setting the pace and controlling the depth of the experience. I want to see you hope and despair and relish and beg, and I want to see on your face your knowledge that I am the one doing this to you. I want to see the war between instinct and fear, which tells you to flinch away, to make it stop when it is too intense—and the desire to please me. I want to win that war—win your surrender, and with it, your renewed adoration.
>
> I want to feel the fervent gratitude as your lips press against my feet. That expression of power—no matter how scene specific and temporary—encapsulates in a perfect crystalline drop my ability to affect things; my ability to impact life and people. That sense of ability, and of power, provides a rush better than any drug. Not secondarily, it encapsulates the depth of trust possible between people of integrity. Trust that while the journey may be frightening in its intensity—that there is confidence in my integrity; absolute knowledge that I will not willingly damage you in any way. And that trust, that confidence, is entirely two ways: I have to trust that you will not stop me during nor hate me afterwards; that you will not find some subtle way of punishing me emotionally for the things that I have done to you. That two-way trust is concrete proof that we do not have to be entirely alone nor do we have to settle for people unworthy of that level of trust.'"

What activities or roles do you have in your life that are designed solely to show affection?

What do other people do as an expression of love for you?

What experiences would you want to further explore, either within yourself or with others?

Do you ever carve out time with your partner with the intention to focus on each other, specifically to create interactions that are sensual and erotic without necessarily becoming sexual?

Story #10

Kink is messy, isolating, taboo, creativity, really submissive, really dominant, liberating, open, and natural.

> "I am a very sexual woman and in most of my partnerships with straight men they have found me too sexual and also too wet. (I do have trouble sometimes finding men who are really, really into female ejaculation. All men love it the first few times and can't get enough. But then it can get messy at times. Rarely, but sometimes in a good session i can soak through 2 towels.) They were excited about female ejaculation but then quickly felt overpowered. I think sometimes they felt emasculated—I, a woman, was more sexual and wanted more sex than them, came more (amount wise), ejaculated farther, and much, much more often. In the kinky world I have met men who truly revel in a woman's sexuality and never put her down.
>
> I am also adding some copies of an email conversation I had with a friend. It will be disjointed because it's only my side but it might explain more …
>
> I find myself isolated from many women in regards to sex. I was raised Catholic but have really made progress in terms of getting away from some of the repressive and backwards ideas about sex. I still have work to do but I am definitely in a more healthy place than I was at 19 let's say. Why [do] I feel isolated? Many women don't want to talk about it as much as I do. As with many taboo issues, I like to talk about everything and keep an open mind. Many women and men just don't want to talk about the real issues but stay in a superficial conversation.
>
> I also feel much more sexual than my friends. I have been very comfortable with my body since a young age and have been having orgasms on my own for years. I know my body and how it works which is not the case for many women. I have never rushed into sexual intimacy because I was determined to never be a woman in a relationship where she wasn't fulfilled sexually. I had too many friends like that. I choose to go slow and 'perfect' each step. Because of my experience with my body I find it hard to relate to women who do not understand their body or are willing to settle for sex where they aren't fulfilled. I also feel that few women can give me advice. I am usually the one doling it out.
>
> Anyway … rambled too much above. I apologize. I think the point I was trying to make before I got distracted is that I am very different than

most women. So, when you ask me questions … I am not speaking for most women.

I am bisexual or I prefer pansexual. I hate the stereotypes placed on women such as we don't enjoy sex as much, we're not as horny, we are always faking. I have never faked in my life. Except once to prove a point but I told him right after so that wasn't really faking. Or I hate the stereotypes placed on genders—that men have to act and look a certain way and that women have to as well. I like to be really submissive sometimes, really dominant sometimes.

Anyway, I think what I am trying to say is that I am different than most women and more open-minded. I do find the idea of two men together very very hot. I also do like to watch a man masturbate and do like a man's cum.

Oh an[d] in regards to your question about female ejaculation. I can get exhausted from a session and will feel spent and not able to produce more. Or I feel sore in the glands and muscles that squirt. However, the amount I ejaculate has nothing to do with not cumming for a while. There are weeks where I ejaculate lots (up to 6 feet at times) and soak through towels and then a rather dry spell. It mostly depends on if I am in the right mood for it and how much clitoral stimulation I am getting to fill up the glands. G spot just releases it.

I don't find female ejaculation to be the ultimate orgasm. I love it but it is not necessary to have really mindblowing orgasms. Often, it's not present or just a little bit. Unfortunately, it is portrayed as such and might make couples feel they're not achieving their potential as lovers, etc.

Anyway, usually men are fine with it. But it can be a bother. The towels aren't romantic. And when you soak through towels and it gets into the new mattress, and there's so much it never dries properly … it's like spilling a cup of water on your bed at times.

I have found the kinky world much more open to sex and what goes with it. Many (not all) people are more open-minded. I have met some men and women who truly enjoy talking about sex (I don't feel like a weirdo or an outsider anymore). Everyone understands female ejaculation and consider it natural. No one has ever made me feel too sexual or dirty or unwomanly at one of the few kinky events I've been to.

get back to you soon! just a bit busy but for now i'll tell you about what happened at my training tonight for *(Redacted)* [Organization]—a feminist run transition house.

Went to training for the volunteer job with [Organization]. I can't remember if I explained to you but they're a bit radical feminist and tonight were arguing that pornography is bad. Which is fine to say because a lot of it is male dominated but I pointed out there's good stuff out there, ethical, etc. They pretty much told me I was brainwashed by the patriarchal system into liking it and enjoying it.

The group leader recounted being 16 and watching porn to learn about sex and how disastrous that was. She was like: 'The porn industry has bad stuff like tying women up and trying to tell me that women were to like facial cum shots' (she was obviously trying to shock the women there because no one else had used such explicit language yet). I then said: 'Well some women like to be tied up and enjoy facial cum shots.' SILENCE. Absolute SILENCE.

oops. now I'm the big brainwashed whore of the group :)

I do love to delve into sub and dom. I'm a bit kinky. Actually, this Monday I was with a kinky friend that I am seeing. We both got really into it. It wasn't the kinkiest stuff I've done (because we're still new partners) but he's the kinkiest partner I've been with. And it was good. My other partners were more willing vanillas that I convinced into pushing their boundaries. But he's pretty kinky and it was good. Got into a good sub-space and he was very good bringing me down from it. Actually, the first time I truly enjoyed a long, repeated spanking. Other times it's been one here or there but he continuously drove me to my limit. And the whole slut/sir dynamic is awesome. Begging, pleading, thanking etc. Forcing legs open. Making me lick his fingers clean. That was new. No one has made me ever. It's just that creativity missing from vanillas, right? The bruises from the first time were a problem! I get questions. So i asked him to not leave any. He seemed disappointed. :)

Actually, I first got into submission through fantasies of slavery and being tied up as a child. Then with my first boyfriend I asked him to do more kinky things. And he would get into it at times. Oblige, etc. Call me a whore, Slap my face, etc. But he still wasn't kinky enough, He broke down once when I was tied up and then asked him to slap me. He slapped me. But I guess the picture of my face contorted, tied up helplessly was too much and he broke down saying he couldn't do it. I looked too pitiful. I was having a ball though!! And he knew but he couldn't do it. :(I felt bad. But he was just not kinky as me.

But recently, I've felt more confident and am enjoying the dominant side. It started with the first guy once when he was kissing my breasts. And then I started guiding him. And then telling him to say my name etc. But it never got farther than that. And then once I ejaculated on a guy by accident when I was above him. We were young, just 20 and he was shocked. Just froze all of a sudden. He went to wash his face and I thought it was over. I kind of chuckled too my self and wasn't ashamed which was cool. And I got off on the power. And then he came back for more. :)

Then when I rode a partner's face full on for the first time, I loved the power. He wasn't so into it I think. He confessed a week later he didn't like that my ejaculate was all over his face. It was also potent at the time as I was ovulating.

And then I rode a woman once and she was so good at it. Grinding her chin into me at times. That's when I really realized I like this dominance. And when she came in my arms under my control and then fell asleep in my arms. That's when I liked that dominant feeling.

So, I'm excited to learn more about myself! And I love delving into these sub/dom stuff. The mind fucking is better than the fucking sometimes! And unlike heteronormative society where a man fucks the woman and a woman gets fucked by a man. I feel for myself that I've been fucked by a man and I've fucked a man too. I've also fucked a woman and been fucked by a woman. How much more fun than just the former!

I also agree that sex just can't happen. I've been with partners that took a very long time to get intimate if at all. And with others I felt that intimacy quickly and things flowed naturally.

I tend to do a lot of manual/finger fucking rather than sex. Before oral sex (which i consider sex) or sex there should always be a safe sex discussion.

Actually, people often think that I've had a lot more sex in the heteronormative definitions of sex (i.e. vaginal penetration with opposite sex and strap on with same sex). I think it's because I'm so open about it, masturbated so much, demand my pleasure is on par to my partner's, etc. But I lost my virginity at age 19. And of the approx. 14 people I've been sexual with (9 men and 5 women) I've only had penis-vaginal penetration sex with one man and strap on sex with one woman. The rest have been oral sex or just manual.

But my definition of sex encompasses anytime there's orgasm or something close to it (if someone has difficulties reaching orgasm). And once I orgasmed when an ex and I were making out fully clothed including thick jeans and he was between my legs, our bodies rarely touching. But the music was dead on, the feeling was there, one exceptionally passionate kiss and bam! He was shocked, Me too a bit!

I think that the women at [Organization] have seen a lot. The effects of sexism and classicism are still alive and well. But it's not always so black and white and they have to realize that. I think sometimes they also don't realize that they need to accept all women's point of view and not just what they think is for the greater good.

So, you've been fucked in the ass? How did you like it? All the sub/dom stuff you described sounds like stuff that i'm into. I like being ordered about, name-called, humiliation, etc. I think those are all fairly common kinky fantasies.

I think both are interesting roles to play. I consider myself a switch. It is fun to let go as a sub. It's also fun to be creative as the domme. The sub is the one in control because they can say stop whenever. But a dom also has control in leading the session and also can say stop. I think in the end, both are in control. I mean both are playing together in the end. As a domme you control how it goes. But a sub you can encourage it to go in a certain way and end it as well.

I agree that more people might incorporate sub and dom, but it's also not for everyone. However, i do agree that most people need to try more things. There's so much to try. Sex is really a chance to open up and play.

I like *(Redacted)* [American Author] a lot too even though he is a bit biphobic but i think he's getting better. His views are awesome. And men really do need to get over their gay hang ups. And women have to get over their general sex hang ups. One brilliant thing that [American Author] taught me is that oral sex is sex. Its last name is Sex. Mr/Mrs Oral Sex. First name oral, last name sex. :) He said that a lot more straight people would be happy if they realized that oral sex was sex—something the gays fully realize. :)

I like the idea of fantasies in many categories. It's ok to fantasize about stuff you would NEVER do. 1 Fantasies about stuff I've done. 2 Fantasies about stuff i'd like to do. 3 Fantasies about stuff i might do. type 4— Fantasies about stuff i'd never do. Those are good ways to look at it. And I like how you said that there are fantasies that you actually don't want. It's just when taken out of context have a highly erotic component.

As a child I was excited by ideas of slavery, also playing as animals, being controlled, kept in pens, obeying, etc. Later on, they were more developed stories when I was 13 or so. Usually human or animal slavery, sometimes medical. I've also been very excited by the idea of breeding, used for sex clinically, etc. and since I read Margaret Atwood's *The Handmaid's Tale*, have often had fantasies about being used for that, or a breeding slave of some sort. I would re-enact some of the ideas alone in my bedroom or in the bathroom where i could lock the door. I've also always enjoyed the fantasy of being sold/captured into slavery, collared, leashed, prodded, humiliated, used for sex, treated like a piece of property/meat, given as a gift to another person, courtesan/whore scenarios, etc. As I've gotten older some of these fantasies have grown to include, rape and gang rape and spit-roasting, mistress and master scenarios. Just crazy what our minds think up, eh?

I'm definitely ok with these fantasies. And thanks for listening! It's the first time i've told anyone the full extent of my fantasies.

Panties and pantyhose are common for some men I think. It's just such a taboo. I mean there's no item of clothing that's truly forbidden for women. But for men? Skirts and dresses and pantyhose, etc. I think piss can be erotic. I don't think I'd like to incorporate it. But the feeling of pissing is a release kind of related to orgasm I think. I like the feel of my own warm pee on me. Have never tasted it though. (yet) :) I have also peed on partners a bit. Not intentionally. But at certain points post-orgasm and usually post-ejaculation when i'm relaxed and trying to reach another orgasm i might let a little out. oops. In the three times it's happened no one has realized it yet, Especially because I'm so wet/squirter etc.

I think fantasies are strange too. But they are a window into the deep scary parts of our inner minds/subconscious. I think when we hear horrible stories in the news and we wonder how could people do that ... you just need to look inwards at some of the stuff you're into. And then you understand more about how some people are consumed by that dark stuff and let it take control without respect to sanity and consent.

I think our society is too focused on vaginal sex. Also, they're too focused on the end and not the journey. I agree about the kissing/touching/mutual masturbation. People don't put enough feeling or sensuality or value in it. Which is a gosh darn shame.

And about having an orgasm when making out. It was super hot. But not some mind-blowing, 2-minute screaming orgasm. It was more of a full body shudder and release with a small moan. I think people don't realize that there are so many pleasurable feelings and different types of orgasms. Good sex comes when you enjoy each moment and ride through each pleasurable feeling or little orgasm. I think sometimes what I consider orgasms, some people wouldn't b/c they have the Hollywood version in their head.

Who knew I had a prostate? :) I find that the more I explore with men and women I see that there is much more diversity within a gender than between the 'two' genders—really disqualifying the great emphasis society places on classifying people differently due to gender. (Same idea when it comes to race! Much more diversity between humans than between the supposed 'races.')

I actually just made out plus some with a friend of mine over the weekend. She is transgendered and it was a neat experience. But I feel like she is a woman. The more I meet different people and genders the more I just think of people as people. That's why I like being pansexual. :) It's so open and liberating and freeing.

Is it bad that I think it's the evolved state? The most liberated and natural state? Being able to be attracted [to] people regardless of genitals? I think so but you can barely go about saying it right? And you have to respect people's choices and feelings in our world.

I like that the woman said that to you. You can't fuck her until she fucks you. Awesome. I have only been with one man long enough to get tested. Actually, I was watching a video on a liberal sex education site and it says that every woman should be the first person to penetrate herself (sad how often this is not true!). And every man should penetrate himself before penetrating others. Makes good sense to me!! If more women were used to the idea of penetration and introduced themselves slowly to it [then] vaginismus might not be a problem for some women.

It has been one of my deepest fantasies for ages to watch two men fuck, any which way everything from kissing to anal to oral etc. When men kiss it gets me all hot. I was at the theater once and all I could think about was this hot couple to the left of me. I couldn't stop imagining them kissing and fucking each other. I used to watch gay porn with a bisexual ex of mine. :) There's actually a term for this on Wikipedia. :)

Thanks for the invite for watching you but I don't feel comfortable yet with that. We'll see if that can change over time.

This weekend I went to my first 'public' kinky gathering. It was a rope bondage workshop-turned play party at someone's apartment with about 12 people. I was involved in some minor things but was mostly an observer. There was no sex in terms of the narrow heteronormative and male-based definition of sex—underwear stayed on. (I however, I think sex is everywhere. Even walking barefoot in the grass is foreplay to me.) So, I got a rope harness tied onto me for a bit. Later I got into a full spandex bag thing and hood (completely breathable all over) that left me semi-motionless and I was touched/spanked/cropped/smacked/vibrating gloved by 3 or so people while I could not see anything. Awesome!

Observing was great too. I feel my dominant side growing. To see a woman dominate a man was wonderful and I yearned to be that sure of myself one day. To see a man dominate another man was great too.

And a woman was hog tied and had orgasms via vibrator right in front of me. I love a woman's orgasm face. So awesome and beautiful. Overall, the open environment was refreshing! I no longer felt the most sexual or hyper-sexual—everyone was! And to hear so many women talk about female ejaculation as if it was normal and not something they never heard of/thought was gross or a myth was so wonderful. And such a respectful environment! I felt more respected there as a woman and a person despite/or because words like slut were being bandied about and women were hogtied.

Afterwards I went out with a friend to her boyfriend's place to watch the hockey game. There were a bunch of his friends and they just seemed unable to speak to women or treat them as equals. I mean they weren't rude or anything, they just obviously preferred speaking with the men in the room and kind of ignored us a bit. Maybe it wasn't gender, maybe the fact that I was new or the hockey game was on? But the other two girls there weren't new at all. I just felt there was a gender divide in socializing in the room and it irked me.

You should be your own first lover. And if you learn how to love yourself from someone else … that's wonderful and radical as well.

I think that we need more comprehensive sexual education and at the very least frank and open and instructional discussion.

These kinky gatherings and sex positive environments are very radical political statements in some ways and it really feels awesome. I actually went to one 2 weeks ago that was actually more sexual. People having sex with many people. BDSM, cuddling and making out going on. So much love and energy and affection. That's what was cool. I described the party to my friends and they usually jump to the conclusion that it's just crass porn fucking. It is so much more than that!! so much more—if it did not have such a sensual energy I would not be able to stay in the environment.

Anyway, I surprised myself in how I let go at the party. Like I mentioned before I only had sex 'fully' with one man despite having sex with about 15 men and women. So i was not ready yet to leave that guilt and shame regarding sex and paranoia of pregnancy and STIs (but I've done a pretty good job telling myself over the years it's ok to do everything else but penetrative penis/vaginal sex!) So, I wasn't sure if I was even going to be able to stay and I thought I only might play with my friend who invited me to this, the trans woman. But within an hour I was making out with a pregnant woman (how awesome!) and it was her first time too at something like this so we bonded. Then her fiancé joined in and it was hot. I ended up naked except for my heels lying on a massage table with two people working on me and eventually another man joined in … the one who was running the event … who is actually bisexual. Ha. So, I lived a fantasy and was completely orgasmed and squirted out by the end. How empowering! They reveled in my ejaculation unlike some partners I've had in the past. And when a guy asked if I would like to suck his cock, I wasn't ready for that and I just shook my head and he immediately backed off. Absolutely NO pressure. What a respectful and liberating environment.

And when I was really having strong orgasms one of the men came over and held me and supported me. Very respectful and caring and perceptive!

Soon after I ended up making out with two men who I had become friendly with at the other event (and at one point there were 4—the two from the other session joined in for a bit). I was on the couch making out slowly and gently and eventually they fondled me and went down on me bringing me to lovely gentle orgasms though I was exhausted. And then i asked (this is a big step for me making sexual requests!) I asked them to tie me up as I had talked over the week with one friend about it. The two guy friends of mine agreed and I ended up suspended from the ceiling, bondaged in rope, in the middle of another room being fondled, cropped, slapped, and vibrated with while people around me had sex. AWESOME. new feelings and a high like I've never experienced. Overall, the experiences were phenomenal and liberating. i would describe them as healing too.

Stripping away negatives. Lovely!"

What Does It All Mean?

Do some of these stories surprise you, move you, or disturb you? Was it the woman's passion, intellect, daring, experiences, or was it something else?

In which of the stories did you find pieces of yourself, your life, and your loves? Which stories will you share and discuss with other people?

We all come from different walks of life and have different opinions which influence our thoughts, feelings, and behaviors. These perspectives shape our dreams, wishes, and goals in life. Yet, one thing we all have in common is wanting to share our lives and experiences with one another.

Every person in the world has their own story, unique to them. It's one of the beautiful aspects of humanity that binds us all together.

Find some quiet time and think about your special story. Write it down and put it away for a few days, then take it out again and expand on it. There's no hurry.

Remind yourself of what makes you special, of your own passion, intellect, daring, experiences, and something else. Remind yourself how astonishing you are, of what you've accomplished and what you will achieve. Write a sentence or write a book. Keep your story to yourself or share it with loved ones, or even the world.

You don't need kink to be wonderful; you really just need to be you.

Conclusion 7

Wow! These wonderful women showed us that there are many aspects to kink, including sex, pain, the mind, spirituality, community, safety, consent, exhibitionism, voyeurism, role play, fetishes, and money. They revealed that their engagement with kink can be fantasy, private, a hidden lifestyle, a casual indulgence, or a core identity. They taught us so many things about being single, married, and polyamorous, and what it means to be in chosen families. We learned that they participate in kink activities for personal reasons and sexual reasons, and as a way to better relate to people. Women can engage in kink activities and not identify as kinky, and they can identify as kinky yet lead vanilla lives.

Kink is quite a phenomenon, isn't it? FetLife, a social network for the BDSM, Fetish, and Kinky community, has over 9 million members as of this book's publication. Using Google to search for "kink" returns about 78 million results, and "BDSM" returns over 420 million results.

Part of our responsibility in writing this book is to provide you, our reader, with perspective, knowledge, and understanding to help you be a better you. Therefore, we must clarify something important: kink will not solve all of your problems, bring happiness and good fortune, or turn your sex life into a non-stop orgasm.

Let's take a moment and consider a hypothetical analogy.

If we had read that travel is a male-only phenomenon and not a natural state for women, we might have surveyed women who travel. We're sure they would have shown us that there are many aspects to travel and that their engagement with travel was casual, a core identity, or something else. They would have told stories of different relationship styles because of travel, and of having travel families spread across continents. The women from that study would likely have traveled for personal reasons and sexual reasons, and as a way to better relate to people.

TripAdvisor, the world's largest travel platform, has 4.6 billion unique visitors each year who submit 147 million reviews and opinions annually. A Google search of "travel" returns over 5 billion results.

Wow! Involvement in travel dwarfs involvement in kink!

But that's not the point.

The number of women involved in kink doesn't matter. What matters is that each quotation in our book tells of how that particular woman uses kink to help solve her own problems, bring happiness and good fortune to her own life, or ignite her own sexuality, information that was unknown just a few years ago.

You can easily find travel magazines revealing first-person narratives of women's adventures as they journey through unknown paths, making fascinating friends, and learning new ways of living. *Women and Kink* has done the same, revealing first-person narratives of women's adventures as they journey through unknown paths, making fascinating friends, and learning new ways of living.

That is the point.

We hope you found inspiration from the quotations in our book to begin to discover your own adventures, fascinating friends, and new ways of living. We hope you were emboldened to examine your own life, loves, relationships, hobbies, activities, dreams, and desires, and perhaps discover a new spark of joy in yourself. Kink is not the goal. Kink is a device, a venue, or a process to get you where you want to be, a place that we call "you."

The purpose of being kinky is not to be kinky. The purpose of being kinky is to be.

The Problem with Labels

Throughout the book, we remind you that words have usage, not meaning. For example, when someone says they are (or are not) a swinger, there is no specific behavior we can associate with that word. Even though we categorized ideas for organizational purposes, we recognize that those very categorizations may be misleading.

> "There is no true label. There is no title that you can put on the kinkster that will explain them and their desires. The largest 'kink' i have seen in the community is the desire to explore more."

Remember all the remarkable stories we just asked you to think about? There are more. This book does not contain all the stories from all the women. There is too much content, too much emotion, too much life and love. We had to find ways to organize the stories so that we could understand them and you could understand them. We had to exclude stories simply because they didn't fit into the neat little categories we were trying to stuff everything into. Yes, we are guilty of the exact thing we are fighting against.

> "I hope that your research gains a depth in its evolution that I am not seeing so far in the 'laundry list' of questions. I believe that women, perhaps more than men, have a fluctuating organic approach to sexuality, what turns us on changes depending on our partners, circumstances and according to our time of month, and time of life. Men seem to fixate much more rigidly in their sexuality, so it is easy for a man to give you a list, even a script of what gets him off. I am making a sweeping generalization of course, but I do hope that when you publish your work, that there will be more to it than a dirty list of what kinky women do to get off. I'd also like to think that you receive a little bit of voyeuristic pleasure from your work and these survey answers and that your interest is not merely academic. If that is the case it can be our little secret :)"

> "I wish these sorts of studies weren't disproportionately about women's sexuality. It reaffirms a bunch of wrong and harmful ideas:
>
> 1) That women's sexuality is complex and mysterious, whereas men's is so simple that it goes without saying.
> 2) That men are the default 'person,' included in general 'people who like BDSM' studies, and women are an outside category.
> 3) That women are something to be studied anthropologically, like some distant tribe. I appreciate that you're studying BDSM from what appears to be a pretty informed perspective and that you probably had good, even feminist motives for limiting your survey to women, but I'm just so tired of the idea that female sexuality is a delicate mysterious beautiful unfolding flower that humans are only beginning to understand, and male sexuality is two pumps and a grunt."

These two quotations deserve an entire chapter. Each sentence should be examined for the power of the idea.

Yet, we did not do that. The two quotations above present unique and perhaps unsettling ideas, and part of the purpose of *Women and Kink* is to find commonality. We recognize that there are many more profound ideas in the words our women provided us besides the ones you've read in our book. We are honored that we could finally include these two.

In actuality, some important themes didn't make the final cut. It wasn't because they wouldn't have added value; it is because they were too complex for a subchapter or even an entire chapter in this book; they deserve an entire book dedicated to them in order to give them real justice.

For example, on the theme of kink and gender, we found that many people talk about the gender of their partners, the genders they are attracted to, how they self-identify their gender, role playing with different genders, the power dynamics of gender, and more. However, gender was not a primary focus of this research; these were unintended findings. And we recognize that this discussion is so rich that a new research study should be conducted with a focused attention on how gender affects kink and how kink affects gender. *Kink and Gender* needs its own book!

Another important theme that we did not discuss too deeply is kink and trauma. Some respondents state that they have never experienced trauma, and others explain that they have experienced trauma and describe how they coped with it. Again, since trauma as it relates to kink was not the focus of the study and because there is so much depth to explore, it needs better treatment than we can give it. This is a huge topic for research and would therefore also deserve an entire book dedicated to *Kink and Trauma*.

Other themes that did not make it into this book include age of partner, length of relationship, relationship transitions, past and future relationships, or the interplay between identity and relationship. These are all interesting topics worth discussing, but they were outside of the focus of this project.

Don't worry; what that means is that there are still more gems remaining in our treasure chest!

The Joys with Research

One of the key goals of our research was to collect quantitative data rather than qualitative data. We wanted yes or no answers to direct questions, objective rather than subjective responses, activities that could be counted instead of emotions measured with an imprecise scale.

That goal seems straightforward, but it isn't. Many words have nebulous meanings or specific meanings within certain groups. We can't ask if you've done an activity if you don't know what the word describing that activity is. As we explained earlier, the initials of "BDSM" have multiple meanings. In fact, the word "kink" is not authoritatively defined.

The thesis is titled *The Occurrence of Unconventional Sexual Behaviors of Women*, the journal article is titled "Sensual, Erotic, and Sexual Behaviors of Women from the 'Kink' Community," and this book is titled *Women and Kink*—yet we must acknowledge, there is only a consensus on what the word "woman" means. Many people have definitions and ideas that are influenced by educational background, social and cultural experiences, religious and political beliefs, personal experiences and philosophies, and more.

We cleverly solved this problem. We decided that we would not define "woman," "female," "man," or "male"; we would allow each respondent to find their own definition. After all, most of these terms in the survey required the subjective interpretation of the meanings, and gender is a complex idea that doesn't have universal definitions. There was no reason for us to go down that rabbit hole.

Our sense of cleverness did not last very long. While most of our respondents were able to work within the scope of our generalities, other respondents felt the lack of clarity prevented them from accurately sharing their experiences.

> "… A less-offensive means of categorization would be to have 'male partner,' 'female partner,' and 'partner who identifies outside the gender binary.' If it's actually relevant and necessary for you to know the gender histories of participants, you could break things down into 'cissexual male partner,' 'transsexual male partner,' 'cissexual female partner,' 'transsexual female partner,' and 'partner who identifies outside the gender binary.'"

We'd already considered these ideas, but did not know how to include them in the survey without adding excessive complexity. We recognize that if we had included all of the possible options, we would likely not have received many completed surveys. It was a difficult decision to make, but that level of complexity was simply beyond the scope of this thesis. We acknowledge an opportunity to expand and dive even deeper for future studies.

Having undefined terms did cause some issues, but we were able to learn more about women just because we left those terms undefined.

> "It was a little difficult to answer this survey correctly as a gender-queer, lesbian-identified woman married to a transman. Some of the categories

> don't entirely apply, i.e. were these things done to you by a woman or by a man? My partner rejects being identified as 'transsexual' but that was sometimes the only option. Also, like many lesbians, I have a heterosexual/bisexual past. The questions don't discriminate between now and the past, so it's not clear from reading these answers that at present, I do NOT play with cysmen/malebodied persons at any time, in any way, or any context."

Also, as you may have noticed, some of the terms used in the survey may have fallen out of usage in some communities, and may now be considered offensive by some; however, they were the accepted terms when the study was conducted. This is another example of how difficult it is to create a study that will satisfy everyone.

We did our best to ensure that there was no judgment or bias in our questions, but we were still caught off-guard by some of the women's reactions. It reminds us that there can be negative emotional connections to activities and relationships we love. We are indeed complex creatures.

> "I really wonder if your thesis committee really APPROVED this ridiculous survey. It really doesn't tell you much of anything about female sexuality. I'll be in touch with SFSU about this."

> "The being naked et al in front of unsuspecting people? Or the other activities? You need more clarity here. You sure this is for a 'thesis' and not your wank fodder?"

> "I have already said that I am disappointed in this survey. I am wondering who you pre-tested it with and how they responded …"

Why did we include these quotations in a book about women and kink? We did it to illustrate just how much we learned and how much more information is waiting to be discovered!

What if we had been able to craft our questions to be less offensive and include all the subcategories of a person's history? Imagine if we could have found better ways to encompass even broader notions of kink, sensuality, eroticism, and sexuality so that everyone's kink activities were included? Consider what else we may learn if we could discover why asking questions about activities and relationships caused discomfort for some people?

The women in our survey had a lot to say about the survey itself. The additional insight from their feedback is appreciated. And as you can see, even the topic of the survey instrument has very strong and opposing opinions.

"I enjoyed taking this survey—the questions encompassed the range of my sexuality far better than I expected."

"Most of my kink activities were not covered in the survey list."

"I'd never really done a survey like this before. I sound like a total slut. Even though I'm NOT."

"I'm really in an in-between right now. Looking for who i am. Am i Sub? Domme? Switch? I've always been a very sexually open person … but this survey has made me feel a bit dirty honestly …"

"Many experiences are very difficult to classify, and you have done a great job of labeling as effectively and efficiently as possible …"

"There are so many variations of my lifestyle and none of them are exactly like anyone else. Good luck with your survey!"

Our survey was exploratory; we did not know how deeply into the shadows we would be able to peer, what knowledge we would bring into the light. We were rewarded both by those women whose range of sexuality we were able to encompass by our questions, and we were rewarded by those women who pointed out that there is still more to discover.

Sample Size

Think of all the remarkable quotations you read in the previous chapters, the ideas that titillated your imagination or prompted a long discussion with friends.

Consider that there are almost 8 billion people in the world, and all those amazing quotations arose from only 1,580 women! What other marvels will be revealed when we can delve into more people's stories? What fascinating accounts of adventure and daring would we discover in your story?

Final Thoughts

We opened our treasure chest, and the light from myriad jewels and gems illuminated the dark and shadowed wilderness! Strangers came forward and elaborated on their life, their loves, and their experiences, and we were struck by the candid sharing of pain, joy, fear, growth, tenderness, and strength these women felt. After a while, we realized they weren't strangers at all, but simply friends we hadn't met, their stories revealing a little part of themselves and a little part of ourselves.

We hope that these personal stories of love, relationship structures, and reasons for participating in the "unconventional" fascinated you, galvanized you, and encouraged you, and they affirmed that you are not alone in your yearnings. If you are curious, we have included the survey instrument (Appendix A) as a tool that you may use to fill out for yourself, to discover your own passions and share with those you love. Feel free to add columns and rows as needed for your own personal use. We have also created a list of resources[1] if you are interested in learning ways to find community, events, knowledgeable professionals, training, and other support. Our vision is to inspire you to explore yourself and the world around you, to define what we could for you, and then wave "bon voyage" to you as you embark on your own adventure to discover your own hidden treasures.

There are no real rules to the game. These women taught us that for every "you must!" there is a "you mustn't!" and both are as true and as proper as you desire them to be. We learned that there is no one-size-fits-all way of living or creating relationships and that there is always someone who loves you just the way you are. We learned that weakness is strength if it helps you be you, and strength is useless if it doesn't.

You are who you are. You are beautifully complex. We all are. The label that fits you best is "you," and you'll need that person as you find your way through life, love, and adventures.

We'd like to leave you with our last quotation from the thousands of responses we've shared, a final message that is simple yet so important to remember:

"Isn't life grand."

Note

1 A Resources list is in the References section.

Appendix A
The Survey

Women's Sexual Behavior

1. Where did you hear about this study?

2. In which State do you reside?
   If outside the USA, in which country do you reside?

Activities

This section will refer to activities you have participated in or observed. The column "Observing Activity" can include watching live or through other media (TV, movies, Internet). If any question is unclear, please use the text box at the bottom to clarify your response.

3. Which of the following activities have you willingly participated in for your own sensual or erotic pleasure?

	Doing Activity to Others	Activity Done to You	Observing Activity
Touching (caress, cuddle, massage, tickle)	☐	☐	☐
Kissing, Licking, Sucking	☐	☐	☐
Grooming (shaving, manicure, pedicure, brush hair, etc.)	☐	☐	☐
Applying ____ (body paint, chocolate, oil, food, etc.)	☐	☐	☐
Using Feathers/Fur	☐	☐	☐
Biting	☐	☐	☐
Hickeys	☐	☐	☐
Scratching/Leaving Marks/Abrasion	☐	☐	☐
Hair Pulling	☐	☐	☐
Pinching	☐	☐	☐
Spanking	☐	☐	☐
Paddling	☐	☐	☐
Ice Play	☐	☐	☐
Candle Wax Play	☐	☐	☐
Fire Play/Fire Cupping	☐	☐	☐
Wrestling	☐	☐	☐
Boxing/Beating/Kicking	☐	☐	☐
Flogging	☐	☐	☐
Whipping	☐	☐	☐
Genital Play: slap, kick, clothespins, etc.	☐	☐	☐

(Continued)

Breast Play: slap, clothespins, etc.	☐	☐	☐
Electrical Play (Violet Wand, TENS unit, etc.)	☐	☐	☐
Using Clothespins/Clamps	☐	☐	☐
Caning	☐	☐	☐
Corset Training	☐	☐	☐
Branding/Burns	☐	☐	☐
Catheterizing	☐	☐	☐
Genital Torture (piercing, stretching, stitching, hooks, dilation, etc.)	☐	☐	☐
Breast Torture (piercings, breast press, stretching, hooks, etc.)	☐	☐	☐
Foot Torture	☐	☐	☐
Anal Torture	☐	☐	☐
Other Torture	☐	☐	☐
Knife Play/Razors	☐	☐	☐
Attaching Weights to body parts	☐	☐	☐
Impact Play/Percussion Play: using blunt or heavy instrument	☐	☐	☐
Piercing: Permanent	☐	☐	☐
Piercing: Temporary, Needles, Pins, Injections	☐	☐	☐
Tattooing: Permanent	☐	☐	☐
Tattooing: Temporary, cell-popping, red-lining	☐	☐	☐
Cutting/Artistic Cutting/Scarification	☐	☐	☐
Blood Play	☐	☐	☐

(*Continued*)

Breath Play, Chocking, Strangling, Hanging	☐	☐	☐
Water Torture	☐	☐	☐
Vacuum Pumping	☐	☐	☐
Physical Humiliation (face-slapping, begging, crawling, etc.)	☐	☐	☐
Verbal Abuse/Humiliation (yelling, calling names, etc.)	☐	☐	☐
Obedience/Training	☐	☐	☐
Punishment: Emotional	☐	☐	☐
Punishment: Physical	☐	☐	☐
Objectification (use person as an object (human furniture, human doll, human ashtray, etc.))	☐	☐	☐
Deprivation (forced chastity, blindfold, bathroom use control, orgasm control, sensory deprivation, etc.)	☐	☐	☐
Forced Cross-Dressing	☐	☐	☐
Other Forced Activities (eating, exercise, masturbation, sexual behavior, nudity, etc.)	☐	☐	☐
Service-Oriented Submission/Domestic Service	☐	☐	☐
Imposed Feminization	☐	☐	☐
Imposed Masculinization	☐	☐	☐
Urine Play (Golden Showers/Water Sports)	☐	☐	☐
Feces Play (Brown Showers/Scat/Excrement/Enemas)	☐	☐	☐

(Continued)

Light Bondage (Able to get out if you wanted to)	☐	☐	☐
Moderate Bondage (Can't get out on own, but with body mobility)	☐	☐	☐
Stringent/Extreme Bondage (Immobilized)	☐	☐	☐
Use bondage toys (chains, gags, cuffs, rope, etc.)	☐	☐	☐

Additional comments regarding the activities on this page:

4. Which of the following Role-Play scenarios have you willingly participated in for your own sensual or erotic pleasure?

	As the Trainer	As an animal	Observing
a. Animal Play (Pony, kitten, wolf, etc.)	☐	☐	☐

	As the Caretaker	As someone being taken care of	Observing
b. Age Regression Play/Guardian: child (baby, toddler, teenager, brat, etc.)	☐	☐	☐
Age Progression (elderly)	☐	☐	☐
Medical Play (Doctor or Nurse:Patient)	☐	☐	☐

	As Someone in Charge (e.g. boss)	As a subordinate	Observing
c. Jobs/Occupation Play (Boss:Secretary, Maid, Teacher:Student)	☐	☐	☐
Religious Play (Priest/Nun, Priest/altar boy or altar girl)	☐	☐	☐

	As the Top (i.e. Abductor, interrogator, initiator)	As a bottom (i.e. victim)	Observing
d. Danger Fantasy (abduction, execution, impregnation, interrogation, rape, kidnapping, prison scene)	☐	☐	☐

(Continued)

Appendix **189**

Incest Play (fantasy)	☐	☐	☐
Sex with Corpse (fantasy)	☐	☐	☐
	As the Master	As a slave	Observing
e. Master/slave Fantasy	☐	☐	☐

f. Other Role Play: (Specify below):

5. Which Role-Play scenario is your favorite? (Describe below):

6. Which of the following activities have you done (in front of unsuspecting people) for your own sensual or erotic pleasure? (Check all that apply)
   - ☐ Showing bare breasts
   - ☐ Showing genitals
   - ☐ Acting out sexual fantasy/Role Play
   - ☐ Being Naked
   - ☐ Engaging in public sex

   Other (Describe below):

Questions About Activities

This series of questions refers to the activities in the previous section. This refers to your responses to questions 3–6.

7. What was your PRIMARY reason for participating in your most recent activity from the previous section?
   - [ ] At the request of a male partner
   - [ ] At the request of a female partner
   - [ ] At the request of a transsexual partner
   - [ ] For money
   - [ ] For self-discovery/personal pleasure
   - [ ] To find a partner

   Other (please specify):

8. What other reason(s) (if any) did you participate in your most recent activity from the previous section?
   - [ ] At the request of a male partner
   - [ ] At the request of a female partner
   - [ ] At the request of a transsexual partner
   - [ ] For money
   - [ ] For self-discovery/personal pleasure
   - [ ] To find a partner

   Other (please specify):

9. For the activities you checked in the previous section, who have your partners been? (Check all that apply)
   - ☐ Women
   - ☐ Men
   - ☐ Transsexual/Transgender (MTF)
   - ☐ Transsexual/Transgender (FTM)

   Other (please specify):

10. For the activities you checked in the previous section, how do you meet new people to participate with you? (Check all that apply)
    - ☐ Internet
    - ☐ Professional Dominatrix/Professional Submissive
    - ☐ Support groups
    - ☐ Magazine ads
    - ☐ Friends
    - ☐ BDSM/Leather Bars
    - ☐ Informal Social Events/Munches
    - ☐ Dungeons/Play Parties
    - ☐ Not applicable

    Other (please specify):

11. Can you ONLY attain an orgasm only by participating in the activities you checked in the previous section?
    - ☐ Yes
    - ☐ No

12. In the previous 12 months, have you paid money to someone for performing any of the activities you checked in the previous section?
    ☐ Yes
    ☐ No

13. In the previous 12 months, have you been paid money to perform any of the activities you checked in the previous section?
    ☐ Yes
    ☐ No

14. For the activities you checked in the previous section, what is your favorite activity?

    (Feel free to combine activities to form one scenario.)

15. For the activities you checked in the previous section, if there is anything else about your experiences that you would like to add, please do so below.

Erotica

16a. Are you sexually aroused by any of the following?
- ☐ Clothing (lingerie, shoes, corsets, etc.)
- ☐ Fabrics (leather, rubber, vinyl, etc.)
- ☐ Uniforms (military, medical, occupational, etc.)
- ☐ Specific Body Part(s)
- ☐ Body Fluids

Other (please specify):

16b. If you answered yes to any of the categories in question 16a, please specify what kind of clothing, fabric, uniforms etc. are sexually arousing to you:

17. Which of the following activities have you willingly participated in primarily for your own sensual or erotic pleasure?
- ☐ Pose for erotic images (photography, video, audio)
- ☐ Take erotic images of others (photography, video, audio)
- ☐ Share erotic images of yourself with others
- ☐ Share erotic images of your partner with others

Other (Please specify) or if you wish to elaborate on your answers above, please do so here:

18. Which of the following have you created or observed primarily for your own sensual or erotic pleasure?
    - ☐ Erotic Literature (books, poems, magazines)
    - ☐ Nude paintings, sculptures, or statues
    - ☐ Performance (strip-tease, burlesque, belly dance)
    - ☐ Sexual pornography

    Other (please specify):

19. What is your favorite theme for erotica? (Describe below):

Sexual Activities

20. Which of the following sexual activities have you willingly participated in?

	Doing Activity to Women	Doing Activity to Men	Having Activity Done by Women	Having Activity Done by Men	Observing Activity
Cunnilingus (Stimulating a woman's genitals with mouth)	☐	☐	☐	☐	☐
Ingesting vaginal fluid	☐	☐	☐	☐	☐
Passing female vaginal fluid from mouth-to-mouth	☐	☐	☐	☐	☐
Using a strap-on dildo to penetrate vagina	☐	☐	☐	☐	☐
Stimulating vagina with other sex toys (Vibrators, Ben Wa Walls, Speculums, etc.)	☐	☐	☐	☐	☐
Sucking/Licking dildo with mouth	☐	☐	☐	☐	☐
Vaginal Fisting	☐	☐	☐	☐	☐
Mammary Intercourse (rubbing phallic object or penis between breasts)	☐	☐	☐	☐	☐
Fellatio (stimulating a man's genitals with mouth)	☐	☐	☐	☐	☐

(Continued)

Ingesting Semen	☐	☐	☐	☐	☐
Snowballing (passing semen from mouth-to-mouth)	☐	☐	☐	☐	☐
Penetrating vagina with penis	☐	☐	☐	☐	☐
Stimulating penis with sex toys (Cock rings, Sheath, etc.)	☐	☐	☐	☐	☐
Stimulating anus with fingers or penis	☐	☐	☐	☐	☐
Rimming (stimulating anus with mouth)	☐	☐	☐	☐	☐
Felching (licking semen out of anus)	☐	☐	☐	☐	☐
Using a strap-on dildo to penetrate anus	☐	☐	☐	☐	☐
Stimulating anus with Sex Toys (Beads, Butt plug, vibrator, Speculum, hooks, etc.)	☐	☐	☐	☐	☐
Anal Fisting	☐	☐	☐	☐	☐
Hand job (stimulating genitals with hands/fingers)	☐	☐	☐	☐	☐
Foot job (stimulating genitals with feet)	☐	☐	☐	☐	☐
Genital to Genital contact: non-penetrative	☐	☐	☐	☐	☐

(Continued)

Using semen or vaginal fluid in mixed-drinks or cooking/baking recipes	☐	☐	☐	☐	☐
Worship (kissing, licking, smelling, enjoying a specific body part):	☐	☐	☐	☐	☐

Other sexual activities (Please describe below):

Miscellaneous Erotic Activities

21. Which of the following activities have you willingly participated in for sensual or erotic purposes?
    - ☐ Masturbation (solo)
    - ☐ Mutual Masturbation (with a partner)
    - ☐ Swinging (Mate Swapping)
    - ☐ Group sex (including orgies, gang bang, bukkake)
    - ☐ Anonymous sex/sex with strangers
    - ☐ Sex with inanimate objects (not designed as sex toys)
    - ☐ Sex with a dead person (real)
    - ☐ Sex with domestic animals (real)
    - ☐ Sex with wild/non-domestic animals (real)
    - ☐ Prostitution (real)
    - ☐ Cyber sex (webcam)
    - ☐ Phone sex

    Additional comments regarding the activities on this page:

Relationship

22. What is your current relationship status?
    - ☐ Single (Never Married/Domestic Partnership)
    - ☐ Divorced/Separated
    - ☐ Widowed
    - ☐ Casual BDSM relationship(s)/play partner(s)
    - ☐ Long-term relationship
    - ☐ Married/Domestic Partner
    - ☐ Monogamous
    - ☐ Polyamorous/open relationship/Polyfidelity
    - ☐ Swingers
    - ☐ BDSM Family
    - ☐ 24/7 BDSM relationship

    Other (please specify):

Final Question

23. If there is anything else you'd like to add about your sexual lifestyle, or if anything in this survey was confusing and you'd like to clarify your response, please do so below:

Follow-up

Thank you for your participation!

Appendix B
Additional Sensual, Erotic, and Sexual Behaviors

The following describing additional BDSM-related activities, miscellaneous erotic activities, and overt sexual behaviors were provided by fill-in text responses. Some categories include contributions from more than one person. Duplications were removed and grammatical and spelling errors were corrected.

BDSM-Related Behaviors

- Other anal play including:
  - Anal fisting
  - Anal sex
  - Anal stretching
  - Anal toys (plugs, "ass pick," anal hooks)
- Enema play (not feces play)
- Doing activities to self, including:
  - Candle wax
  - Choking with belt
  - Clothespins
  - Cutting
  - Mild self-bondage
  - Mousetraps
  - Using clamps on labia and nipples

- Use of physical force, including:
  - Being held down by partner (not wrestling)
  - Defending self from dominant partner/being "taken"
  - Physically forceful to, and be forced/pushed with sexual partners
  - Takedowns
- Breath play (mild), glove over face, briefly covering the nose and mouth
- Other blood play including:
  - Drinking partners blood
  - Using menstrual blood
- Other bondage including:
  - Bondage photo shoots/demos/performances
  - Saran wrap
  - Wearing and watching others wear corsets: form of bondage
- Other additional/uncategorized:
  - Being observed
  - Boot kissing
  - Choking on cock
  - Cupping (without fire)
  - Crawling—not for "physical humiliation, bit for some level of control/dominance"
  - Energy exchange
  - Face slapping: non-humiliation, not hard
  - Forced bi-sexuality
  - Forced orgasms
  - Genital piercings
  - Golden showers—peeing when demanded, either for their amusement or on them
  - Humiliation or degradation play—not in activities listed
  - "I like the milder things"
  - "I've only watched feces play because of 2girls1cup—not sure if that counts"
  - Leather sex
  - Making artistic arrangements on the body with clothespins, then follow with candle wax
  - Massage and suckling to induce lactation
  - Objectification—not in the activities listed
  - Other foot play (bastinado)
  - Reading about these activities
  - Receiving physical abuse without humiliation or verbal abuse
  - Strap-on

- Tickling/Tickle torture
- Vaginal fisting
- Waxing—for purposes of painful, forced hair removal

Miscellaneous Erotic Activities

- Cybersex without webcam
  - Text-based
  - Instant message
  - Chat
  - SMS/MMS/Text message
  - E-mail
  - With virtual avatars, e.g., Second Life
- Sexting (sexual text messaging)
- Threesomes
- Part of a very serious and secure fluid bonded safe-sex circle of 24
- Poly (open relationship)
- Guided masturbation
- Not allowed to masturbate in current relationship
- Sex with inanimate objects: using candles and vegetables to learn to relax my inner muscles to allow fisting
- Blind fondling by strangers i cannot see and can only reach me through a hole in a box
- Given to others (by my Owner) to be used sexually
- Sex in front of strangers at a club
- Sex with my husband in the same room as another married couple
- Stripping/live sex shows/lap dance
- Watching others
- One-night stands
- Sex with a stranger only once. We are friends now

Overt Sexual Behaviors

- Masturbation
  - Activities done to self
  - Anal stimulation to myself, not done by others
  - Female ejaculation—self
  - Masturbation using stream of water in pool or hot tub
  - Vibrator used on self

- Mutual activities
    - Doing an activity WITH someone
    - Mutual masturbation
- Stimulating body part not specifically mentioned
    - Armpit stimulation
    - Cunnilingus on menstruating woman
    - G-spot stimulation
    - Stimulating clitoris
    - Stimulating nipples
    - Stimulating vagina with breast
    - Strap-on cock sucking
- Multiple partner sexual activities
    - Cuckold—forcing partner to watch me play while he's unable to participate
    - Double penetration
    - Fellatio or cunnilingus while having sex with a different person
    - Group sex, group scenarios
    - Multiple partner sexual play (penetrative and non)
    - Triple/multiple penetration, vagina, anal, mouth, etc.
    - Used a man to fuck a woman vaginally
- "Forced" activities
    - Being "forced" to drink out of animal bowls/sleep on animal bed (have had done by a man, observed)
    - Forced bi scenarios
    - Forced masturbation
- Activities previously categorized as "kink" or BDSM
    - Boot fucking
    - Boot licking
    - CBT (cock and ball torture)
    - Choking—all with female partners
    - Cock worship
    - Diapers (wearing/putting others into them, using them for their intended purpose)
    - Play rape
    - Using a leash (Have done on a man, have had done by a man, observed)
    - Using my nightstick as a double dildo in a uniform scene
    - Using unusual objects for penetration
    - Verbal humiliation
- Body fluid play
    - Drinking from filled condoms
    - Drinking my own ejaculate and splashing it on my face and breasts

- Drinking/squirting of breastmilk
- Lactation/adult breastfeeding/adult erotic nursing
- Semen play—facials, swallowing, pearl necklaces, etc.
- Sniffing, scenting and body rubbing
- Squirting vaginal fluid
- Swallowing and playing with my own vaginal fluids (not ejaculate)
- Urinating on men and women
- Using urine as a drink
- Watersports (golden showers, watching voiding, voiding for others)

- Uncategorized
  - Asexual
  - Dirty talk
  - Extended foreplay/body worship, extended eye contact, dirty talk, smacking
  - Face-fucking (had done by a man, observed)
  - "One time the family dog licked my pussy. Kinda unexpectedly"
  - Orgasm control … being required to "not cum until my top gives me permission"
  - Perform fellatio on a trans woman
  - Sexting
  - Teach another how to properly touch me
  - Urethral sounding on a penis

Appendix C
Exhibitionistic Behaviors

The following additional exhibitionistic behaviors were provided by fill-in text responses. Some categories include contributions from more than one person. Duplications were removed and grammatical and spelling errors were corrected.

- Arranged scenes with "strangers"
    - Being a glory hole
    - Gangbangs
    - Playing on webcam / Webcam sex

- Covert bondage (bound under clothes in public)
    - Being bound under clothes while out
    - Covert bondage (light to moderate)
    - Covert bondage (worn underneath clothing while in public)—rope harness, PVC harness, chastity belt, waist chain, waist-cincher, or corset
    - Covert bondage: being bound in some form underneath your clothing
    - Discrete bondage (having some part of me bound beneath my clothes, occasionally allowing it to be seen)
    - Hidden bondage & restrictions they can't easily see but my partner is acutely aware exists
    - Wearing rope bondage under my clothes

- Discreet/covert public sex
  - Balcony sex
  - Discreet public sex
  - "Had sex in an airport family bathroom with the door locked. I'm sure people heard us"
  - Having a quickie at the park at night
  - Parking lot sex
  - Public sex in unseen areas
  - Secretly engaging in public sex
  - Sex behind a curtain in empty hotel ball room
  - Sex in public
  - Sex in front of windows
  - Sex on the elevator
  - Sex outside of clubs or house parties

- Nude for art
  - Nude for peace public nudity art "stunts" and performances
  - Nude modeling

- General public (not done directly in front of people, but in public where there was a certain risk of discovery)
  - Being nude on a balcony
  - Discrete/covert power exchange in general public:
    - "Have taken off under pants in a restaurant while seated in a booth across from the person directing me to do so"
    - "Never overt, more like wearing a skirt w/no panties underneath & not being allowed to x [cross] my legs. Highly unlikely anyone actually saw anything, but the possibility exists"
  - Driving with no top or bra
  - Being nude on the beach
  - Walk around the house/fenced yard naked and have an adult voyeur neighbor that watches in glimpses around the back of the fence

- Public displays of D/s or M/s dynamic/power exchange
  - On rare occasions, I would be asked to do something by my Master/Top in semi-public situations
  - Beaten and made to give oral to my Master
  - Being topped in public, being led around by my hair or being spanked while shopping, etc. Aggressive play while at dinner

- Control games (being required to ask to use the restroom, not being allowed to carry my own cell phone, not allowed to use keys to unlock doors)
- Discreet D/s and role play in public spaces
- Dominating subs
- Engaging in D/s "protocol" such as calling my partner "sir" if that is the particular game we are playing
- Engaging in Master-slave dynamics in a public place
- Forced orgasm
- I have had boys have to buy 3 tubs of lube and several different sized cucumbers
- I have worn a butt plug in public by the orders of my Master
- Leading a sub/slave on leash in a shopping center
- Engaged in "low impact" (to others) gestures of dominance to my boyfriend, Held his wrists tightly in my hand, discretely held his hair in a dominant way etc. I like it to be discrete though
- Master also likes for me to flash at vanilla sites, parks, forts, etc. Master has made her pull pants down and masturbate as they go by 18-wheelers
- On road trips i am naked in the passenger seat and fingered by my master, or made to masturbate, for his amusement and that of observing truckdrivers/motorists
- Public discipline
- Public display of BDSM activities
- Public displays of ownership are fun like bringing her out to eat in handcuffs. Verbal reinforcements of who is in charge in some public settings. (away from minors)
- Public humiliation
- Serve my Master, defer to him and call him Master or Sir in public
- Showing submission in public, i.e., kneeling
- ... to please my Sir for His sensual or erotic pleasure (at His request, not because i thought of it)—showing bare breasts, being naked in front of other people, going in public without a bra or in a see-through shirt, not wearing panties

- Other kink behaviors in public places
    - Abduction
    - Being pinched, bitten, and fingered
    - Bondage in public

- Breath play
- Cross-dressing
- Bondage and flogging play
- Flogging someone in a public place
- Gender transgression
- Golden showers play in public
- Golden showers … recipient
- Humiliation in a public place
- Humiliation play (consists of name-calling and face slapping)
- Urinated for my own pleasure in front of unsuspecting people, usually after consuming alcohol
- Mild hair pulling, faux chocking, rubbing against each other with clothes on, quick groping in crowed bars or on the dance floor
- My husband and i enjoy performing psychodramas on the unsuspecting public, which may or may not be sexual in nature, but are always disturbing. he is much younger than i, and we can very convincingly roleplay mother and teenage boy in public
- Non-sexual topping in public
- Peeing
- Playfully spanked
- Public flogging
- Public humiliation by way of wearing a revealing shirt that clearly displayed that she had "slut" written on her chest in permanent marker
- Public whipping on a dance floor at a semi-vanilla event
- Receiving a spanking in public with my skirt up, panties showing
- Spanking in public
- Stealth scening
- Taken my play partner out for a walk on a leash and in a big dog collar many times, with both hidden underneath thick winter clothes but easily accessible for me to hold onto the leash and pull on the leash and collar inconspicuously
- Taken a submissive who was dresses in women's clothing and wearing piggy accessories out in public (vanilla setting) for a public humiliation scene
- Taking people tied up for a walk to a restaurant, and have them eat with their mouth only. I told people they lost a bet
- wearing a remote-control egg in public with Mistress controlling the remote
- Worn and used diapers for their intended purpose

- Other sexual activities (non-coitus) in public places
  - A female friend of mine occasionally go[es] out in public and act[s] as if we're dating (holding hands, snuggling, kissing, occasionally making out if we have a receptive audience)
  - Been groped in public but under clothing but at a distance from the public
  - Blowjobs:
    - In the car
    - In movie theater (during an R-rated movie)
    - In parks
  - Cumming
  - Enjoy being watched performing blowjobs in vehicles as people drive by
  - Engaging in "group" making out with several men at the same time in a public situation
  - Engaging in conversation with unsuspecting people to work up the mood or dirty talk in public
  - Fondling, but not so far as public sex
  - Frottage
  - Have had to wear devices attached out in public, on the train and at the hairdressers, as well as pleasure myself in a park with my toe so that only the Dom and myself knew what was going on
  - Having an object hidden in my vagina while out socially at a vanilla venue
  - Having sex toys in use underneath clothing while out in public (like nipple clamps or an anal plug)
  - Having spontaneous orgasms (albeit fully clothed)
  - Naked on beaches and given oral sex there and in alleyways, taxicabs, etc.
  - It wasn't to the point of hav[ing] intercourse, but being fingered in public
  - Kissing and fondling
  - Kissing another woman, nuzzling her hair or whispering in her ear
  - Making out and petting on the lawn of a friend's house during a party they held with a woman and a t-girl
  - "Making out" with a person of the same sex in a straight environment
  - Masturbation
  - Masturbated in a movie theater ... in the dark, nobody could see
  - Masturbating in public, but without their knowledge

- "Masturbating (usually to climax) in front of unsuspecting people on the highway. Since everyone has cell phones now, that's not safe to do anymore"
- Masturbating as 18-wheelers pass
- Masturbating in my car
- Masturbation in public
- Only once in the back of a cab; cab driver consented by his actions (turning the rear-view mirror so that he could see a full-length image of me in back seat) after activity began; otherwise, always get consent first
- Oral sex/mutual masturbation in library/on long distance bus trip
- Riding the motorcycle with due balls or remote vibe eggs in, etc.
- Touching myself erotically in a way people can't see, while engaged in non-sexual activities like work, being out to dinner, etc.
- Upskirt
- Used a vibrating egg while in public
- Wearing toys under clothing (remote vibrators, for example)
- Wearing sexy lingerie under my clothes

- Sex in front of others (not strangers)
    - Group sex
    - Had sex while a friend was in the same room
    - Swingers, orgies, 3somes 4somes

- Wearing kink-related items in public
    - Also wearing unusual fetish items in public—corsets, rubber, bondage accessories, gas masks, etc.
    - Clubbing with a sub with collar and leash at vanilla places
    - Collar and cuffs in public
    - Corset training in public
    - Dressing provocatively … short leather skirt, corset, thigh high leather boots, etc.
    - Exhibiting fetish wear
    - Wearing latex
    - Wearing nipple clamps under clothing
    - Wore wrist cuffs and collar in a public restaurant

Appendix D
Additional Forms of Erotica

The following additional forms of erotica were provided by fill-in text responses. Some categories include contributions from more than one person. Duplications were removed and grammatical and spelling errors were corrected.

- Forms of erotica via images
    - Drawings and CG (computer generated) art
    - Photography (bondage photography, pictures of piercings)
    - Non-photo erotic art
    - Painting
    - Porn site model
    - Pose as a life model for drawing class
    - "Web camming"

- Kink-specific
    - BDSM fantasy
    - BDSM scenes not involving sex (floggings, spankings, cuttings, needle play, pony play, medical play, electrical play, etc.)
    - Directing others to do SM activities over the telephone
    - Dungeon equipment (sawhorse, spanking bench, etc.), toys (canes, floggers), symbolic items (collar)
    - English tea service with nude servers in a small-group setting

- I have written SM erotic stories and shared the stories. I have written reports of a play session and shared that with the people I played with (and in one instance) published it (using a pen name) in a BDSM newsletter
  - Leather/uniform gear with flogging
  - My own life sub dressed up in latex
  - Rope performances, improvisation performances mixing rope work and butô dance
  - Watching BDSM games i.e., others play sub/dom, sensation/pain play

- Other media
  - Japanese dating sims
  - Movies/video
  - My female nudes are very sensual, usually close-focused pieces. I find them sensually pleasurable to create. They sell very well, too, which is a bonus!
  - Online play
  - Phone sex
  - Writing erotica
  - Yaoi pictures (Japanese drawn guy on guy porn)

- Uncategorized
  - Ballroom dancing
  - Orgies and play parties
  - Owner of adult website
  - Relating, in person, of sexual fantasies by/to a partner

Appendix E
Additional Role-Play Scenarios

The following additional role-play scenarios were provided by fill-in text responses. Some categories include contributions from more than one person. Duplications were removed and grammatical and spelling errors were corrected.

- Age play:
    - Bottoming/forced orgasms
    - Child
    - Cougar age play—playing the role of an older women who pursues much younger men
    - Daddy/little girl (NOT as incest play; to take care of me, dress me, feed me, bathe me, diaper me, etc.; It is loving, sweet, caring, comforting, submissive, and safe)
    - Daddi/grrl
    - Daddy/Little Princess
    - Dutch Daddy/little femme girl
    - Girl scout/older guy selling cookies to
    - Good girl/bad girl role reversals
    - Have played with/had pets/subs who were into role play as children/school girls
    - Head Mistress/school girl
    - Incest play:

- Aunt/naughty nephew
- Brother/Sister
- Older Sister/younger brother
- Daddy/Babygirl with forced anal
- Daddy/Boy—"Little Camper"
- Father/daughter (with impregnation, rape play, teenage seduction, molestation, naughty teenager, Dad's friends forced rape, teaching to be a good girl/slut, spanking, anal, oral play, forced oral, vaginal sex, taking virginity)
- "Incest, with me as the corrupting mother"
- Mommy/little girl (being controlled, punished, and used)
- Mother/son
- Sister/sister
- Rape
- Step-Daddy/step-daughter
- Uncle/niece
- Madame/domestic
- Mommy/boy (Also noted as "Mommi/boi but without the incest aspect to it")
- Naughty school girl caught with other boys and punished by priest
- Neighbor Lady/teen boy
- Older, more experienced cowboy and a new rather inexperienced cowboy
- Regressed to (5-years-old, 4-year-old boy, bratty little kid)
- Runaway
- Schoolyard bully

- Animal play:
    - Bear
    - Being a cat (wild, domestic, or kitten)
    - Canine play
    - Me as pet (crawling on my hands and knees through the house, eating out of a bowl, begging for attention, whining, curl up on owner's lap, being taken care of)
    - Primal/animalistic play
    - Pony play (training, show ponies, work ponies)
    - Wolf/bunny

- Anonymity:
    - Faux anonymous sex encounter play (sexy stranger game)
    - Gangbang/anonymity play

- Cosplay
  - Pop culture costumes
  - Anime characters
  - Video game characters
  - TV and movie characters

- Danger fantasy
  - Abduction with abuse of power (religious/medical), anonymity, bondage, confinement, forced behavior, gang bang, hard take-down, held captive, gun, knife, physical punishment, rape, held down, moderate abuse, leave marks)
  - Captor prisoner
  - Being victim of a vendetta
  - Damsel in distress
  - Deity/sacrifice
  - Gang rape (where I am directing my boys on what to do to the "victim")
  - Goddess/worshiper
  - Hunter/prey
  - Home invasion
  - Kidnap (grabbed, wrestled down, restrained, used, raped)
    - from a bar
    - kidnap witness
  - Serial killer/stalker
  - Rescue
  - Torture play
    - Nipple torture
    - Water torture

- D/s- or M/s-related fantasy
  - Being submissive in blackmail role
  - D/S power exchange
  - Female Master (Switch)
  - Mistress/slave (FemDom, Dominant slave, Demanding Mistress, Sex slave, sexual slave, domestic slave, forced service, and cross-dressing)
  - Mistress/sub (forced nudity and arousal, exhibitionism, orgasm denial, verbal humiliation)
  - Owner/puppy
  - Owner/toy
  - Owner/pony
  - Sir/boi

- Toy Keeper/toy
- Uppity Slave
- Unsuspecting maiden in a barn

- Fantasy world play:
    - Alice lost in Wonderland
    - Being an alien or something strange: alien abduction/alien interrogation
    - Big Bad Wolf/little red riding hood
    - Demon/Demonic
    - Fairy play (fairy tales, faery)
    - Fantasy world like magician and victim
    - Macrophilia
    - Part animal, part human (usually a human body with features or attributes of a cow or pig. Specifically, multiple breasts/udders, pig nose, curly tail, animal ears, and large belly)
    - Superhero play
    - Supernatural (werewolf attack, vampire attack, demon/incubus attach, submission to gargoyle)
    - Vampire bleeding victim dry
    - Vampire or werewolf and prey
    - Vampire role play but without blood play
    - Witch hunt

- Inanimate object play—one or both partners pretending to be objects
    - Made into human furniture (fucked)
    - Made into artwork
    - Ragdoll (put to sleep and made love to)
    - Using man as an ironing board

- Jobs/occupations:
    - Caricatures of political figures
    - Construction Worker/Passer By
    - Cowpokes/Ranch Hands
    - Cop play
        - Cop and perpetrator
        - Cop and bad guy
        - Cop or SWAT and arrest
        - Cop/prisoner/inmate
        - Cop/robber
        - Crooked cop who is punished

- Drill sergeant and recruit
- Fed Ex delivery person and customer unable to pay for package
- Hypnotist/subject—assistant
- Interrogation/Prison Scenes
- Lord of the Manor/Farmer's Girl
- Mad scientists (may or may not involve one of us in the lab assistant role)
- Maid:
  - Cleaning
  - Master of the House/lowly maid
- Massage therapist/patient
- Medical play (exams, enemas, catheterization)
  - Doctor/patient (observes, sticks, and probes patient)
  - Gynecologist/patient
  - Nurse/patient
  - Dentist/patient
- Military, army scenes (interrogation, abduction)
  - Military/prisoner
- Naughty librarian
- Pimp/whore
- Police play
  - Police/prisoner
  - Police officer/hooker
- Prostitute/customer (john)
- Religious play
  - Priest/school girl
  - Priest/nun
- School room play (getting caught passing notes, smoking, get sent to principal, get paddled at school)
  - Teacher/student/schoolboy (bondage, knife play, hot wax, flogging, slapping, feather/soft mitt, pin wheel)
  - Assistant Principal/student
  - Coach/gymnastic, cheerleader
  - Headmistress/student
- Subordinate role as a Dominant character (i.e., being taken advantage of, spanked, paddled, belted, choking, breath play, light bondage)
  - Boss/worker
  - Boss/secretary (punished for mistakes, forced molestation)
- Supervisor/supervisee
- Test object of an evil scientist or doctor
- Vet/pet

- Period and or historical play, acting out dynamics as practiced in specific times and places in history
    - 40s gangster brothel take over
    - 18th-century highwayman happening
    - British soldier
    - Bodice-ripper romance
    - Domestic 1950s household
    - German Prince (kidnaps monk and seduces him)
    - Governess/head of household
    - Governess/school marm
    - Medieval play
        - Medieval Inquisitor/heretic
        - Harem girl
        - Middle-Ages torture play
    - Nazi/prisoner military interrogation
    - Pirate play
        - Pirate wench
        - Pirate/Innocent Victim
        - Captive stowaway/maiden (tied to ship's mast, flogged by the bosun, rape, captain rescue)
    - Playing Verzingettorix [Vercingetorix], a Gaulish king
    - Racial play: (examples: white Mistress/black slave (racial play), black slave revolts and punishes white owner, black SS officer interrogates prisoner, reverse slavery, black dominate/female sub)
        - Inter-racial breeding, impregnation
        - South Mistress/uneducated male slave in South
    - Ronin/geisha
    - Seduced by Julius Caesar
    - Viking pillaging a convent

- Royalty play:
    - Knight/servant
    - Lord and lady plus servants
    - Monarch/harem slave
    - Princess/pet tiger
    - Queen, King, and court (group scene)
    - Queen/court jester
    - Queen dominating slaves
    - The princess/the slut

- Uncategorized role-play scenarios:
  - Being "coerced" into doing more and more sexual/BDSM activities
  - Being "taken advantage of" while in immobilizing bondage or while unconscious/sleeping
  - Being tied to a cross
  - Being sold as cattle to another person
  - Breast inflation/lactation fantasy
  - Different genders, characters
  - Dress up in specific outfits that partner finds sexy
  - "Fag Sex"
  - Fat admiration and erotic weight gain. Fantasy and role play (specifically acting out being fed and gaining weight)
  - Feminization and humiliation of boyfriend
  - Gender fucking
  - Gender play ("ex being dressed as male ... and packing for my female lover ... or vice versa ... and one calls on phone to say coming home and you better be ready for me etc.")
  - Intersex Person
  - Ilsa Krebb interrogating/torturing James Bond for [unspecified] information
  - Lactation/milk slave
  - Living as a gorean slave for six years
  - "More equal based role play games ... eg 'chatting up stranger,' slave girls, wrestlings, less to do with one dominant to [an]other"
  - Mutual animal play/mutual incest play
  - Naked and sex with an audience
  - Online role play
  - Other role play threatened as punishment
  - Predator play (where one is a tiger and the other is a human or a fairy)
  - Sexual object to be used as prize
  - Sexy Slytherin student of Professor Snape from Harry Potter
  - Sorority
  - Tied on hands and knees with sign on my back that says $5 per use and be sold/used by others
  - The bogeyman
  - Uniform (priest cassock)
  - Virginity: both virgins; teaching virgin; whore and virgin boy
  - Victorian-era man accidentally walks in on a woman undressing and becomes obsessed with her
  - Vulvoid transformations

Appendix F
Additional Fetishes

The following nine categories describing additional causes of arousal were provided by fill-in text responses. Some categories include contributions from more than one person. Duplications were removed and grammatical and spelling errors were corrected.

- Attitude/personality traits
    - A dominant and very sensual man
    - A good fashion sense
    - A proud submissive attitude in a sub; "i don't like doormats"
    - A strong confident mental "Attitude" of the Top is the biggest & main turn on for me
    - All of the above and none of the above. It depends on the mind inside the body
    - Arousal in others
    - Attitude
    - Compassion
    - Confidence
    - Consideration and caring
    - Dominant energy
    - Dominant men
    - Dominant enthusiastic men with confidence but NOT arrogance
    - Masculinity in women

222 Appendix

- ○ Sexually aroused by a person
- ○ Intelligence
- ○ Partner(s) brain
- ○ People
- ○ People's minds and mind states
- ○ Personality
- ○ Sense of humor and intelligence
- ○ Sexual passion by my partners. Getting turned on the right way
- ○ Status
- ○ Strong Dominant women in almost anything they are wearing
- ○ Submission
- ○ Wit

- Bodily
  - ○ Arms: bare arms, forearms, lightly muscular arms and legs, lower arms, masculine arms and hands, muscular arms or legs or back, strong arms, strong biceps in both men and women
  - ○ Body fluid: blood, female and FTM ejaculate, Male and female cum/ejaculate, pre-ejaculate/precum, saliva, semen, spit, squirt, and vaginal fluid (the smell and taste), sweat, urine, vaginal secretions: female ejaculation, lubrication, wetness
  - ○ Breasts: a woman's chest—the space just above her breasts and just under her neck, all shapes and sizes, especially when they're quite sensitive (although I'm not fond of breast implants), Beautiful breasts, big natural breasts, natural large breasts especially if they are lactating, Nipples, small tits, the curves of a woman's breasts, the under curve of the breast
  - ○ Buttocks: a firm ass, ass/tight buns, big arses on women, large round butts, men's and women's buttocks, rear end, the ass
  - ○ Eyes: brown eyes, his eyes and smile, lovely eyes and a warm smile, Trusting Eyes
  - ○ Fat deposits
  - ○ General body: All parts of a woman, his entire body really, I prefer the whole person, Men's bodies, on butches—breasts, shoulders, arms, necks, belly, the curve of a female, the general shape of a woman, the whole person, women who are NOT skinny. I like big butts and boobs;o)
  - ○ Genitals: a hard penis push against my body, A wet cunt, balls, BBC, butch and ftm cock, circumcised penis, large male or female genitalia, Large testicles, I love them, they are great for clothes pins but i love to kick them, men's cocks, penis (limp or hard), Sacred Yoni,

transmen's cocks, uncircumcised penises, women's mons/labia/clitoris/vagina
- Hands
- Hair: a woman with a very hairy pubic/anal region and hairy armpits, Bald heads, body hair, light hair on chest of a man, hair color, hair cuts, hairless body, his hair, long hair, dyed hair, hair
- Head: Honest Smile, jaw, mouths and lips, really straight teeth, and clean teeth, sexy full lips, the beauty of the jaw, the curve of his ear, tongue
- Hips/hip bones
- Legs: calves, long, well defined legs, men's legs, Strong legs, the line of the hip that runs along the top of the leg joint, women with thick thighs
- Men that have height
- Muscles
- Neck: back of the neck, nape of the neck, the line of the neck ears
- Skin coloring
- Skin
- Torso: a bare chest, a little belly, a man[']s naked back, abs, armpits, bare backs, Collarbone, lower back, men's stomach, muscular chests, shoulders, that deep groove down the center of a man's back, the back of a woman's shoulders, the curve a woman's back, the curve of a female waist, tummy

- Clothing
  - 1950s' lingerie
  - A fat femme in leather
  - A girl with hips I can grab hold of
  - A long black leather coat
  - A skirt my master can put his hand under while in public
  - A strong black belt with a silver buckle
  - A-shirts ("wife beaters"—a terrible name)
  - Animals or furry costumes
  - Any clothing that's badass and revealing at the same time, and as long the woman looks fit and strong
  - Boxer briefs
  - Boots: big kick ass boots on men, brown cowboy boots with blue jeans, combat boots, fuck me boots, high heeled boots, Motorcycle boots, tall healed leather boots, work boots (Dr Martens, military boots etc.)

- Business suits
- Clothes that reveal sexy boy parts
- Corsets
- Corsets which leave the breasts open
- Corsets: tight vintage with boning
- Costumes
- Cowboy hat
- Daddy in his suit and tie, (or) in his sleep pants and robe
- Denim
- Dress ups of any sort when associated with my beloved … and bits of her showing seductively!
- Dresses of any type
- Dressing up in a nice way, looking the best you can (and corsets almost always do)
- Fetish wear
- Fishnets
- Footwear
- Gloves
- Great-fitting jeans, jeans with rips in them, great boots, some typical femme trappings (great lingerie, strappy sundresses with straps falling down), white shirts with black bras underneath, thousand-dollar insane french feels that should be in museums leather
- Her regular clothes (which are "men's" clothes)
- High heel slutty shoes
- High heels with bobby socks
- High heels, stilettos
- High heels, tight pants of any kind, sexy silky lingerie (no tassels, feathers, and not too much lace)
- Hosiery
- Hot high heeled shoes
- Latex gloves
- Leather and formalwear, especially women in suits
- Leather clothing (gloves, hood, skirts)
- Lingerie ("especially panties, satin corsets, silk stockings, chiffon or other flowing translucent materials")
- Leather or patent leather shoes high heeled, mary janes, come fuck me pumps. Cotton or satin gloves. I am aroused wearing leather or

uniforms, priest's garb soft cottons with a stiff collar some wools arouse me as well.
- Low cut tops and mini skirts
- Men bikini underwear
- Men in women's clothing
- Men who wear kilts
- Menswear: clothes: briefs, dress shoe, formalwear, underwear
- Motorcycle clothing
- Neck ties
- Nylon, silk, or lace underwear/bra
- Over the knee socks
- Panties
- Pencil skirts
- Sexy high heel shoes
- Sexy rubber on femmes
- Sexy shoes on a femme
- Shoes—leather
- Short revealing skirts and dresses
- Socks
- Soft silkies
- Something soft and sensual feeling that makes me feel attractive and sexy
- Stockings
- Stockings/garters
- Suits
- The feel of denim on my bare bottom
- Thigh high stockings or socks, especially striped socks
- Thigh high tights
- Tight lacy lingerie
- Tight shirts
- Traditional leathermen style of dress
- Tutus
- Uniforms: Almost any kind of uniforms, any law enforcement, Anyone in a position of power i.e. Police, military, anyone who can carry a weapon or restraining gear, boyscout uniform, business attire (Suit/ suit and tie), complete Santa outfit, construction work clothes, cops, Cosplay, FBI jacket, etc., firefighter, librarian, maid uniforms (french maid outfits and high heels), medical (certain medical uniforms/doctor/nurse), military uniforms (a woman in a military uniform/army fatigues with the boots and hat/especially fatigues), Nazi

and other dangerous looking authoritative uniforms, nun costumes, Police uniforms (cops), school girl uniforms, steampunk attire, the 1960's female star trek uniforms, the high collared priest outfits
  - Very masculine and/or dominant pieces of clothing
  - Vinyl tops
  - Wetsuit
  - Women and transmen in men's clothing or uniforms
  - Women dressed as dykes in dress shirts or white tank tops with dress jackets

- Dominance/submission
  - Being dominated by a man (my DOM) is what arouses me the most. All the things He does, says to me and the things He makes me do
  - D/s dynamic
  - Dominance and submission
  - Forceful and specific demands given by partner
  - Power
  - Power and control
  - Power and control exchange
  - Situations, bondage, power exchange, i.e., Dominatrix—sub
  - The power difference with the other person
  - Severe bondage

- Fabrics
  - Any Fabric That Holds His Scent And Body Heat
  - Canvas
  - Feathers
  - Fleece
  - Fur
  - Lace
  - Latex
  - Leather
  - PVC
  - Rubber
  - Satin
  - Silks
  - Spandex
  - Spandex/Lycra
  - Suede
  - Velvet

- Kink toys/sex Toys
    - BDSM toys (floggers, paddles, needles, etc.)
    - Bondage furniture
    - Bondage with rope and chains
    - Chains
    - Diapers
    - Dildos, strap-ons
    - Gas masks
    - Handcuffs, hot wax, canes
    - Insertable foreign objects (bottles, beer cans, pylons, etc.)
    - Leather bondage cuffs and manacles
    - Pussy slapping
    - Restraints
    - Rope
    - Rope on a bare body
    - Rope—soft and rough
    - Scratching with hands/fingernails
    - Sex toys (dildoes, vibrators)
    - Strap-ons, women who pack
    - Toys

- Objects
    - Cars
    - Certain masks
    - Desks/office spaces
    - Electricity
    - Fangs
    - Food (like chocolate)
    - GLITTER!
    - Guns and weapons
    - Old Frederick's catalog drawings
    - Semen in a condom
    - Leather, silk, or nylon sheets
    - Semi-precious stones
    - Some photos/movies/books
    - Spikes
    - Upgrades in electronic technology (new computer, for example)
    - Victoriana
    - Weapons

- Personal Care
    - GQ haircuts—on really tall men
    - Lipstick, mascara
    - Makeup
    - Piercings
    - Tattoos
    - Well-tailored clothing

- Scents/smells
    - A certain sent of cologne
    - Body smell
    - Certain colognes
    - Certain smells
    - Good natural body odor
    - Her husband's scent
    - Smells: leather
    - My master's cologne
    - Perfume
    - Scent of orange
    - Scent of leather
    - The smell of my primary partner and me having sex, my fluids plus his fluids. If I still smell it the next day I am all over him
    - The way my master smells

- Sounds
    - Accents—especially British and Australian
    - Breathing or whispering in ear
    - Certain sounds
    - Heartbeats
    - Some spoken words and music
    - Sounds as in aural noises
    - Sounds of pleasure
    - Sounds of sexual pleasure
    - Sounds, music
    - Strong voice
    - Talking dirty
    - The sounds of an aroused person
    - Voice
    - Voices in the ear

- Tactile
    - Ice
    - Pain
    - Textures
    - The feel of leather
    - Warmth

- Uncategorized
    - Acts
    - a sub wearing cheap make up that runs down their face
    - Bukkake
    - Butch on butch
    - Exhibitionism
    - Fear
    - Female orgasm
    - Gender variance
    - Aroused by a person in certain clothing, fabrics, uniforms and then consequently with that person, specific body parts, and their body fluids
    - Non-sexual massage
    - Nudity
    - Science
    - Scratching with hands/fingernails
    - Specific roles/activities
    - Specific sexual acts
    - Technology
    - The enjoyment my partner gets from my discomfort or pain
    - The leather collar master locked onto my neck
    - Thoughts
    - Threat of violence
    - Tickling
    - Violence
    - Watching others masturbate

Resources

Community and events:

    FetLife: www.Fetlife.com
    Leather Archives & Museum (LA&M): http://leatherarchives.org/ca/
    Leather Pride (check your local area for specific leather pride events)
    Society of Janus Suggested Reading page:
        https://soj.org/resources/suggested-reading/
    The BDSM Events Page:
        http://www.thebdsmeventspage.com/events.html

Directories to find knowledgeable professionals:

    American Association for Sex Educators, Counselors, and Therapists (AASECT) directory of Certified Sex Therapists:
        www.aasect.org/referral-directory
    Bisexuality-Awareness Professionals Directory:
        www.bizone.org/bap/locate.php
    Kink And Poly Aware Professionals Directory (KAP):
        www.kapprofessionals.org/business-directory-2/
    Open List: https://openingup.net/open-list/
    Pineapple Support Society:
        https://pineapplesupport.org/pineapple-support-therapists/
    Poly Friendly Professionals: www.PolyFriendly.org

Academics and trainings:

    Community-Academic Consortium for Research on Alternative Sexualities (CARAS): www.carasresearch.org/
    The Alternative Sexualities Health Research Alliance (TASHRA): www.tashra.org/
    Kink Academy: www.kinkacademy.com/
    Kink Knowledgeable: www.kinkknowledgeable.com/
    Sexual Health Alliance (SHA): www.sexualhealthalliance.com/
    World Association for Sexual Health (WAS): https://worldsexualhealth.net/

Additional support and outreach:

    Female sexuality:
        OMGYES: www.omgyes.com/
        Dipsea: www.dipseastories.com/

    LGBTQ+:
        American Civil Liberties Union (ACLU): www.aclu.org/
        Gay and Lesbian Medical Association (GLMA): www.glma.org

    Sex positive:
        The Center for Positive Sexuality (CPS): https://positivesexuality.org/
        National Coalition for Sexual Freedom (NCSF): https://ncsfreedom.org/

    Sex worker support:
        Free Speech Coalition (FSC): www.freespeechcoalition.com
        Adult Performer Advocacy Committee (APAC): www.apac-usa.com
        Sex Worker Outreach Program (SWOP): https://swopusa.org

References

Addis, I.B., Van Den Eeden, S.K., Wassel-Fyr, C.L., Vittinghoff, E., Brown, J.S., Thom, D.H., & Reproductive Risk Factors for Incontinence Study at Kaiser Study Group. (2006). Sexual activity and function in middle-aged and older women. *Obstetrics and Gynecology, 107*(4), 755–764. doi: 10.1097/01.AOG.0000202398.27428.e2

Alwaal, A., Breyer, B.N., & Lue, T.F. (2015). Normal male sexual function: Emphasis on orgasm and ejaculation. *Fertility and Sterility, 104*(5), 1051–1060. doi: 10.1016/j.fertnstert.2015.08.033

American Psychiatric Association. (2000). *Diagnostic and statistical manual of mental disorders* (4th ed., Text Revision). Washington, DC: Author.

American Psychiatric Association. (2013). *Diagnostic and statistical manual of mental disorders* (5th ed.). Arlington, VA: Author.

Breslow, N., Evans, L., & Langley, J. (1985). On the prevalence and roles of females in the sadomasochistic subculture: Report of an empirical study. *Archives of Sexual Behavior, 14*(4), 303–317. doi: 10.1007/BF01550846

Cambridge Dictionary. (n.d.). Aspect, consent, cuckold, fetish, marriage, orgasm, resilience, self-discovery, sex, sex organs, spiritual, trust. In *Cambridge.org dictionary*. Retrieved September 14, 2020 from https://dictionary.cambridge.org/us/

Masters, W.H., & Johnson, V.E. (1966). *Human sexual response*. Boston, MA: Little, Brown and Co.

Meston, C.M., Levin, R.J., Sipski, M.L., Hull, E.M., & Heiman, J.R. (2004). Women's orgasm. *Annual Review of Sex Research, 15*, 173–257. https://pubmed.ncbi.nlm.nih.gov/16913280

Moser, C., & Levitt, E. (1987). An exploratory descriptive study of a sadomasochistically oriented sample. *Journal of Sex Research, 23*(3), 322–337. doi: 10.1080/00224498709551370

The National Coalition for Sexual Freedom (NCSF). (1998). *BDSM vs. abuse statement*. Retrieved September 1, 2020 from https://secureservercdn.net/198.71.233.68/9xj.1d5.myftpupload.com/wp-content/uploads/2019/12/BDSM-vs-Abuse-Statement.pdf

Rehor, J. (2011). *The occurrence of unconventional sexual behaviors in women.* AS36 2011 HMSX. R44 [Master's Thesis, Human Sexuality Studies, San Francisco State University.] Leonard Library Scholar Works. http://sfsu-dspace.calstate.edu/handle/10211.3/116924

Rehor, J. (2015). Sensual, erotic, and sexual behaviors of women from the "kink" community. *Archives of Sexual Behavior, 44*(4), 825–836. doi: 10.1007/s10508-015-0524-2

von Krafft-Ebing, R. (1906). *Psychopathia sexualis with especial reference to the antipathic sexual instinct: A medico-forensic study* (F. J. Rebman, Trans.). New York: Rebman. (Original work published 1886).

Index

abuse: backgrounds 114, 152; as stereotypical background 75, 142, 155; vs. kink 38–39
adult nursing relationship/adult breastfeeding (ANR/ABF) 123
aftercare 138, 143–144
age play 50, 63, 77, 78, 90
Archives of Sexual Behavior 2–3, 9
arousal 11, 22, 46, 52, 53, 55, 59, 138–140, 144
ashamed 83, 155, 168; *see also* shame

BDSM behaviors 5, 184–192; as career 61–64; and consent 39–40; and identity 75–76; motivations for 20, 23–24; need for to orgasm 7, 15, 17, 18, 141; novices to 68–70; and submission 15; without sex 19–22, 151–153; *see also* Dominant/submissive (D/s) dynamics; masochism; power exchange; sadism
BDSM communities 20, 28, 89, 99; changing 157–158; experiences in 31–32; perceptions of 30–31
BDSM families 113–114, 161–162
behaviors: included in the survey 184–192; and meanings 11
body parts, and fetishes 56
bondage 9, 11, 21, 31, 33; and safety 35
bottoming 40, 47, 70–71, 120, 134, 136, 157
boundaries 70–72; setting 36, 40, 72, 133–134; *see also* privacy
Butches 50, 78, 108, 154, 156–157

casual relationships 88–89
celibacy 21, 73, 102
childhood, and kink discoveries 80–81, 155, 167
chosen families 113–115, 161–162
closed relationships 95–96
clothing 52–57; lingerie 53–54; *see also* uniforms
collars 73, 91, 94–95, 152
communication, importance of 40, 49, 78, 134–135
Community-Academic Consortium for Research on Alternative Sexualities (CARAS) 2, 5
community events 29, 30, 33–35, 71, 171–173; voyeurism/exhibitionism 11, 44–46; *see also* kink community
consensual non-monogamy (CNM) *see* polyamory
consent 35–36, 38–41, 43, 47, 65, 134–135; consensual nonconsent 48, 51; *see also* safe, sane, and consensual (SSC)
corsets 53, 56–58; *see also* clothing
cuckolding 102

desire 15, 17, 52, 138, 140
The Diagnostic and Statistical Manual of Mental Disorders (DSM-5) 41–42, 52
Dom/Domme relationships 86, 104
Dominant, identity as 76

Dominant/submissive (D/s) dynamics 25, 40, 157; and clothing 54–55; community events 29, 171; Daddy/girl 50, 54, 67, 93, 106, 151, 156; predatory 37–38; in relationships 92–94; and rules 133–134; service 93; and trust 135–137; *see also* BDSM behaviors; Master/slave relationships; power exchange; slaves; submissives
dungeons 20, 25, 28, 29, 38, 45, 61, 70, 82, 128, 131, 147, 157, 159

education, in communities 29–33
endorphins 23, 24, 25–26, 128; and pain 23–24, 77, 78, 128, 131
engagement 104–105; *see also* marriage
enjoyment: of connection 130; as kink motivation 120–124, 131
erotic humiliation 136
erotica 5, 48, 60, 212–213
exhibitionistic behaviors 5, 41–48, 77, 206–211; *see also* public sex

fantasies 48, 67–68, 73, 80–81, 155–157, 169–170, 188–189; *see also* role-play
female ejaculation 165–168, 170, 172–173
fetishes 11, 29, 52–60, 61, 62, 142, 161, 175, 193, 221–229; and BDSM 53–54, 57; *see also* clothing; uniforms
fetishistic behaviors 5, 46, 47, 52–60
FetLife 30, 128, 152, 175
fibromyalgia 23
fire cupping 123
fisting 123, 157,
flogging 9, 22, 23, 44, 49, 58, 99–100, 126, 136, 157

genitals, and arousal 139
grief 112, 126, 128–129

headspace 25, 143
Human Sexual Response (Masters and Johnson) 138

identity 66, 72–80, 84, 175–176, 178
"in service" 93; stories about 159–160
intimacy 156–158

Johnson, Virginia, *Human Sexual Response* 138

kink 14, 65, 175–176; definition 12; importance of 75; as love 161–162; new to 68–70; without sex 19–22, 151–153
kink behaviors 117–118; definition 11; outside attitudes towards 167; personal reasons for 119–129; relational reasons for 129–137; sexual reasons for 137–144
kink community 28–35; changing 157–158; definition 12; importance of 33; online 29–30; and stereotypes 33; *see also* community events
kink professionals 29, 61–64, 159–160, 182
kink studies 177–178
Kinky Women Research Study 2–3, 6–7, 9–10, 177–179, 181; demographics 5–6; inclusion criteria 5; and labels 179–180; reactions to 179–181; survey 183–229

labels 176–177, 179, 182
latex fetishes 29, 46, 58–59
leather 12, 29, 31, 43, 44, 52, 53, 55, 57, 58, 74, 77, 99, 154, 156, 157
leather families 113–114
lifestyle 78

making out, stories about 168, 170, 172–173
male partners: payment from 7; requests by 7–8
marriage 96, 104–107; engagement 104–105; non-legal 108–109; and other relationships 107; platonic 107–108; polyamorous 106; *see also* relationships
masochism 142; definition 21; and identity 77; *see also* BDSM behaviors
Master/slave relationships 49, 74, 93–94; stories about 147–148; *see also* Dominant/submissive (D/s) dynamics; power exchange; 24/7 relationships
Masters, William, *Human Sexual Response* 138
masturbation 9, 17–18, 61, 130, 138, 170
media depictions 68–69; of families 116; and sensationalism 14; and stereotypes 40
mental stimulation: and power exchange 25; vs. physical 24–27
monogamy 10, 19, 37, 68, 77, 82, 86, 96, 98, 101; closed kink relationships 91; stories about 151–153; *see also* closed relationships; relationships

motivations: considering 117–118, 117–119, 144–145; enjoyment as 120–124; relational 129; resilience 126–129; and role-play 49; self-discovery 124–26, 155, 161–162; sexual 137–144; stories about 161–162; for various activities 10–11
munches 29–31, 33, 38, 62, 70–71; definition 12
mutual pleasure 131–133
myths, about women and kink 3, 7, 23, 27, 46

National Coalition for Sexual Freedom (NCSF) 38–39
needles 127–128

The Occurrence of Unconventional Sexual Behaviors of Women (Rehor) 3, 179
open-mindedness 30, 72, 165–166
open relationships *see* polyamory
oral sex 20, 37, 86, 118, 147, 151, 167–169
orgasms 23–24, 28, 39, 58, 138, 140–143, 170; kink required for 141; and masturbation 18, 142

paganism 27
pain: and altered mental states 26; and chronic pain 23; and connection 131; and endorphins 23–24; giving 21–22, 57, 76, 122, 99; and power exchange 23; receiving 21–22, 99–100, 142, 149; stories about 149–150
"pain pleasure principle" 21, 24
pansexuality 72, 107, 166, 171
parenting 91–92
personal discoveries/evolution 80–83, 124–126
personality traits 56–57
perverse, definition 8
pet role-play 50–51, 94, 132
physical disabilities, adjusting for 127, 151–152
play, definition 12
play partners, definition 12
pleasure, mutual 131–133
polyamory 15, 17, 37, 86, 90, 94–95, 97–104, 112; chosen families 113; non-consensual non-monogamy 97, 102–103; open relationships 98, 100; polyfidelity 106; stories about 147–148, 154; *see also* relationships

power exchange 18, 20, 40, 136–137, 139–140; chosen families 114–115; and mental stimulation 25; and pain 23; and relationships 91–97; stories about 147; total power exchange (TPE) 95; *see also* BDSM behaviors; Dominant/submissive (D/s) dynamics; Master/slave relationships
primary-plus 97–104; *see also* polyamory
privacy 70–72; *see also* boundaries
Pro-Dommes 61–63, 100, 155
protection 31
public/private lives 70–72
public sex 43–44, 46; *see also* exhibitionistic behaviors; voyeuristic behaviors

rape scenes: fantasies about 170; role-playing 48, 51
Rehor, Jennifer 2–4; *The Occurrence of Unconventional Sexual Behaviors of Women* 3, 179; "Sensual, Erotic, and Sexual Behaviors of Women from the 'Kink' Community" 3, 179
relationship statuses 10, 89–91, 198–199; divorced 85, 86, 109–111, 112, 113, 115, 161; widowed 85, 89, 109, 111–113, 115; *see also* marriage
relationships 115–116; casual 88–89; chosen families 113–115; closed 95; describing 86–87; Dominant/submissive 92–94; importance of 59; Master/slave 93–94; new relationships 87–88; and power exchange 91–97; total power exchange (TPE) 95; variety of 85–86; vs. play 99, 105, 111; *see also* monogamy; polyamory; single-plus relationships; 24/7 relationships
religion, and kink 20, 26–27, 30, 52, 123
resilience 120, 126–129, 144
risk-aware consensual kink (RACK) 37
role-play 5, 23, 43, 48–51, 74, 188–189, 214–220; *see also* fantasies
roles 154; defined 133; and respect/authority 12, 93

sadism: defining 11, 12, 21; and identity 76; *see also* BDSM behaviors
sadomasochism 22, 99–100; *see also* masochism; sadism
safe, sane, and consensual (SSC) 35–37; *see also* consent

safe sex 17, 36–37, 100, 102, 156, 168
safe-words 21, 23, 36, 37, 95, 135
safety 35–38, 143, 159, 175
San Francisco State University, Human Sexuality Studies program 2
scenes 31, 32, 44, 50, 50, 71, 123, 156–158; definition 12; stories about 159–160
Schiffman, Julia 4
self-discovery 124–126, 155, 161–162, 168
"Sensual, Erotic, and Sexual Behaviors of Women from the 'Kink' Community" (Rehor) 3, 179
sex magic 27
sexual activity 195–197; definition 15, 137–138; enjoyment of 16–17; and kink 17–18
sexuality 59–60, 84, 140, 177
shame 46, 126, 128, 172
single-plus relationships 89–91; *see also* relationships
slavery relationships 91–92, 94
slaves 39–40, 73, 76, 91; *see also* Dominant/submissive (D/s) dynamics; submissives
spanking 8, 17, 18, 22, 27, 28, 29, 54, 68, 80, 92, 99, 167, 171
spirituality 14, 27–28, 64, 175
stereotypes 33, 166, 177; female submissives/slaves 39–40

submissives 39–40, 76–77, 79, 81; professional 159–160; *see also* Dominant/submissive (D/s) dynamics; slaves
swingers 12, 29, 92, 97, 98, 100, 107, 112, 178
switches 76, 80, 100, 136, 156, 165–169

trust 135–137, 150, 163
24/7 relationships 10, 19, 32, 49, 62, 73–74, 79, 92, 94–96; *see also* Master/slave relationships; relationships

uniforms 55–57, 59; *see also* clothing

vanilla relationships/sex 15, 17, 78, 102–103; definition 12, 19; desire for 160; as not enough 18, 79, 82–83, 106, 142, 154; stories about 147–148, 167
virginity 147, 168; and kink 20–21
von Krafft-Ebing, Richard 8
voyeuristic behaviors 10, 41–48, 177; *see also* public sex
vulnerability 76, 125, 135–137, 149–150

Wiccan religion, and sexuality 27
woman, lack of definition for 179
women-only kink events 3, 29, 157